Archbishop Tutu

Archbishop Tutu

Prophetic Witness in South Africa

Edited by
Leonard Hulley
Louise Kretzschmar
and Luke Lungile Pato

HUMAN & ROUSSEAU
Cape Town Pretoria Johannesburg

Layout and design by Annelize van Rooyen
Typeset in 10.5 on 12 pt Berkeley by Human & Rousseau
Printed and bound by Printkor, Kinghall Avenue, Epping

ISBN 0 7981 3607 3

Contents

Foreword

Archbishop Desmond Tutu has been a towering figure in South African church and political life for over twenty years. From the time he wrote that open letter to Prime Minister John Vorster as Dean of Johannesburg in 1975, South Africa has had to take notice of this cleric who has been a stern critic of apartheid as well as a priest of deep spirituality, much loved for his ability to tell jokes as easily against himself than against the stupidity of white racial prejudice. I know him as a pastor devoted to those in his charge; a preacher with an ability to translate deep theological insights into the language of ordinary people. At the height of the international campaign against apartheid, Fr Desmond shot into international prominence when he called for the boycott of South African coal in Australia. In time he was honoured with the Nobel Peace Prize and countless honorary degrees from universities around the world.

These essays attempt to capture the being of Desmond Tutu through the insight of a few of his friends and scholars who have observed his progress over the years as well as those whom he mentored like this writer. To all of us Desmond Tutu presented a different and fascinating character. It is hoped that, though this is not a biography, the breadth and depth of his intellectual and practical interests will come under the spotlight. And so, we have here essays on his contribution to theological education both as a teacher, an administrator at the ecumenical Theological Education Fund based in London and as a bishop, his lifelong contribution to African Christianity and African Theology and, of course, his contribution to the political developments in our country. We are given insight into his spiritual life and his ethical exploration. We read here about the influences, both theological and political, that shaped his life. In all these instances, his was a complex role. A role which he entered into both reluctantly and as a participant who excelled in what he did. One was always struck by how much he kept protesting that he was not a politician and yet thrived under the spotlight that was cast upon him in order to expose the injustices of apartheid and to be the spokesman of the voiceless millions whose political leaders were either incarcerated or in exile. One could not but notice how he took to the world stage, interacting naturally with monarchs, heads of state and the rich and famous. It must be very hard for Desmond Tutu to be obscure and humble.

There are some excellent vignettes of Desmond Tutu's life here and some recollections from personal friends. What I miss, though, and I know it's through no fault of the editors, is a contribution in relation to Fr Desmond's ecumenical commitment. After all, not only was he on the staff of an important ecumenical agency, the TEF, he was General Secretary of the South African Council of Churches and, currently, he serves as President of the All Africa Conference of Churches. An evaluation of his contribution to ecumenical theology would have been in place although most can attest to the fact that his time at SACC was obscured by the necessity to campaign against apartheid and to organise on a large scale for the support of victims of apartheid. One can say that during that time, the SACC as such was able to unite the churches against apartheid but never quite refined the challenge to visible and organic unity which the WCC's Commission on Faith and Order and South Africa's Church Unity Commission have been struggling with for a long time. Some matters were more urgent. However, the witness to justice and liberation which Archbishop Desmond Tutu championed is also an important contribution to ecumenism.

Today, Archbishop Desmond Tutu is Chairperson of the Truth and Reconciliation Commission. That came within months of his retirement as Archbishop of Cape Town. With the support and understanding of his fellow bishops, formal retirement from the national stage has been shelved for another two years. That is the measure of his commitment and magnanimity. He is entrusted with this very sensitive task that is very much at the heart of the South African project of democratisation. Through the Truth and Reconciliation Commission a delicate balance has to be achieved in dealing with the gross human rights violations of the apartheid era, and clearing the way for healing and reconciliation to take place. The Truth and Reconciliation Commission is the culmination of a life's work for Fr Desmond: pastor, priest and reconciler.

This volume of essays comes with the best wishes of many of his friends and the gratitude of many who can never be named for his witness to Christ in our land. This writer commends this work as yet another contribution inspired by Desmond Tutu's leadership.

N. Barney Pityana, PhD
Chairperson
The Human Rights Commission
Good Friday, 1996.

INTRODUCTION

Leonard Hulley and Louise Kretzschmar

Not without honour:
Reflections on the life and
witness of Desmond Mpilo Tutu

In 1986 a previous *festschrift* for Desmond Mpilo Tutu entitled *Hammering swords into ploughshares* appeared. This was at a time when the country was experiencing enormous political conflict and the government had earlier resorted to a declaration of a State of Emergency in order to seek to compel its rebellious citizens to comply with the official policy of apartheid. This volume, appearing in 1996, has a rather different context. Although problems still abound within the country, especially those of a socio-economic nature, a large measure of political stability has emerged as a result of the multiparty negotiations of the early 1990s, the national elections of April 1994 and the subsequent establishment of the Government of National Unity under President Nelson Mandela.

In the earlier *festschrift*, edited by Buti Tlhagale and Itumeleng Mosala, it was said that Desmond Tutu was "a much maligned person" (1986: ix). He was regarded by the authorities as a threat to the well-being of the country and was portrayed in the government-controlled media as untrustworthy, even as a dangerous communist. Anyone who sought to portray Tutu in a different light was equally perceived as a risk to the security of the government. This was illustrated in the case of the television interviewer, Pat Rodgers. In the late seventies he interviewed Desmond Tutu on national television. Because Tutu came across in a positive way during that programme, the interviewer's contract with the SABC was terminated. Such was the paranoia in government circles that they could not allow Tutu to be seen in other than a negative light. They used all the means at their disposal to communicate a negative message to the populace at large. He was maligned at every opportunity.

But why was Tutu so much maligned by those in power? Was it not

11

precisely because the powerful realised that his message, if widely accepted, would fatally undermine the entire structure of apartheid? He opposed apartheid because it was based on the idea that the biological feature of colour, which was part of God's creation, was made into a criterion for discriminating against certain people. He argued that because we are all created in the divine image we should be treated equally (in Tutu 1985: 17). He opposed apartheid because it was fundamentally unjust and, therefore, unchristian. As such, his was a prophetic witness, a spirituality of struggle.

Within the black community, Tutu was faced with the situation that "the Church of God must sustain the hope of a people that have been tempted to grow despondent because the powers of this world seem to be on the rampant" (Tutu 1983: 119). He had to convince these people that God cared for them when they were marginalised, exploited, poor, hungry and ragged. This he was able to do because he believed that God was a God of liberation. The only question was when and how this liberation would take place, a liberation which he hoped would be peaceful rather than accompanied by the shedding of blood (Tutu 1983: 85; see also Tutu 1982: 3).

When both international and internal pressure on the apartheid regime was mounting and repressive measures were increasing within the country, Tutu was one of those who campaigned for international economic pressure to be applied to persuade the government to negotiate with the "authentic leaders of all sections of the South African population" (Tutu 1983: 82). He did this in spite of the draconian laws that had been passed which stated that those who advocated an economic boycott for any reason were guilty of high treason. He was well aware that some people would suffer as a result of economic pressure, but saw that as a preferable alternative to violence. He chose the option of a boycott rather than that of bloodshed because he was a man of peace (Tutu 1977: 116 and Tutu 1985: 17ff).

It would be wrong to think that as a man of peace Tutu has been a quietist. For him peace was a goal that could only be achieved once the demands of justice had been met. It was his passion for justice that made certain individuals and groups perceive him as a threat to the continuance of the status quo whilst others, the poor and disenfranchised, perceived him as a champion of truth and equity.

In an analysis of various statements Tutu made during the period 1977 to 1992, the authors of a new book on Tutu's sermons came to the following conclusion:

A theological interpretation of our analysis of Tutu's sermons, speeches and other texts reveals to us a modern liberation theologian who stands steadfastly in the central faith of the great Christian tradition. He thinks from the classical theory of salvation – the revelation of God's grace and love in Jesus Christ, the victory over Evil and sin on the cross through his resurrection and ascension. He is a committed pastor and theologian who discovered in his context of oppression and suffering the Liberator God, who loves and cares for us, who promises – on the basis of Jesus' victory over Evil – liberation for his people. He also discovered an active God who involves his people in the praxis of the struggle for liberation (Pieterse 1995: 55).

Tutu's ongoing commitment to justice and peace was confirmed in two recent events. On 9 February 1996 at a book launch of a publication which analysed a selection of Tutu's public utterances Bishop Richard Kraft, who received the book on Tutu's behalf (Tutu was unavoidably detained by his involvement with the work of the Truth and Reconciliation Commission) spoke about Tutu's deep spirituality and concern for reconciliation. This was evident also at a service held on 11 February in Pretoria during which various dioceses bade him farewell on his impending retirement. In his quest for reconciliation he asked those who were present to forgive him if his actions in the past had caused them hurt. He said that what he had done was done in the context of extremely difficult circumstances within the country and seemed very necessary at the time, although he was aware that it might have caused deep wounds in some people.

At that same service the bishops present commissioned him to continue the ministry to which God had called him, as chairperson of the Truth and Reconciliation Commission. The bishops of the Church of the Province believed that it was because of his spirituality and his concern for reconciliation that he was the appropriate person to head such a commission. He would seek to promote healing and transformation in the whole process. Transformation was also central to the theme of Tutu's sermon at that service. He saw what had happened in the country within the space of a few years as a miraculous transformation. Tutu interpreted it as transfiguration, a transformation that was beyond mere human capacity but was possible only with divine assistance, when "God does God's thing", to quote the Archbishop. So

13

instead of retiring from his onerous task as Archbishop and taking up an academic appointment as visiting professor at Emory University (Georgia) in the United States, he will be seeking to participate in the healing of the wounds of the past. Whereas previously he was denigrated and vilified as a monster, he now is seen as a man of peace who will contribute significantly to the healing of the wounds in our society. He has come in from the cold; instead of being "much maligned" he is now feted and honoured. A symbol of this new-found acceptability is the honorary doctorate bestowed on him by the University of South Africa in 1995, the institution where he earned his first degree.

Many people in a variety of walks of life were approached by the three editors to participate in this venture. For a number of different reasons, several people were unable to produce contributions. Fr Trevor Huddleston, for example, was keen to participate but, due to his increasing frailty, reluctantly declined. Although supportive of the idea, even enthusiastic, several other people were unable to send in their contributions due to prior commitments. Ironically, some of these commitments include the demands made on them because of the positions which they now hold within the government; a possibility that seemed remote to many of us in the dark days of the mid-1980s.

A number of issues are raised in this volume in the three main sections entitled: "Who is Desmond Mpilo Tutu?"; "Life and faith in an African context"; and "Morality, religion and society". The last contribution, by Luke Pato, seeks to draw the various themes together in a concluding postscript.

The first subsection consists of a number of biographical essays and personal tributes. To begin with, we reproduce the citation which was read in 1984 when Desmond Tutu received the Nobel Peace Prize in recognition of his contribution to the non-violent struggle against apartheid. This is followed by an insightful personal tribute written by the now retired Dean of St George's Cathedral in Cape Town. As someone who has worked with Father Desmond for many years, Dean King is well placed to give us an intimate glimpse into what drives Desmond Tutu. Dr Francis Cull's contribution similarly shows how Father Desmond's spirituality is at the root of all he is and does. His is a spirituality rooted in the Benedictine tradition of "rest, prayer and work, *and in that order*". This spirituality, says Cull, has enabled him to engage in a ministry of service, prophecy and compassion, and it is what makes Tutu a priest rather than a cleric.

Charles Villa-Vicencio shows Tutu's concern for obedience to what

14

he perceives to be the divine will, rather than being politically or theologically "correct". After the release of Mandela he had hoped to leave politics to the politicians but found that the needs of the people summoned him to intervene again on their behalf not as a party politician but as a pastor. Tutu's concern for integrity rather than correctness has had an impact beyond the borders of this country. Deep spirituality and theological acumen are important characteristics of Tutu as a person. At present, Tutu's primary concern is to break the cycle of violence in the country.

In "The transfiguration of politics", John de Gruchy, the well-known Professor of Christian Studies at the University of Cape Town, draws a distinction between a "political priest" and "the true pastor and prophet" who has been drawn into performing a political role for the sake of the poor and suffering. Tutu, in his view, is a priest and pastor who has exhibited a deep and abiding faith in the "redemptive power and purpose of God". Tutu's life and ministry have been driven by his theological convictions, not by political ambition.

Livingstone Ngewu compares Tutu, the champion of the people, with Geoffrey Clayton, who was also regarded in his day as a champion of the people. Ngewu argues that Clayton, like most liberal church leaders of his era, thought that blacks were not yet ready to exercise proper political discretion. Following Augustine, he also advocated obedience to the state. He only balked when Verwoerd proposed preventing blacks and whites from worshipping together, saying that he would disobey and counsel his clergy to do the same if the Bill became law. Although he too followed Augustine, throughout his ministry Tutu was willing to challenge the unjust laws of the apartheid regime. Whereas Clayton abhorred activism, Tutu was an activist seeking social justice. Ngewu concludes "that Tutu does not stand . . . in the tradition of Clayton".

The first contribution in the next subsection of the book, "Life and faith in an African context", is written by Njongonkulu Winston Ndungane, Anglican (CPSA) Bishop of Kimberley and Kuruman. He speaks of Tutu as "*ngumntu lowo*", that is, "the one in whom full personhood is manifested". One of Desmond Tutu's most significant achievements, he argues, has been the restoration of the dignity of the African person. It was his conviction that all are created in the image of God that caused him to resist the evil of apartheid and, in the present context, causes him to stress that the poor and marginalised need to be involved in the process of reconstruction. In this regard, says

Ndungane, an African Christian spirituality needs to develop, a spirituality which is God-centred, rooted in a deep sense of community, and "that has been purified by the experience of pain and suffering that is rooted in the cross of Jesus Christ which exhibits forgiveness, compassion, tenderness and a loving and a caring disposition towards the other. For Africans are a people whose identity is founded on Ubuntu."

Simon Maimela, previously Professor of Systematic Theology at UNISA and now a vice-principal at the same institution, outlines the uses and misuses of African culture within colonialism, within the political struggle of the African people, and within the Bible itself. He makes the point that "God's gift of racial and cultural diversity should be seen as a source of strength and enrichment"; in this way cultural and ethnic diversity can become a source of blessing rather than a curse. A question that arises from Maimela's discussion is: How can the people of South Africa, indeed of Africa, escape the poverty, conflict, corruption and oppression that is so prevalent in our continent? How can we combat the combination of exploitation from external countries as well as those forms of exploitation that are generated from within African countries themselves in order to give expression to a life-giving form of African culture?

Michael Battle argues that Tutu's theology must be understood in terms of the African concept of Ubuntu. Though the word is difficult to translate, there are signs that this concept is beginning to be understood and used outside its African milieu. It suggests that we are fully human because we are in community, and it is only in community that justice can be done to individuals. Furthermore, in Ubuntu there is an "absolute dependence on God and neighbour". It is significant that several authors within this volume mention Ubuntu.

Whereas Battle sees Tutu's theology functioning in African terms, Janet Hodgson shows that in many parts of Africa the residual influence of negative missionary views on African culture remains strong. This heritage has prevented the wholehearted acceptance of indigenous resources within the church. She suggests that the Anglican Provinces in Africa "can only experience renewal by sharing in the African church's struggle to reclaim her liturgical genius". Here Tutu has been in the vanguard in calling for a "radical spiritual decolonisation". Hodgson's chapter shows that although Africa has been liberated politically, the conservatism of many churches has prevented it from using the rich resources at its disposal. Her contribution is a clarion call to the churches to do just that.

Neville Richardson takes this stress on the resources of Africa one step further. He makes a significant attempt to facilitate the use of African "customs, concepts and time-honoured wisdom" in Christian ethical thought. Indeed, he says that "the time is ripe for Africa to make a rich contribution to Christian ethics". Instead of Western individualism we should use the African idea of communality; whereas in the West we have largely severed the connection between worship and the moral life, in Africa religious ritual and morality are held together. Richardson also states that the mutual caring and sharing captured in the term Ubuntu could also make a contribution to ethical thinking and actions. Richardson links African ethics with his own interest in the community ethics espoused by the writer Stanley Hauerwas.

The third subsection of this book deals with issues related to "Morality, religion and society". Here a number of interesting, even controversial, contributions appear.

Denise Ackermann tackles the problem of "violence [which] is an endemic reality in our society". She identifies both social violence, such as that which results from a social system like apartheid, and domestic violence, which results in actions such as rape, wife battering and incest. She then focuses on "rape [as] a case study of violence against women in South Africa". She argues that traditional theology has contributed to the powerlessness and silent suffering of women both through its legitimation of male power and its avoidance of the fact of rape in its preaching and pastoral ministry. The church has all too often been silent on the matter. She goes on to say that people "do not choose acts of violation . . . But equally clearly human beings have the capacity to choose: either to be crippled by violence, or to use the power of human agency to resist unto healing together as believing people". With the widespread violence in our society and the high incidence of rape and the molestation of children, Ackermann's chapter is a call to the church to enter the fray on the side of the victims.

In "Children, sexism and the church" Caroline Tuckey shows that the whole question of the subordination/subjection of women, which Ackermann shows to have such negative implications, is something which is part of the process of socialisation in both the church and society at large. From an examination of what is taught to children in Sunday schools, she concludes that women are seldom if ever shown as doing things for God; the heroic figures about whom the children are taught from the Bible are almost without exception men. Instead of the church helping both men and women to fulfil their potential as

17

human beings created in the divine image, men alone are held up as paradigms of that to which believers should aspire. Instead of both consciously and unconsciously perpetuating female subordination, the churches ought to "more closely reflect what it truly means to be the female and male body of Christ".

Libuseng Lebaka-Ketshabile's chapter takes this debate one step further. As a black woman she is concerned about the plight of black women "the majority of [whom] . . . are at the bottom of the socio-economic ladder and living in extreme poverty". She acknowledges that in the new dispensation some women are making their mark but, although this is a sign of hope, there is still a long way to go. She argues for equality in terms of relationships and labour. She shows that even when men are engaged in work which is antisocial and unproductive they are perceived to be working, whereas women who work from morning to night in caring for their families by gathering food, fuel and water are not regarded as being economically active. This is reinforced by the negative attitude towards women in the church which is largely patriarchal. She proposes that "women 'must defeat the Bible as patriarchal authority by using the Bible as liberator' ". Doing this would free women to "effectively challenge what needs to be changed" in both the church and society.

The contributions by Ackermann, Tuckey and Lebaka-Ketshabile provide the community of believers with much food for thought. They all reveal that the church discriminates against people on the basis of the way God has created them, something over which they have no control. Tutu himself has argued that in the same way that we need to fight racism and poverty, we need to fight against the exploitation of women and children.

Liz Carmichael, who has been heavily engaged in attempts to bring about justice, peace and reconciliation in the township of Alexandra near Johannesburg, writes authoritatively on the subject of the "spirituality of reconstruction". This is entirely appropriate in a book honouring Tutu, whose spirituality is the source and strength of his social concern. She argues that "reconstruction assumes both a need and a vision". She finds this vision both in the description of *shalom* found in scripture and in the Reconstruction and Development Programme (RDP). "The word 'reconstruction' reminds us that something has been seriously wrong and there is literally a need to reconstruct and develop something new." Here she has in mind the need to pay attention to unemployment, the high incidence of crime, and the lack of houses, education and skills. The realisation of this vision, she argues, must not be divorced from its spiritual source. Quoting from Tutu she says: "Prayer shows its authenticity when its fruit is 'some of the all-embracing generosity and compassion of God for all his children', expressing itself in actual service." This chapter could inspire those church members who are passive spectators to go out and actively serve people, that is, if they are truly followers of Jesus Christ.

Beverley Haddad, from the University of Natal, Pietermaritzburg, has written a most interesting essay on the interface between issues of gender and development. For a vast number of women, she says, the key issue is not liberation, reconstruction or even transformation, but survival. "For the church to be a transformative agent in the development process," she concludes, "the church structures themselves need to be transformed."

It is quite appropriate that Simon Gqubule, an erstwhile colleague of Tutu on the staff of the Federal Theological Seminary (FEDSEM), should examine the development of theological training in the Church of the Province. He describes the significant contribution that St Peter's made to the level and quality of education within the Anglican communion in this country. Alpheus Zulu, the first black bishop in the Church of the Province, and Tutu himself were products of that august institution. Gqubule goes on to lament the demise of the Federal Theological Seminary which trained ministers for its partner churches in an ecumenical framework. He avers that: "Training should be ecumenical and non-racial and should be in close proximity to a university." Unfortunately, Gqubule does not go on to ask what forms of theological education ought to be encouraged within contemporary South Africa, nor how new ecumenical ventures can be successfully pursued.

Concerns related to theological education are closely linked to the way in which the Bible is interpreted and applied. Jonathan Draper says that Tutu draws on the Bible a great deal in his preaching and argues that he uses liberation as his "fundamental principle of biblical interpretation". He then sets out to interpret the story of the ten lepers who came to Jesus for healing, using liberation as the hermeneutical key. The purity laws excluded certain people from society, the lepers being one such group. In their excluded state the lepers overcame barriers between the Jews and the Samaritans and formed a community, but when "the ten realise that they have been healed, that the oppressive effect of the purity laws has been lifted from them, their human solidarity breaks down . . . A new marginalisation takes place and the Samaritan is excluded and alone." In South Africa, various groups excluded because of their colour found a "commonality in 'blackness'". In the new South Africa there is the potential both to develop an inclusive solidarity or to "return to the old divisions, then the healing will be only superficial". Draper's article thus raises a very important question about who are now the "outsiders" and the "insiders".

In recent discussions on the issue of homosexuality, at least four basic approaches have emerged: the rejecting-punitive; the rejecting-compassionate; the qualified acceptance; and the full acceptance stances. John Suggit's paper, "Gay liberation: In scripture and theology", adopts the approach of full acceptance as long as such relationships are governed by faithfulness rather than permissiveness. However, Christians are still widely divided on this issue and some of the key areas of dispute which remain are: is homosexuality "natural" or is it "unnatural"?; how can it be reconciled with Christian teaching about humanity being either "male" or "female"?; how ought the relevant biblical verses to be interpreted?; and ought the notion of "homosexual orientation" automatically make homosexual behaviour or acts morally acceptable?

Gerrie Lubbe shows that even as a student Tutu was interested in other religious faiths. On the basis of a few available sources, he sketches an outline of a theology of religions as held by Tutu. While Tutu says that "Jesus Christ is the full and final revelation of God. I will not compromise my belief in His absolute uniqueness," he nevertheless holds that something of the "divine splendour" can be found in other faiths. A secular state in which religions are treated equally is, in his view, desirable. This means, for example, that they should have access to the national radio and television. In terms of the freedom of religion guaranteed under the new constitution, the state nonetheless should accept "that religious communities [may still] feel called to act as watchdogs of social justice".

In his postscript, Luke Pato outlines some of the challenges that arise for religious communities, particularly the churches, from the contributions contained in this book. Representing a theological training institution, Pato pays particular attention to the ways in which Christian communities need to understand, formulate and live out their faith within society as a whole. In order to achieve their goals, churches need to pay close attention to theological education. In all of this, Pato says, "we need inspiration from [people like Tutu] if we are to have any hope of changing the dominant and oppressive models in theological education, church and society . . ."

"Where are we going?" This is a question that is often on people's lips. Depending upon their circumstances, people tend to be either apprehensive about the future or they eagerly anticipate it. But this contrast may be too sharp. The prevailing feeling may be a complex combination of hopeful expectation and anxiety. In order to have the strength, courage, veracity and commitment to give practical expression to the vision of a democratic, nonracial and nonsexist South Africa, we can learn much from the faith and integrity which have been exemplified in the life and witness of Desmond Mpilo Tutu. Archbishop Tutu would be the first to acknowledge that he is by no means perfect but, then, neither are we. Nevertheless, he is a living example to our country and the wider world of what it means to have personal integrity (in the sense of both honesty and wholeness). He has sought to live out the practical consequences of the Christian faith in the context of the struggle against apartheid. Now he is engaged in the struggle to renew the church and reconstruct our broken society. Can we do anything less?

BIBLIOGRAPHY

Hulley, L.D. (1996?), "Liberation theology and beyond: The contextual ethics of Desmond Tutu", forthcoming in *Journal of Theology for Southern Africa*.

Kretzschmar, L. (1996?), "A holistic spirituality: A pre-requisite for the reconstruction of South Africa", forthcoming in *Journal of Theology for Southern Africa*.

Pieterse, H.J.C. (ed.) (1995), *Desmond Tutu's message: A qualitative analysis*, Kampen: Kok Pharos.

Tlhagale, B. and I. Mosala (1986), *Hammering swords into ploughshares: Essays in honour of Archbishop Desmond Mpilo Tutu*, Johannesburg: Skotaville.

Tutu, D.M. (1977), "God intervening in human affairs", *Missionalia*, Vol. 5: 2. pp. 111-117.

Tutu, D.M. (1982), *The Divine intention*, SACC: Johannesburg.

Tutu, D.M. (1983), *Hope and suffering*, Johannesburg: Skotaville.

Tutu, D.M. (1985), "Wall of fire", *Trinity Seminary Review*, Vol. 7: 1, pp. 17-24.

Who is Desmond Mpilo Tutu?

Citation for the Nobel Peace Prize – October 16, 1984 Received by Desmond Mpilo Tutu

(Used with the permission of Geir Lundestad, Director of the Norwegian Nobel Institute.)

The Norwegian Nobel Committee has chosen to award the Nobel Peace Prize for 1984 to Bishop Desmond Tutu, General Secretary of the South African Council of Churches.

The Committee has attached importance to Desmond Tutu's role as a unifying leader figure in the campaign to resolve the problem of apartheid in South Africa. The means by which this campaign is conducted is of vital importance for the whole of the continent of Africa and for the cause of peace in the world. Through the award of this year's Peace Prize the Committee wishes to direct attention to the non-violent struggle for liberation to which Desmond Tutu belongs, a struggle in which black and white South Africans unite to bring their country out of conflict and crisis.

The Nobel Peace Prize has been awarded to a South African once before, in 1960 when it was awarded to the former president of the African National Congress, Albert Lutuli. This year's award should be seen as a renewed recognition of the courage and heroism shown by black South Africans in their use of peaceful methods in the struggle against apartheid. This recognition is also directed to all who, throughout the world, use such methods to stand in the vanguard of the campaign for racial equality as a human right.

It is the Committee's wish that the Peace Prize now awarded to Desmond Tutu should be regarded not only as a gesture of support to him and to the South African Council of Churches of which he is leader, but also to all individuals and groups in South Africa who, with their concern for human dignity, fraternity and democracy, incite the admiration of the world.

Archbishop Desmond Tutu
– a personal tribute

I have a sense of having met Archbishop Desmond before. Perhaps it
is partly because he presents himself as a fascinating mixture of the
archbishops who have preceded him. He has the restrained flamboy-
ance of Joost de Blank, the search for holiness of Taylor and Burnett
and the pragmatic mediating gifts of Philip Russell. Above all, he has
a strong slice of Geoffrey Clayton's sense of the absurd, without which
a man cannot be saved. Anybody who can remember being reduced
to tears of laughter late at night, and often after a good meal, by
Geoffrey Clayton, a fag hanging on his lips, and as he told stories of
his early days or of naughty clergymen he had known, will recognise
the explosive humour that can overtake Archbishop Desmond, often
at serious moments in Synod or Chapter.

Like so many people, I have known Desmond Tutu as a rising star
in a dark sky. He seemed even in the seventies to be destined to lead
the Church in a time of increasing need. When a telephone rang late
in 1981 and he invited me to go to America in his place, with a small
group of South Africans, and at the invitation of the Diocese of
Connecticut, I gratefully accepted and benefited from the experience,
although I was a makeshift replacement. But he had no passport.

Earlier in the year I had telephoned him asking if I might nominate
him to the forthcoming Elective Assembly in Cape Town. There were
some of us even then who believed that this was the moment for him
to lead and guide us through those difficult years. But the voice of cau-
tion prevailed and his response to my call correct. "I haven't got a
snowball's chance in hell," he said. He has a limitless supply of these
lucidly corny expressions which come out endearingly in sermons and
talks. To me, they are the jargon of another age – but he seems to think
they are the bee's knees. Sermons get spattered with "You can bet your

bottom dollar" (or Kruger Rand). We are told that we are the cat's pyjamas.

In all my association with him I have never felt that I could call him "Desmond", although I count him a dear friend and he thinks I am the cat's whiskers. I think this is because I feel I am in the presence of someone who never forgets his priestly character or indeed his episcopal status, who carries it with an inner dignity, quietly and firmly. Well, the snowball melted in 1981, but not so easily and quickly as expected. There was considerable support for him. It was noticeable that even in the speeches which were critical of him as a candidate for election, tribute after tribute was paid to him – but "the time was not right". So, after the Assembly, like a mighty army moved the Church of God at least a few centimetres. When at last he was elected Archbishop in 1986, we knew that a prophet had come among us. Elective Assemblies can be divisive and acrimonious. His entry to the Assembly on his election, accompanied by his brother bishops, was a time of rejoicing and holy clamour. He loves an occasion and uses all the attributes of a good actor, studies his audience and rarely misses a punch line. His enthronement was a great day, where the bodyguards of Mrs Coretta King, Japanese Archbishops and mayors of American cities brought the necessary excitement and angst to the organising committee. We missed Bill Cosby; and the Archbishop of Canterbury told us that we had placed him (the Archbishop) in such an exalted position in the Cathedral that he never heard a word of the sermon.

What do we expect of an archbishop? I have served on a number of committees concerned with the election of an archbishop and each time the consensus is that they are looking primarily for a pastor and a man of prayer. They are also looking for an administrator and a financial wizard – but always a prayerful man and one who, seeing the multitude, has compassion on them. In all this, the Anglican Church in South Africa has been doubly blessed. Disciplined prayer has always been at the heart of Father Desmond's ministry, and as a scriptural man, he has always believed in prayer and fasting. And "Father Desmond" is the form of address that he prefers. There have been times when prayer and fasting have been deeply necessary. Times when the government, those in power and their media have tried to persuade us that this is a dangerous man, a stirrer-up of violence, a crypto-communist. Under such misrepresentation it has surely been hard to pray "to forgive our enemies, persecutors and slanderers, and to turn their hearts". A dangerous man he certainly has been, and the

Bible, as he says, is a dangerous book. So being a father to a family in distress has been hard work for him and he has gone into the holy of holies, like Aaron, bearing the people on his heart. Few bishops can have had the slightly odd idea of compiling a large picture album of all his clergy, as well as their wives and families, with details of who they all are, and using this large tome as a handy intercession book. He gets upset and angry if people do not supply all this material for his intercessions. He needs his family.

His training as a priest by the Community of the Resurrection fathers placed him in a firm Anglo-Catholic mould and he has never left it. Bishop Charles Gore was one of the founders of the Community, with its stress on preaching the Resurrection and the search for holiness, and it is in his preaching that Father Desmond gives himself away. Words like "love", "compassion", "caring" can become devalued by the constant use we make of them in sermons. With Father Desmond they ring true. He is no theological laggard – but neither are his sermons cluttered with quotations from theologians, and certainly not with the latest theological excitements. His words are simple, and he just reminds us of how great a God we have and how much we owe in thankfulness to him. The ease with which he speaks is in itself a temptation of which he is perhaps aware, and he is capable of relying too easily on what he feels, without perhaps enough preparation under a busy schedule. But when he speaks of the love of God, and of the Cross, you can often just hear him at prayer, and it can be very moving because it is so simple and heartfelt. On one Good Friday, at the Cathedral, when we were approaching the part of the Liturgy of the Day called "The Adoration of the Cross", he left his throne, where he had been sunk deep in thought, and moved down to join the long line of worshippers who were slowly moving forward to kneel and venerate the cross. I don't know why I felt particularly moved – perhaps it was because he had removed his shoes, and he just seemed to melt away among the people.

What more is there to tell? He has an immense sense of fun, and his laughter keeps bubbling out to embrace us all. He is a man of great generosity, a spin-off of which is his sending all his clergy wives flowers on their birthdays (he has a special sympathy for clergy wives) and many hidden acts of kindness. Above all, it is his humanity: he touches people where they are and has no predigested words. He is at the opposite end to the parsonical.

Has he no faults? Of course he has, and those who are specially near, and counsel him, would know them. He longs to be loved and accepted by people, and this in itself is not without dangers. I believe that he would agree with something Thomas Merton wrote: "There is one root truth: that God calls human persons to union with himself, and with one another, in Christ." To that conviction he has unsparingly given of himself. To have shared part of the Christian pilgrimage with him, known his friendship, heard his voice, has been heartwarming. To be the beneficiary of his gifts has been humbling. And it has been great fun.

Desmond Tutu:
Man of prayer

A priest is one who mediates to others what otherwise they could not have; and so the priestly function is wider than the ordained ministry: a woman carrying a child has a priestly function, as does the artist expressing a truth, the surgeon with skilful hands, the nurse, the architect shaping spaces – skilled workers in many fields all exercise a priestly function, mediating to others what otherwise they could not have. The test of priesthood is its authenticity. The action of the priestly person is the outward and visible expression of an inward and spiritual reality which in Christian terms will be rooted in an experience of Christ, the Great High Priest. Where this authenticity is absent the priest puts on the outward trappings in the hope that "the apparel oft proclaims the man" – in this case making a false claim. John O'Donohue[1] draws a useful distinction between "cleric" (appearance) and "priest" (reality).

> A cleric is someone who attempts to be a priest from the outside in. He assumes and adopts the uniform, behaviour and language of the institution. Ultimately even his perception and thought become institutionalized. The role creeps deeper and deeper inwards until it houses at the heart of his identity.
>
> In priesthood priestliness becomes explicit as a commitment. A vocation to the priesthood is a calling to the realisation of one's own priestliness in the service of the implicit priestliness of all people.

1. John O'Donohue, "The priestliness of the human heart" in *The Way Supplement*, No. 83, 1989, pp. 46, 47.

The priest in our more ordinary use of the word is one who is aware of his or her own inadequacy, or his or her sinfulness, and is in touch with the shadows and the feelings which are facts of our humanity – but equally he will know the grace of God that responds to the cry for mercy and forgiveness. The priest will know that priesthood is a sharing, however humbly and however faulty, in the priesthood of Christ which is expressed in the fourfold role of prophet, shepherd, priest and ruler.

Desmond Tutu is a priest, not a cleric, though like all of us he has had to resist the temptation to be the latter with its obvious worldly advantages and its lesser demands. Because he is a priest he will be seen to fulfil the fourfold role of the great High Priest. As one who has been accompanying him on his interior journey as spiritual director and confessor for the past nine years, I feel I have a certain qualification not perhaps shared by others, to write of him as a man of prayer who through his life of prayer fulfils these Christ-given roles.

A publication such as this, which seeks to give thanks for all that Desmond Tutu has done for South Africa, ought not to need any justification for considering the interior life of the man. But reflection shows that over and over again to those who were aware of his inner life of prayer and worship, that it was precisely these things which not only motivated the Archbishop as preacher, campaigner for justice in the widest sense, wise counsellor to many in high places and so on, but these things were in fact the strength and stay whereby he was able to be all that he became and remained for Church, Land and World.

I propose therefore to focus on the life of the Archbishop as the man of prayer and to suggest that his particular approach has a vital bearing on the many issues discussed in this publication.

Spirituality is somewhat of a buzzword today, and it is necessary to define what is meant by it in all that follows. By the spirituality practised by the Archbishop I mean the lifestyle which is rooted in his Christian beliefs. These beliefs stem from his conviction, shared by all who take the Bible to be God's Word, that "Jesus is Lord". But his own spirituality is rooted in a particular ecclesiastical tradition, that of the Anglican Church. Behind the life of prayer and worship which actuates him lies the long Benedictine tradition which is central to Anglican spirituality. As I ponder on the prayer life of Desmond Tutu I see the three fundamental Benedictine demands that there shall be: rest, prayer and work *and in that order*. It is a remarkable fact, and it is one reason at least why he has been able to sustain the burdens he has

31

carried, that he has within him a stillness and a need for quiet solitude. He is able to relax and regularly takes a quiet day and an annual long retreat. We live in a climate of anti-silence, which is a condition totally foreign to the life of the church over the ages. The Archbishop knows that he cannot survive in the world unless he can withdraw from the world. He has learned the truth of the demand: *"Vacete, et videte quoniam ego sum DEUS"* ("Empty yourself, and see that I am GOD", as found in the Vulgate version of Psalm 46:10). The "rest" of which St Benedict speaks is not a mere switching off; it is a positive attempt to fulfil the age-old command to rest in God, which was given so long ago in the desert journey of Israel. Similarly, the annual retreat is an opportunity to understand the need for solitude. Human life can be very lonely; as Thoreau said, "most men live out their lives in quiet desperation". At its worst that loneliness turns to isolation: from self, from others, from God. But to accept loneliness in a positive way is to turn it into a solitude which has a profoundly healing and wholifying effect on those who seek it. In the retreat experiences in which I have had the privilege of accompanying the Archbishop, it has become clear how vital these times of withdrawal have been for him to grow on the inward journey. For without that growth the priest becomes the saddest of all creatures, the cleric. And here again he has pointed the way for the Church. It was due to his encouragement that the members of the synod of bishops have made eight-day individually guided retreats. The pattern of Jesus which he follows here: "Come apart and rest awhile", is an urgent need for all those who are caught up in the busyness of church and world.

It is convenient to link the Benedictine call to pray and work together. Before I examine the nature of the Archbishop's type of prayer and how it impinges upon everything he says and does – especially upon his grave public utterances – it is necessary to identify two kinds of spirituality he has avoided. These were prevalent across the whole spectrum of religious life during the apartheid years and continue to plague the scene today. The first is pietism; an attitude so other-worldly that it is of no earthly use at all. It is an attitude that has dismissed not only any hope of changing the world but would positively state that to involve the church in the world of politics and social betterment is a delusion and that all that the individual can do is act generously to the poor and whoever suffers from the·evils of the world. The result in the church structure is what has been called the "holy huddle". Quite naturally it is rejected by those who feel that change is a part of the task of the church. But in their reaction against pietism many fall into an activism which, in spite of its generous motives and often costly suffering, because it rejects pietism, so often rejects the role of the church altogether. This inevitably leads to an activism which in turn is likely to be at the whim of passing needs and leads to a humanist view which puts the actor in the centre in the place of God. The long tradition of the praying church places *contemplation* in the place of pietism and *action* in the place of activism. The contemplative – and Desmond Tutu's prayer has become more and more contemplative over the years – finds its source of strength in his or her God and longs to take that experience out into the world. But out in the world the contemplative longs to bring the world back to God. Because the contemplative constantly seeks the vision of God, she or he will tend to capture, as far as any human being may, something of God's vision for his world. We have here something far beyond meditation; in meditation we take thought and care; in contemplation we are beyond thought and care. The contemplative heart is perhaps well expressed in the delightful story of the French peasant who, upon being asked what he did when, on returning from the fields, he went into the village church, replied: "He looks at me and I look at him and we are both happy." But, of course, there is much more than this to contemplation, because as the contemplative seeks to enter into the vision of God, he or she is aware of the compassionate, suffering God, and it is this experience that sends the contemplative into the world with his or her own compassionate heart to speak for and to raise up the outcasts and rejects of society, and especially those who have no-one to speak for them in the harsh world in which we live. And because the contemplative seeks to live in the Presence, the Presence tends to be carried into the world with the maximum effect and without the dangers of activist extremism. It is here that I believe we can find the source of the wisdom, charity, compassion and balance that has informed so many of Desmond Tutu's pronouncements. So his prayer informs his work; his work is an expression of his life of prayer.

It is a natural corollary for the contemplative person to see the immense value of intercession. Aware of Christ, the great Intercessor in heaven, his contemplative prayer will also be intercessory. But the Archbishop, quite apart from that, keeps up a constant stream of intercession for a wide range of persons and causes. It is encouraging and salutary to arrive in the chapel at Bishopscourt and find him already turning over the pages of his book of intercessions. "If only we could get people praying again," he said in the dark days when he came back to be Bishop of Johannesburg, "we could save the day." No-one can measure the effect of his constant intercession. And behind it there lies an immense gratitude. On one occasion when I was directing him in an individually guided retreat he asked me whether he should continue with his intercessions. "They mean a lot to you," I said. He replied, "Well, you see, I have so many people praying for me."

He carries his prayer into the very ordinary moments of life: starting a journey with prayer before the car moves off; not rushing in to the business of a meeting with those who come to see him without a prayer. Often he uses the prayer of the Institute for Christian Spirituality[2], which has found its way into his book of prayers. It represents so much of what he is and so much of what he would be. "I do so want to be holy!"

Others will, no doubt, speak of the Archbishop as a preacher and communicator. I would add here the way he communicates his love of God in church at worship. His celebration of the Eucharist is without fuss, quiet and with the utmost reverence. There is no pressing of his persona on the congregations. All is directed to draw all together to the wonder of the Mystery. So quiet is he at the heart of the service that if one did not know him one might suppose him detached. But it is that very quiet which is the mark of his devotion to the Sacrament of the Altar. It is here that he expresses himself in his priestly function, totally subordinated to Christ the High Priest. So too his regular recitation of the daily offices of the church has been an example to us all and a challenge to those who feel we have outlived this form of worship. Here again his sense of being a part of the church comes out strong and clear. He is of that long line of priests who, true to the Benedictine ethos of Anglicanism, know the value of the Offices of Morning and Evening Prayer. Here too he has been a sign to the whole church, for these Offices are meant for the whole church and they are one of the greatest gifts we can offer to the whole Christian Body. It is significant that many people of other denominations are asking for information and even for instruction in this way

2. Holy Father, make us holy;
   Holy Jesus, make us holy;
   Holy Spirit, make us holy;
   Holy God, make us whole.

of punctuating the day with worship and intercession and dedication of the whole life to God.

It has not only been my privilege to walk with Desmond Tutu as a spiritual friend, but I have also been his confessor. About this I can say little. Only this perhaps: that like us all, he faces the constant attacks of the evil one, constantly seeks the grace of absolution and thus grows in holiness. He values the sacrament of penance highly. It may be the greatest offering he brings to the church as we seek reconciliation among the peoples of this land that he knows that all reconciliation must start with penitence, sorrow for sin and a new life of joyful praise, amendment and service.

Tough and compassionate[1]: Desmond Mpilo Tutu

Twenty years ago Desmond Tutu was seen by some as no more than a meddlesome priest. The majority of South Africans must have inwardly feared that he would suffer the fate of so many other courageous opponents of the apartheid state. Today Archbishop Tutu is, together with President Nelson Mandela, among the best known and most respected South Africans in the world.

His journey to recognition and influence can conceivably be traced to a letter he wrote, while Dean of St Mary's Cathedral in Johannesburg, in May 1976, to the then Prime Minister, John Vorster. He warned of his "nightmarish fear" that violence and bloodshed would envelop the country. Five weeks later, on 16 June, the shooting of Hector Peterson in Soweto triggered a bloody revolt against the state in dozens of townships, leaving scores dead.

> I write to you Sir, because like you I am deeply committed to real reconciliation with justice for all, and to peaceful change to a more just and open South African society in which the wonderful riches and wealth of our country will be shared more equitably.

Ten years after writing that letter, Desmond Tutu was enthroned as Archbishop of Cape Town. Today he is chairperson of the Truth and Reconciliation Commission. I asked him how he felt about the appointment. He spoke earnestly about the need to close that chapter of

---

1. This essay is a revised and updated version of an interview with Archbishop Tutu, first published in Charles Villa-Vicencio, *A spirit of hope: Conversations on politics, religion and values,* Skotaville, 1993.

the country's history which brought suffering to so many thousands of people: "the Truth and Reconciliation Commission is the middle path between two extremes," he suggested. "Some say, let us forget the past while others want revenge . . . Nobody claims the commission is the perfect solution. It does, however, give us a chance to deal spiritually, psychologically and politically with the problem. There are tough times ahead . . ." The Archbishop smiled: "Ek is moeg, man. Ek raak oud. (I am tired, man. I am getting old.) I was hoping to retire . . . But this thing is too important to turn away from. We need to be tough and yet compassionate . . ."

POLITICS AND RELIGION

The Archbishop disarmingly responds to suggestions of political unpredictability: "I have my idiosyncrasies the same as anyone else, and sometimes probably speak up when I should let things go. I try to think things through. I pray about matters. Obedience to God is very important for me. Perhaps it is my attempt to respond to the living, dynamic God that makes me appear unpredictable. Maybe this makes me ungovernable!" He laughs. "What I am suggesting is that the church must sit a little loose on political ideology and never be too concerned about being 'politically correct'. Our task is to be agents of the Kingdom of God, and this sometimes requires us to say unpopular things."

The Archbishop's theology is equally capable of suffering the charge of "incorrectness". He has managed to upset some Christians by suggesting that God is not a Christian! "If you say God is a Christian, what happens to God's relationship with the Jews? What about devout Muslims? The Dalai Lama is a person of unquestionable holiness. I've experienced God in a Buddhist temple." "The Archbishop is correct," an elderly parishioner observed. "The initial impact of what he says is, however, sometimes a shock to the system."

Nelson Mandela spent his first night of freedom at Bishopscourt, after twenty-seven years in prison. The next morning the Archbishop escorted Mr Mandela to his car, prayed for him and sent him on his way. "I can now get on with the work of the church," the Archbishop told reporters. Three years later his words still concern some Christians who struggle to discern the role of the church in the present political situation. "Before we simply got out there and disrupted things . . . we made the place ungovernable," observed a young member of a township church. "Now we are not sure what we ought to do."

I asked the Archbishop to revisit the February morning in 1990 when Mr Mandela left Bishopscourt. "I had hoped that the release would mark the normalisation of the political process in South Africa, and that I could take a far lower profile in the political arena," he observed. "Prior to February 1990 we often held political rallies under the guise of church services. Such actions were politically necessary and theologically correct. Then, with the unbanning of political organisations and the release of Nelson Mandela I believed the church should render a different kind of service to the community. I had hoped to leave the overtly political work to the politicians and to minister to the spiritual and material needs of people."

The Archbishop spoke of a practice he has followed for several years as a means of regaining his spiritual and physical strength:

> I often meet with a solitary in England. This wonderful person had for some time counselled me to become more contemplative. As I bade Mandela farewell, I thought that perhaps that moment had come. I wanted to have more time for meditation and more time to give to people who are hurting, to visit the so-called informal settlements and squatter camps on a more regular basis and to use my resources to renew the lives of the poor. I wanted to get out of the limelight and to enable the church as a whole to contribute in a quiet and effective way to the healing of the nation. I continue to believe that this is an area of ministry which the church has neglected through the apartheid years. We need to empower people to rise above their circumstances, to reclaim their full humanity and to seize the moment in which we live in South Africa. Blacks and whites need to rise to the challenge which God is offering us.

He spoke of the inter-relationship between faith and politics: "Faith is a highly political thing. At the centre of all that we believe as Christians is the incarnation – the participation of God in the affairs of this world. As followers of that God we too must be politically engaged. We need inner resources, however, in order to face the political demands of our time." Returning to the hopes he attached to Nelson Mandela's release from prison, he continued:

Well, things didn't quite work the way I had expected when Nelson Mandela was released from prison. I was hoping for too much. I soon discovered that the poor, to whom I sought to minister in a new way, were continuing to suffer because of the grandstanding and Prima donna behaviour of some of our politicians. So, I once again visited homeland leaders, spoke with the leaders of the national liberation movements and with government representatives. In a polite but often forceful manner I have tried to knock their heads together, tried to persuade them to stop dilly-dallying and to get the democratic process under way. My fear is that if we do not get on with the process the violence that is racking our country will escalate to the point of no return. To an extent I have found myself thrown back into the rough and tumble of the political arena, but playing a new role. Any political role which I played earlier was of a caretaker kind. Our leaders were in prison, church leaders were thrust into political roles. Today our role is to persuade politicians to get on with the job.

Stressing the importance of timing and process in politics, the Archbishop spoke of the facilitating role he had played, together with Bishop Stanley Mogoba, in arranging the meeting between Nelson Mandela and Chief Buthelezi. "My role was that of a catalyst. The idea of the meeting had been in the air for some time. I had just served in a very beautiful eucharist at the consecration of the Bishop of Zululand, Chief Buthelezi was present and the mood was correct. I put the question to him and he agreed. The opportunity to speak to Nelson Mandela was in an equally apt situation. We had participated in the Gandhi centenary celebrations and the unveiling of the Gandhi statue. I put the question to him and he agreed. The task of the church is to facilitate the political process, rather than itself to be overtly political." Several years ago Archbishop Tutu was asked to explain his persistent refusal to espouse political ambitions. "Archbishop Makarios, the Ayatolah Khomeini and Dr D.F. Malan," he replied.

Archbishop Tutu's decision, at the time of the democratic elections in 1994, not to allow his priests to belong to political parties was regarded by some as an example of something he would have done well not to have turned into an issue. "Some clergy were very angry with me. We all have personal political persuasions, but as ordained clergy and repre-

sentatives of the church we have a special responsibility to make ourselves as approachable as possible to all political groupings. We are
required to suspend our personal political persuasions at the level of
party membership in order to facilitate the political process at another
level. Take Natal for instance. It would not only threaten the life of a
priest if it were known that he or she was a member of this or that political party, it would also render the ministry of that priest virtually impossible in some rural and township parishes." The 1995 Synod of Anglican
Bishops rescinded the prohibition of priests belonging to political parties. The matter continues, however, to be a sensitive issue.

Tutu has been more outspoken than most other church leaders in
his criticism of South Africa's post-apartheid government. He suggested that some politicians slowed down the gravy train just long enough
to get on board themselves. Asked what he was going to do with his
salary as chairperson of the Truth and Reconciliation Commission, he
indicated that he would pay half of this into education bursary funds.
Insisting on the need not to get rich from any post-apartheid initiative,
he is equally committed to providing a prophetic stance in relation to
government. "Our task as church," he insists, "is to remind our leaders, including Mr Mandela, that they are not God."

COMMUNISM

We talked about communism. "Some suggest that I am anti-commun-
ist," Tutu observed. "That is not the case. My objection is essentially
theological. Historical materialism, on which communism is based, is
essentially an atheist philosophy." He accepts that there are those who
see a space for God within this philosophy and that there are Christians who belong to the South African Communist Party. His concern
is, however, that communism fails to locate God at the centre of history. "Communism places too much trust and confidence in human
beings. For people to be good and just, they need to be exposed to the
grace and goodness of God. Historical materialism does not do this.
That, in a nutshell, is my problem with communism."

The Archbishop adds that this does not mean he is not prepared to
work with communists: "I immediately need to add," he continues,
"that I have had the greatest admiration for people like Joe Slovo and
Chris Hani. I walked arm in arm with them. Communists and Christians have co-operated in the struggle against apartheid and I see no

reason why we cannot work together for justice in the future."

He spoke of his participation in Chris Hani's funeral, for which he was severely criticised by some. The Archbishop had stated in his sermon: "For us Chris was a hero and great leader, irrespective of whether he was a communist or not. We were oppressed by those who claimed to be Christian." To what does he ascribe the hostility from sections of his church to his participation in the funeral? "White fear and confusion. How can I turn my back on a person like Hani? He has done more for justice than most Christians."

THE CHALLENGE OF AFRICA

As President of the All Africa Conference of Churches (AACC), the Archbishop spoke about the loss of human values in Africa: "There have been the most atrocious violations of human rights in this continent and the church ought to have a very red face for having held its silence." Addressing a general assembly of the AACC in Togo in 1987, the Archbishop pointed to the example of Archbishop Janani Luwan who was murdered after criticising the atrocities of General Idi Amin, suggesting that this might be the awful price that the church in Africa would be required to pay to regain its integrity. Tutu recalls his visit to the 25th anniversary of the AACC in Nairobi in 1988. "In my sermon I referred to the galling fact that there was often less freedom in independent Africa than in the much-maligned colonial days, and that if detention without trial is evil in South Africa it must be evil everywhere else." The Voice of Kenya was present at the rally but his speech featured neither on TV nor on the radio. *The Standard* (a Nairobi daily) quoted the Kenyan Minister of Manpower Development and Employment, who dismissed the Archbishop's criticism, saying that in Kenya detention was "constitutionally gazetted and part of development"! Another minister observed that it was "sad and bad" for the Archbishop to make such remarks in Kenya. Having been welcomed to Kenya by President Arap Moi, the Archbishop's departure was less propitious. "President Moi was not happy with me. But he still allows me to use the VIP lounge!"

At the Harare Assembly of the AACC in 1995 Archbishop Tutu said that Africans were disillusioned with politicians and tired of corruption and repression. "Africa will not be the same again," he told delegates in his opening address. "The so-called ordinary people, God's favourites, are sick and tired of corruption, repression, injustice,

41

poverty, disease and the violation of their human rights. They are crying out 'enough is enough'!" Speaking in words reminiscent of those he has used in South Africa, he remarked: "It is exhilarating when you are able to say to dictators everywhere: You have had it! You have had it! This is God's world and you will bite the dust! They think it will not happen but it does, and they bite the dust comprehensively and ignominiously."

Responding to President Robert Mugabe's opening remarks on the prophetic role of the church in Africa, the Archbishop observed: "I assure you, Mr President, we will want to continue to keep governments on their toes as we seek to be the voice of the voiceless. It is the role of the church to be the conscience of society." Despite this, the Archbishop reports that Mr Mugabe responded warmly and positively towards him. "He insisted that it is right and proper that ministers of religion should speak out clearly regarding the moral and ethical implications of any policies and actions, placing the insights of the church's social doctrine at the service of the wider community. The task of the church in Africa, as everywhere else in the world, is to insist that the government is honest and that the cries of the poor be heard in the highest decision-making structures in the land."

A PRINCE OF THE CHURCH

The character and person of Desmond Tutu is both a contradiction and a challenge to anyone trying to do justice to all that he is. He is at once both a prince of the church and a very ordinary and humble person.

He has transformed Bishopscourt from a place of neglect to a place of grandeur. He has given the office of the Archbishop of Cape Town a status that it has not had in generations. He is perhaps the most celebrated cleric in the world today. "His tenure will be an impossible act to follow," one of his priests observed. He has used his ecclesial dignity to confront presidents, prime ministers and ministers of state, while showing a deep pastoral concern to minister to those occupying high office. To the chagrin of some he has on several occasions gone the second mile to consult with former officials of the apartheid regime – when other church leaders had resolved not to do so. In so doing he has dug in his heels with a resolve and outspokenness unequalled by others. Former Prime Minister Vorster discovered this when the

Bishop terminated his talks with the government several years ago. P.W. Botha was reprimanded on more than one occasion and President F.W. de Klerk has experienced both the charm and the wrath of the Archbishop.

He carries the pomp, ceremony and lavishness associated with high church episcopacy with aplomb. Even a sense of regality. There is also another side to Desmond Tutu. He is a man of the people, a simple parish priest and a son of the soil of Africa. He can talk with all the solemnity and precision of an ecclesiastical teacher of things divine, and laugh, joke and taunt with all the eloquence of the Soweto and Johannesburg streets. A man for all occasions, he can speak to alienated black youth, to the most pious evangelicals, to white nationalist Afrikaners, and to the secular business community. When a friend broke her ankle she received a bouquet of flowers with a note saying, "I'll come and kiss it better". A bereaved family, who had never met the Archbishop, received a pastoral visit after it was reported in the newspaper that their son (who attended an Anglican church school) had been tragically killed. Township kids are invited to Bishopscourt for a picnic – and the Archbishop is there to enjoy it with them. A personable man, always ready to make a phone call or write a personal note, he will step down from a stage in a crowded hall to greet a friend. Desmond Tutu observes: "I like to regard myself as primarily a priest, whose task it is to minister to people, leading them in the ways of the gospel. I am also a bishop whose task it is to be a minister and shepherd to priests and laity alike. I take this calling seriously."

SPIRITUALITY AND THEOLOGY

Those who know the Archbishop best soon recognise that there are two overriding dimensions to his character. He is a profoundly spiritual person and deeply theological in his understanding of life.

His spirituality is profound to a level that some regard as simplistic. Regular in prayer, meditation and fasting, he administers the sacrament to himself during flights across the Atlantic. Few formal or informal meetings take place in his office that do not commence with prayer, and many a hardened reporter has been told to close his or her eyes and pray when all he or she was trying to do was report on an event that involved the Archbishop.

The Archbishop on one occasion withdrew from a conference held

43

at St Peter's Conference Centre at Hammanskraal, after delegates had been struggling all day to agree on a particular statement. He later returned and announced that he had been alone before God, and shared with the conference the insight he had gained. His sincerity earned the response of a delegate who obviously disagreed with his counsel: "You put me at a disadvantage, Father. I would dare to argue with you but not with God."

A subtle form of manipulation, some have suggested. "Whatever Desmond is, he is not a democrat," an Anglican priest told me. "He can be uncompromisingly authoritarian." When he believes he is right it is not easy to change his mind. "It is extremely difficult to know and discern the will of God," Tutu insists. "It involves thoughtfulness, a willingness to search the scriptures, an ability to plumb the depths of the Christian tradition, and consultation. God's will has to do with what is right, just, decent and healing of the wounds of society. To know what this means we need to cleanse ourselves of ourselves – of our fears, greed, ambitions and personal desires. This is where prayer, fasting, meditation and the sacraments play such an important role. Honest prayer and disciplined living is an incredibly illuminating and revealing thing."

The Archbishop is also a theologian. His books, articles in professional journals and conference presentations are enough to make the point. More than that, his thinking and everyday activity is theological. He locates theology at the centre of the political fray:

> Theology is among the most important and crucial disciplines in South Africa today. It reminds us of the worth and potential of people. It tells us that no one is expendable and that the rights and dignity of even those who society regards as insignificant are to be treated with respect. Only when this lesson is learned will there be peace. Theology also teaches us that all people, including the most respected and unquestionably decent leaders are mere mortals, capable of succumbing to the temptations and the blandishments of power. This means we should not become disillusioned or cynical if those who are oppressed should one day become the oppressors of tomorrow. Theology alerts us to this possibility, reminding us that sin is a stubborn, persistent dimension of the human character. We must be vigilant in ensuring that the good that is within all people

triumphs over the evil that is also there. That, briefly, is the task of the church in South Africa and Africa today. We have an enormous responsibility. At a very simple level, we must commit outselves to tell the truth. We must identify evil wherever we see it. The lies in which South Africa is wallowing must end. We must never again tolerate a situation where a General can simply inform a Commission of Inquiry that he has lied and get away with it. There can be no justice and no peace where government and security force officials can tell lies with impunity. The problem is that such things are contagious. If we do not do something about it we could end up as a nation of liars.

CHRISTIANITY AND OTHER FAITHS

Archbishop Tutu has been a patron of the South African chapter of the World Conference of Religion and Peace since its inception. He spoke about religious pluralism:

For me, Jesus Christ is the revelation of God, but I am opposed to proselytisation. Our task as Christians is simply to live attractive lives that are transparent with the gospel. We take ourselves far too seriously when we think that God is relying on our evangelical campaigns to make everyone Christians, in order for them to enter into communion with God.

People sometimes ask me what I make of the fourth gospel which quotes Jesus as saying: "No one comes to the Father except by me" (John 14:6). The question is whether this means it is by the incarnate Christ or the preincarnate Logos that we enter into union with the divine? Surely it is through the eternal creative Word of God that this happens, and there are so many different manifestations of God's Word. If this is not the case, how do we account for the encounter between God and Abraham, Sarah or Moses? Jesus Christ had not yet appeared. I have encountered holiness, spiritual insight and the presence of God in people of many different religions. I cannot be so arrogant as to insist that these people become Christians.

45

Concerned that Christianity is too influenced by imperialist and racist ideas which reject all that does not fit into European and missionary world views, the Archbishop insists that we develop a freedom to use our own cultural metaphors to speak of God. "By encouraging people to do this, we enable them to discern the presence of God in their midst." This, of course, has major implications for the church of Africa. Addressing the question of syncretism and fears of the loss of a Christian identity, the Archbishop comments: "For goodness sake, God was able to look after God long before we were around. It is not for us to decide who God is and where this God is to be found."

LIFE'S JOURNEY

In his own unique way Desmond Tutu entertained and needled the Eloff Commission, appointed by the government in 1983 to investigate the activities of the South African Council of Churches, by explaining, with a touch of irony, how his father Zachariah Tutu, a school headmaster and a somewhat proud Fingo, inexplicably married Aletha Matlhare, a Motswana woman who washed clothes for a white family. "Am I Xhosa or Motswana?" He soon, together with his two sisters, learned to speak Xhosa and Tswana as well as English and Afrikaans. His roots are inherently African. He can be no other. He is intensely South African, and yet for many years his travel documents declared his nationality as "indeterminable at present". A man with a huge sense of humour, he laughs as he observes that it would be no bad thing if a few more of us were less sure of our precise identity – "it might help us to find a new common identity in South Africa".

Born on 7 October 1931 in the township outside of Klerksdorp in the Transvaal, Desmond Mpilo Tutu married Leah Nomalizo Shenxane, a school teacher, and former student of his father. Neither of them could have foreseen the prominence that would characterise their lives. Having earned a Teacher's Diploma from Pretoria Bantu Normal College in 1953 and a correspondence BA degree from the University of South Africa in 1954, he taught at Johannesburg Bantu High School and later at Munsieville High School in Krugersdorp. Called to the priesthood, he earned a Licentiate in Theology at St. Peter's Theological College in Rosettenville, and he was ordained priest in 1961. Proceeding overseas he earned his BD, BD Hons and MTh degrees at Kings College at the University of London. Returning to

South Africa, he lectured at the Federal Theological Seminary in Alice, while serving as chaplain to students at Fort Hare University. From there he was appointed to the University of Botswana, Lesotho and Swaziland, where he taught on the Roma campus in Lesotho. Next came a four-year appointment as Associate Director of the Theological Education Fund of the WCC, which again located him in England. On his return home he was appointed Dean of Johannesburg. He later became Bishop of Lesotho, vacating that position a few years later to become General Secretary of the South African Council of Churches. After serving the SACC in this capacity for several years, he became Bishop of Johannesburg. In 1986 he was enthroned as Archbishop of Cape Town.

His many honorary doctorates, international awards, medals and salutations are too numerous to mention. Among them was the Nobel Peace Prize, awarded to him in 1984. The award was greeted with an official silence from the government. Even the staunchly progovernment newspaper, *Die Vaderland*, thought that while "the man says things that stick in one's craw and sends blood rushing to one's head . . . formal congratulations by the state for one of its citizens who had gained international recognition decidedly would have been in order". On the other hand, Alan Paton, the doyen of liberal thought in South Africa at the time, thought that the Peace Prize should have gone to someone whose concern it was to feed the hungry and not one who called for economic pressure which "could put a man out of a job and make his family go hungry so that some high moral principle could be upheld".

Awards have continued to flow. There is, however, a strange although not an unpredictable irony about his acclamations – not until 1993 did any South African university choose to recognise his achievements. The award of an Honorary Doctorate of Laws by the University of Cape Town came belatedly. Asked to comment, he carefully observed: "In the eighties UCT gave honorary degrees to blacks who were acceptable to the white establishment, in a way that I was not. There was a time when I would have given it back and I don't need it now. But I've decided to accept it as an act of healing." Having declined an invitation to take up an appointment as visiting professor at Emory University after his retirement in June 1996, Archbishop Tutu has accepted the position as chairperson of the Truth and Reconciliation Commission. I suggested to him that his role as chairperson would necessarily require a different set of skills to that of being Archbishop. "Yes, of course. But then I have also developed a certain style of leadership which will be difficult to change."

UNSTOPPABLE

What does the Archbishop fear most about the future? "Violence," he insists. "My greatest concern is how to break the cycle of endemic violence. I am concerned that there are political leaders who may refuse to accept the outcome of a democratic election. I fear the involvement of sinister neo-facist international organisations like the World Preservationist Movement."

"I, at the same time, believe in a great God," the Archbishop continued. "The violence, the resistance to change and the horrible things that we are presently experiencing must not be allowed to stop the inevitable. Peace will take a Promethean effort on our part, but ultimately it will come. I say this because I firmly believe that this is God's world, and God is a God of justice. This is what makes us unstoppable."

The transfiguration of politics

There has been a long tradition in South Africa of priests and *predikants* who have been deeply involved in political issues and struggles. Some names immediately come to mind: John Philip, superintendent of the London Missionary Society and doughty opponent of slavery; John Dube and Zacharias Mahabane, early leaders of the African National Congress; D.F. Malan, leader of the National Party when it came to power in 1948; Joost de Blank and Trevor Huddleston, who were regular thorns in the flesh of the apartheid regime in the nineteen-fifties; and Beyers Naudé, the founder of the Christian Institute. There have been many others, just as today there are a number of ordained clergy who are members of parliament or regional and local government legislatures. Depending on which side of the political fence people stand, the political priest or *predikant* has often been a target of criticism, accused of dragging politics into religion or using religion as a smokescreen for personal ambition and political self-interest. Archbishop Tutu is no stranger to such accusations. Yet in many ways his political role and witness has helped to clarify the difference between a "political priest" and the true pastor and prophet amongst the politicians.

A POLITICAL PRIEST?

Desmond Tutu has undoubtedly been a major political figure in South Africa during the past few decades. But he is not the proverbial "political priest", despite appearances to the contrary. He became a political leader by default when those elected to lead the liberation movement (embodied in the ANC and PAC) were forced into exile, imprisoned, or killed. But it was not Tutu's choice to assume their mantle, nor was he elected to such an office. It was an extraordinary calling to which he somewhat reluctantly responded. He had no alternative but to become a spokesperson for the victims of apartheid and a prophet to the perpetrators of racist oppression. His primary calling, however, was to be a priest, a representative of Christ, a minister in the church of God. He has never wavered from that summons. But there come extraordinary moments in the life of nations when priests have to become prophets and provide leadership on the political terrain. This is not something which they do out of self-interest; it is something thrust upon them in an hour of desperate need. That is what distinguishes them from the "political priest" or the "priestly politician".

There are further reasons why it is inappropriate to describe Desmond Tutu as a "political priest" or even a "priestly politician". Politicians are invariably members of particular political parties whose policies they endorse and which they represent in the public arena. Tutu was certainly identified with the aims and objectives of the liberation movement and has always had close ties with the ANC and its leadership. He was deeply involved in the struggles of the United Democratic Front, of which he was a patron, in the final years of apartheid rule. But he is not a "party man". As much as Tutu may be ideologically aligned with the ANC, he is not a member, and he has always sought to be inclusive in his relationships to political parties, insisting that the Church of the Province is not the ANC at prayer, nor should it be. To the consternation of his friends he is sometimes doggedly politically incorrect. Often this has meant that he has ploughed his own furrow, taken a different stand, and expressed sharp criticism, to the annoyance of party leaders and members. But he has never wanted to lead his own party – as has been the case in some other countries. He quite explicitly eschewed the option taken by Bishop Abel Muzorewa in Zimbabwe of entering politics to achieve his goals.

Tutu has not been a "party man" for the simple reason that he has sought to be a servant of Jesus Christ and his church. That is his party. Sometimes this has meant solidarity with a particular political party platform; sometimes it has meant resistance – but always it has meant critical distance even when in solidarity. It was largely as a result of his efforts that the Anglican bishops forbade priests from belonging to political parties after the unbanning of the liberation movements. How else could they act as the agents of reconciliation within their conflict-ridden parishes? All of this has been fundamental to Tutu's own role as a political reconciler, not only in South Africa but also in the rest of Africa. As a Nobel Laureate, and President of the All African Conference of Churches during the past decade, he has expended much time and energy on trying to help resolve many of Africa's political crises. Whatever his success rate in this regard, there can be no doubt that his role has been significant and widely welcomed by heads of state, politicians and church leaders because of his moral integrity, his concern for justice and peace, as well as his ability to relate meaningfully to the conflicting parties.

Most politicians are glad when their opponents lose face and suffer defeat, and some rejoice when their political enemies suffer physical pain. But that can never be the attitude of the true priest. The true priest as a representative of Christ is always one who seeks to be the vicar of humankind in all its pain and agony. The true priest will not want cheap reconciliation any more than he or she will be a purveyor of cheap grace, but the true priest does not want to see the death of the enemy but his or her conversion. The path of the peacemaker is certainly the struggle for justice; but the goal of the peacemaker is the conversion of the enemy into a friend. The true priest cannot be neutral in the political arena. How can one who is truly called to such a ministry not take sides against injustice, oppression, racism, lies; how can such a ministry not align itself without equivocation with those who are the victims of society and those who struggle for freedom and justice? But taking sides, as Jesus of Nazareth took sides, does not mean rejecting the enemy, the opponent, the oppressor. It means seeking ways to bring opponents to their senses, to help them repent and change, to bring them on board. How often Tutu told us whites to "join the winning side" – not because it was winning, but because it was the side of justice and the only way to peace.

The danger facing all politicians is not just becoming remote from the people they are meant to serve, wrapped up in the world of power play, but that of losing their own souls. That is one good reason why politicians need pastors and prophets. Pastors to care for their souls; prophets to remind them of the demands of justice. The two tasks are inseparable sides of the same coin. Without compromising his stand against apartheid, time and again Tutu tried to relate in a pastoral way to the likes of State President P.W. Botha, despite being rebuffed and maligned. His letters to those in power were tough and unequivocal, but they always sought to provide an opportunity for dialogue and an invitation to find a way forward as "Christian brothers" and members of the "body of Christ". After the dramatic changes which occurred in 1990, Tutu continued his pastoral ministry to the emergent new political leadership. Yet, painful as it proved to be, once the new parliament was elected to power in 1994 he found it necessary to criticise the extent to which former fighters for freedom and justice had jumped on the "gravy train" of power and privilege. He was not only critical because he felt that it was a misuse of public funds, but because he was concerned that it could undermine the integrity and commitment of those elected to high office. Having gained the "whole world" they were in danger of "selling their souls". Could that be, he often asked, what the struggle against apartheid had really been all about?

The litmus test which distinguishes the "political priest" from the priest who reluctantly takes on a political role in extraordinary times is what role he or she assumes when the times become more ordinary, when the exiles return and the prisoners are released. Those who are concerned about political power will seek ways to guard their turf. They will, with some justification, claim that having been political leaders (even if by default) they should continue to play a political role. The priest in Tutu immediately recognised that this was not to be the case. So he signalled a withdrawal from political leadership. That was now the task of those elected by the people. There were some former comrades in the struggle who were critical of Tutu because at this crucial moment of transition he seemed to be withdrawing into an ecclesiastical ghetto and taking all his priests with him; that he was returning to pursue the "real business of the church", the cure of souls. "Why not stay active in politics?" asked a Danish journalist:

Tutu: I am not a politician.
Response: Yes, you are.
Tutu: No, I am a pastor, I am a pastor.
Question: But you are also a politician?
Tutu: Uh-uh, no I am not. I am a church person who believes that religion does not just deal with a certain compartment of life. Religion has a relevance for the whole of life and we have to say whether a particular policy is consistent with the policy of Jesus Christ or not, and if you mean to say that that is political, then I am a politician in those terms. But it won't be as one who is involved in party politics. (Tutu 1994: 204).

PUTTING SOUL INTO POLITICS

A politician has to be politically shrewd to succeed or even survive. "Priestly politicians" are usually very shrewd! But that is not why Tutu has survived long after most politicians who opposed him have left the public arena. Not that Tutu has lacked political insight, or is without "godly cunning". But this arises more from Tutu's spirituality and theological conviction. There is much evidence in his political utterances and actions of what has been referred to as a "second naivety". A "first naivety" is childishness. It is a lack of understanding. A "second naivety" is being childlike. It is an intuitive grasp of reality which arises out of experience, a knowledge of good and evil, indeed, a knowledge of human nature. But even more, it is childlike in its ability to keep hope alive in the future when the political analysts have already determined that there is no future. Being childlike is a gift, a grace if you like. It is not a denial of reality nor an escape from reality – it is a different way of relating to reality. Only the childlike have the faith which moves mountains.

Which leads us to the heart of the matter. Tutu wants to put "soul back into politics". This much is clear simply from his commendation of Jim Wallis's excellent book, *The soul of politics*. "It is riveting stuff", Tutu writes, "just what the doctor ordered for a hardened, cynical, and disheartened and disillusioned world." The book, he added, "shows how it is possible for all of us to become more human, living in an environment that is hospitable to people, where they matter, where justice and compassion and caring are at a premium". If politics is the "art of the possible", Tutu is more concerned about achieving the impossible. This has little to do with political analysis or shrewdness; it has to do with faith in the redemptive power and purpose of God.

In his sermon on the occasion of his enthronement as Archbishop of Cape Town on 7 September 1986 – a few months after the second State of Emergency had been declared, and at a time when resistance and repression were entering a new phase – Tutu gave the rationale for his political involvement:

> If we take the incarnation seriously we must be concerned
> about where people live, how they live, whether they have
> justice, whether they are uprooted and dumped as rubbish
> in resettlement camps, whether they are detained without
> trial, whether they receive an inferior education, whether

they have a say in the decisions that affect their lives most deeply . . . Friends, we do this not because of our politics, but because of our religion. Blessed be God our God for being such a God (Tutu 1994: 117).

Several themes which continually recur in Tutu's sermons and speeches indicate the theological premises on which his political concerns are based. First and foremost is his repeated conviction that the world is God's world, and that God is the God of justice and liberation, as well as peace and reconciliation. Secondly is Tutu's affirmation of the dignity of all human persons as created "in the image of God". We dare not treat others with any kind of contempt or discrimination or cause them to suffer, for then we are denying their importance to God. Which leads, thirdly, to Tutu's belief in the incarnation, for the incarnation is the redemptive outworking of God's love for all men and women and the whole creation. In Christ, God has entered into the human condition, shared its pain and suffering, and brought about our redemption at great cost. At the centre of the incarnation, for Tutu, lies the profound mystery of the transfiguration, a theme which has become ever more prominent in his reflections since his enthronement as Archbishop of Cape Town. On that occasion he declared:

The principle of transfiguration says nothing, no one and no situation is "untransfigurable", that the very creation, nature, waits expectantly for its transfiguration . . . that an erstwhile persecutor can become the greatest missionary of the truth . . . It is the principle of transfiguration at work when an instrument of the most painful and shameful death can become the life-giving Cross which Christians wear with pride and which is traced over them at significant moments in their life . . . (Tutu 1994: 121).

Tutu has known moments of deep despair, and on many occasions during the struggle he expressed his fears about the future of South Africa. Writing to Prime Minister B.J. Vorster in 1976, Tutu spoke of his "growing nightmarish fear that unless something drastic is done very soon then bloodshed and violence are going to happen in South Africa almost inevitably". (Tutu 1994: 10). Tragically his warnings were not heeded and his fears were frightfully fulfilled. Yet, throughout the years of struggle, somehow Tutu retained hope, a hope born out of faith in God and nurtured in prayer. This is what kept him going over the long haul.

This also explains something of his overwhelming sense of gratitude to God and his exuberant joy which has become so much part of his character since the unbanning of the liberation movements and especially since the first democratic elections in South Africa in 1994. His faith in God's ability to transfigure reality through human instrumentality had been vindicated.

Addressing a congregation in Westminster Abbey in celebration of the fiftieth anniversary of the founding of the United Nations, Tutu referred to the many hopeless situations in the world which had been turned around and then, with reference to South Africa, he declared:

> We have seen a horrible-looking caterpillar being transformed into a gorgeous butterfly – the world's pariah welcomed like the prodigal of old back into the fold . . . a nightmare has been turned into a beautiful reality – a spectacular victory, a wonderful success story . . . So let us go forth and celebrate this jubilee and hold before the world the dream of the UN, its vision for a world of peace, of equality, of freedom, of love, of caring, sharing, compassion, of laughter and joy (Tutu 1995).

BIBLIOGRAPHY

Tutu, Desmond (1994), *The rainbow people of God: The making of a peaceful revolution*, New York: Doubleday.

Tutu, Desmond (1995), Address given in Westminster Abbey, 24 October 1995, Anglican News Service.

Wallis, Jim (1994), *The soul of politics*, Maryknoll, New York: Orbis.

Two Archbishops of Cape Town, Desmond Tutu and Geoffrey Clayton: One on a wicked path, the other a true champion of the black cause?

I t was once observed that the triumph of evil is not so much that some people wreak havoc in the lives of others, but that good people do nothing. It is, of course, one thing to do nothing about evil and quite another to appear to be doing something about it. Now that apartheid has been removed from the statute books of South Africa, it is intriguing to compare two archbishops, Geoffrey Hare Clayton and Desmond Mpilo Tutu, to see whether it is appropriate to say that Tutu stands firmly in the Clayton tradition (Villa-Vicencio 1986: 3). Both are recognised as having been opposed to the racial laws in South Africa. What this paper hopes to unravel is the degree to which their actions attest to their commitment to the cause of black liberation.

A comparison of these two ecclesiastics must have some limitations. Clayton and Tutu came from two different worlds. Clayton was born into a white middle-class family in England where he spent twenty-five years as a parish priest. In 1934 he was appointed Bishop of Johannesburg. Tutu, on the other hand, was born of black South African parents who struggled to provide their son with what they regarded as the best education. Despite the limitations of the educational system, he rose to be one of the greatest ecclesiastics that the South African Anglican Church has ever produced. He became the Dean of Johannesburg (1975), General Secretary of the SACC (1978), Bishop of Johannesburg (1985), and Archbishop of Cape Town (1986). His tenure as Archbishop coincided with the "total onslaught" era of P. W. Botha, which could best be described as particularly turbulent. Whilst Clayton saw the ushering in of apartheid, Tutu saw its demise.

In his biography of Clayton, Alan Paton suggests that both the African clergy and people regarded Clayton as "the champion of their cause" (Paton 1973: 63). Blacks believed that Clayton held that it was the duty of the church "to be on guard against any possibility of the State's suppression of individual worth". Whilst Clayton truly championed their cause he was, nevertheless, opposed to "arguments that favoured immediate and full enfranchisement of the whole population" (Worsnip 1991: 17, 21). The majority of South African white liberals believed that a fair number of black South Africans lacked political sophistication. They held that there was still a need for blacks to be fully developed before they could be entrusted with the right to decide for themselves. These liberals were quite content to play the role of chaperons to blacks (see Hulley 1993: 146). There is indeed an element of truth in Paton's observation that Clayton was a champion of the black cause, but one needs to unravel the mystery surrounding this alleged championship. This can be done by examining Clayton's treatment of blacks within the ecclesiastical structures of his day.

CLAYTON'S EPISCOPACY

When Clayton was enthroned as the second Anglican Bishop of Johannesburg in May 1934, the only black priest with the rank of canon was Andreas Rakale. For fifteen years during Clayton's episcopacy in Johannesburg no black priest became a canon. This does not necessarily suggest that the bishop was against the advancement of black clergy; it may mean that no black priests were qualified for such a position.

The Church of the Province of South Africa (CPSA) which Clayton joined in 1934 was steeped in segregation, and this was not Clayton's doing. It was Cecil John Rhodes who laid the foundations of the segregationist legacy on which apartheid was built. Rhodes had wryly said:

> I will lay down my policy on this native question . . . either you receive them on an equal footing as citizens or call them a subject race . . . I have made up my mind that there must be a class [race] legislation . . . The Native is to be treated as a child and denied franchise. We must adopt the system of despotism as works well in India in our relations with the barbarians of South Africa . . . These are my politics and these are politics of South Africa (La Guma 1972: 13).

Clayton's ideas were fundamentally at variance with Rhodes's ideas. But although Clayton's ideas were well ahead of his time, he had to be careful not to estrange some of the stalwarts of the Church.

In fact, the outlook of the majority of the white Anglican membership in South Africa had been conditioned by the then current atmosphere of colonialism. Clayton joined a church whose practice was at variance with its profession. This can clearly be seen in the segregated institutions within the Anglican Church long before the laws forbidding integration were passed. This white exclusivism was highlighted by their refusal to admit so-called coloured pupils to white Anglican schools, an anomaly which Clayton justified (see Walsh 1983: 75).[1] This rejection was mainly due to the fear of being swamped by other races.

In his charge to the 1934 Johannesburg Diocesan Synod, before the apartheid era, Clayton said that "the Jew was not the same as the Greek, and the male the same as female. Neither is the European the same as the African. We are not going to be all alike in Heaven." This conviction drove Clayton to suggest that blacks and whites should not worship together, as this would have a disastrous effect on the development of African spirituality. In the same charge Clayton spelt out that the first duty of the church was to offer God the worship due to his name and the second duty was "the service which she owes to mankind" (Clayton 1934; see also *The Watchman* Dec. 1934; Paton 1973: 50). Clayton, however, never spelt out what service to humankind meant.

Clayton had the onerous responsibility of bridging the apparent chasm between blacks and whites. Two incidents can be cited that prove the point. In 1947 at the Diocesan Synod of Johannesburg a motion asked Clayton to appoint a commission to explore the possibility of dividing the diocese into two separate dioceses, one for the African and the other for the non-African members.[2] Clayton found this motion so bizarre that he asked Geoffrey Fisher, the Archbishop of Canterbury, for advice.

1. This refers to an incident when the governors of one of the Anglican white schools in Cape Town turned coloured pupils away under the pretext that the whites who supported the school financially would withdraw their financial support. Clayton's successor in Johannesburg bemoaned the fact that the Anglican Church in South Africa had not done anything to integrate the institution under her control. See A. Reeves (1962), *South Africa – yesterday and tomorrow: The challenge to Christians*, London: Victor Gollancz, Ltd., p. 147.
2. In August 1947 the Secretary of the Malvern Parochial Council submitted a resolution on the desirability of dividing the diocese on racial lines. (CPSA Archive AB 2013/D1, the CPSA Diocese of Johannesburg Minute Book 1936 -1961.) See also Fisher Papers, Vol. 29, 1947, in the Lambeth Palace Library in London.

The second incident had to do with the translation of Clayton from Johannesburg to Cape Town. When the Diocese of Johannesburg became vacant, one of the names submitted to the Elective Assembly was that of Donald Harris, the Archdeacon of Bedford in England. William Palmer, who was co-ordinating the electoral process in the diocese, wrote to the Archbishop of Canterbury, Geoffrey Fisher, asking whether Harris was a suitable candidate for a diocese "which as far as colour prejudice is concerned is likely to be a storm centre in the next years" (Fisher 1949, Vol. 58). Palmer's letter highlights the polarisation between blacks and whites and his acute concern to have a bishop who would be an effective crusader against the colour bar. Palmer was possibly looking for a sturdy figure to build on the firm foundation laid by Clayton.

It is true that Clayton did criticise the social imbalances in South Africa. He appealed both for the election of African representatives on the City Council of Johannesburg and for the abolition of the colour bar in industry (Paton 1973: 115). But he was ambiguous on issues of social justice. How committed was Clayton to integration in the domain over which he was in charge? After the Second World War, the Rev L. E. Sigamoney submitted a Resolution arguing that since Africans had fought in the cause of democracy, the Church should educate public opinion and agitate for the removal of all legislative restrictions which barred them from enjoying full citizenship in South Africa. This Resolution also stated that blacks who were "the majority of the inhabitants [of South Africa] be given a say in the administration on an equal basis with the minority". Clayton found the Resolution too radical because it did not represent the mind of the majority of white South Africans. The Resolution involved an outright rejection of racialism and that was never Clayton's style of doing things. Clayton cautiously suggested that the Synod should set up a special commission "to make a careful study of the question of the franchise" (Johannesburg Minute Book). Evidence does suggest that the policy Clayton "advocated was essentially of a gradualist and rather paternalist type" (Hastings 1979: 23).

The Rev. Redvers Rouse, who was the Archdeacon of the Native Mission, campaigned to raise the stipends of black priests and to work towards parity of stipends between black and white priests in the Diocese of Johannesburg. This venture had to be abandoned when Clayton declared that "an equalised stipend would in many cases make the African priests the richest man in his community" (Paton

1973: 65). At the time none of the English-speaking churches in South Africa had parity of stipends for their priests.

Clayton spent a great deal of time talking about social problems rather than attempting to find solutions to these problems. In the 1940s he set up a commission to explore ways and means of transforming South African society. This commission had a preponderance of white membership with only two blacks, hardly a representative body. The commission declared that in principle there was nothing wrong with segregation. Clayton felt that any demand for "the immediate removal of the colour-bar was absurd" and a year before he died he told whites at a summer school at the University of Cape Town: "I do not think that we ought to hurry what is called integration" (Paton 1973: 118-119, 266).

The views held by the other bishops of the CPSA, other leaders within the CPSA and the leadership of the other English-speaking churches in South Africa at the time were probably similar to Clayton's. For example, the bishops generally discouraged mixed marriages even though they did not think such marriages were criminal acts. English-speaking whites had a very low opinion of blacks and any white marrying a black would be seen as marrying below his or her station. Whites were victims of a deep phobia called miscegenation. The question: "Would you let your daughter marry a kaffir?" (Beinart 1994: 141) was regarded as unanswerable.

The bishops of the CPSA were quick to rationalise separate worship, exaggerating the linguistic difficulties in integrated worship (Bush 1961: 31: see also Huddleston 1956: 25). South African English-speaking whites, who included the English bishops, detested apartheid intensely. They, however, enjoyed the privileges of segregation and were willing to train their ordination candidates in racially divided seminaries.

CLAYTON AND THE STATE

When the Nationalist Government introduced apartheid laws which denigrated the blacks, Clayton, and the majority of the Anglican bishops, made some spasmodic protests but regrettably did no more. Clayton for all his condemnation of apartheid will be remembered as an accomplice when the Afrikaner sacrificed the education of the black child on the altar of convenience. When Verwoerd introduced

Bantu Education, Clayton suggested that a rotten system of education was better than what black children would pick up in the streets.

Both admirers and critics of Clayton could easily be hoodwinked by the uncompromising stance that he took with regard to the Church Clause 29(c) of the Native Laws Amendment Bill of 1957, whose main intention was to prohibit integrated worship in South Africa. He wrote to the Prime Minister informing him, *inter alia*, that if the Bill became law the bishops of the CPSA would not only be unable to obey it but would counsel their clergy and people to do the same (Paton 1973: 275ff).

Clayton's theology of church and state was largely shaped by his interpretation of Augustine's *De Civitate Dei*. In fact both Clayton and Tutu reflect ideas which seem to come from Augustine. Augustine exhorted his readers to obey all the laws promulgated by the ruler except those laws or commands that run contrary to God's ordinances. Even though a Christian was at liberty to flout the laws and commands that are contrary to God's ordinances, Augustine argued that Christians could not escape the consequences of their actions because the ruler has a right to punish anyone who refuses to obey an impious law. Clayton stated that obedience to secular authority was a command laid upon human beings by God. He felt constrained to disobey Clause 29(c) but, as a staunch follower of Augustine, he knew that he could be imprisoned for his actions. The thought of languishing in gaol made him apprehensive. "The idea of going to prison filled him with a revulsion that was almost fear" (Paton 1973: 278).

Clayton's other major objection against the Clause was that the Nationalist Government was beginning to make insidious inroads on a domain that fell completely outside the jurisdiction of the government. Clayton understood himself to be a "Prince of the Church" and "[i]n one particular sense [he] was the church" (Paton 1973: 208, 242). Throughout his episcopacy he had advocated that the church and the state were distinct realities and he preferred the church to "maintain a certain aloofness from the society from within which it works" (Worsnip 1991: 32). The introduction of this Bill galvanised Clayton into action. He threatened the government that if the Bill became law the CPSA would have no option but to disobey it. Clayton had eschewed any collective resistance but realised that little would be achieved by submitting. He found himself in an invidious position similar to that of Donatus in the fourth century, which led him to greet the two envoys from Emperor Constans: "*Quid est imperatori cum*

Ecclesia" (What has the emperor to do with the church?) (Optatus of Mileve 3,3;7,6).

What is significant in the letter that Clayton was to have sent to the Prime Minister was his observation that issues raised by Clause 29(c) could not be regarded merely as Native Affairs since they affected even those churches attended by Europeans. The question is whether Clayton would have acted if this Clause had referred exclusively to blacks.

It is very clear that Clayton cannot be seen as a political bishop. This is illustrated by the negative attitude he adopted towards Michael Scott and Trevor Huddleston as well as his successor bishop in Johannesburg, Ambrose Reeves. These three men were impressive "political activists". In 1946 Michael Scott left Johannesburg for Durban to join the Indians who had organised a passive resistance movement in opposition to the Asiatic Land Tenure Bill. Scott was arrested under the law of trespass and spent three months in prison. On his release Clayton withdrew his license as a curate, partly because he believed that "passive resistance was incompatible with the Christian faith" (Hastings 1979: 25ff; see also Paton 1973: 151ff). Since Huddleston belonged to a religious order known as the Community of the Resurrection, Clayton had no incontrovertible authority over him. Clayton, however, suggested to Huddleston's superior, Father Raynes, that Huddleston should return to England.

Clayton and his successor in Johannesburg, Ambrose Reeves, were quite incompatible. Clayton's revulsion for Reeves was such that he even considered him to be *non compos mentis*. Clayton perceived Reeves to be obsessed with politics. According to Hastings, Clayton was "unemotional, distrustful of populism [exhibitionism] . . . an English upper-middle-class type who was constitutionally as incapable of identifying with the blacks as with women [he was a renowned misogynist], or with the poor anywhere in his own lifestyle", thus, Clayton never set his face firmly against racialism (Hastings 1979: 23f). Clayton and Tutu both respected church tradition but Tutu was not enthralled by that tradition in the same manner as Clayton. Politically Clayton and Tutu were poles apart. Alan Paton could not have thought of a more appropriate title for Clayton's biography than *Apartheid and the Archbishop*.

DESMOND TUTU'S CAREER

In 1981 an article appeared in one of the English newspapers stating that "the Church does not kill its prophets by stoning them but by consecrating them" (*Church Times* 1981). Tutu has proved to be an exception to the rule. Those who disliked him intensely could only glare at him. Tutu has commented: "If looks could kill, I would have suffered several deaths" (Tutu and Allen 1994: 70).

Tutu's rise in the ecclesiastical sphere is a mystery, because although the churches in South Africa worked hard on the development of schools and hospitals they did very little to groom black clergy for positions of leadership. Black ordination candidates were trained to play second fiddle to white priests. The story of Desmond Tutu is an exception. Trevor Huddleston helped to mould the Tutu we know. It is not difficult to see what particularly attracted Huddleston to Tutu. For one thing, Tutu was a brilliant student. This led the Anglican Church to send him to study in England. One of his lecturers at Cambridge describes Tutu as "an extraordinary student whose entire scholarly deportment repudiated the myth that blacks are bovine".[3] Besides this he was and still is very gregarious. Tutu has an effervescent nature and always radiates joy, giving rise to frequent laughter.

When some people started speaking ill of Tutu, one could not help but wonder whether there were two Tutus, the ogre Tutu being a figment of people's imaginations, an *enfant terrible* for those who were victims of some form of inability to understand.

In 1974 the Bishop of Grahamstown, Bill Burnett, was elected to succeed Archbishop Selby Taylor in Cape Town. One of the names submitted for consideration by the elective assembly of Grahamstown was that of Desmond Tutu. Although Tutu stood head and shoulders above the other candidates, the white electors in Grahamstown were neither prepared to listen to reason nor to the pleas of their black colleagues. It would have been considered somewhat blasphemous to ask why the Holy Spirit has had such overt preferential bias for the white candidates.

In 1975 Tutu was appointed the Dean of Johannesburg and there he ably ministered to the privileged whites who had the capacity of co-opting him to their *Weltanschauung*. Ten years later Desmond Tutu's name was submitted to the elective assembly of the Diocese of Johannesburg. By then he had already served as a Diocesan Bishop of the Kingdom of Lesotho and as the General Secretary of the South African Council of Churches. In Johannesburg Tutu could not get the

3. An interview with Professor William Hugh Frend in Cambridge on 16 June 1995.

required two-thirds majority, but none of the other candidates could either. The bishops decided, quite rightly, to offer Johannesburg to Tutu. When his name was considered for the bishopric in Johannesburg he was already a Nobel Prize laureate. Even so, some white liberals thought that it was a mistake to award the Nobel Prize to him. Alan Paton, who had ensconced himself as the mouthpiece of the blacks, did not hide his disapproval when he suggested that the prize should go to someone whose concern was to "feed the hungry and not one who calls for economic pressure which could put a man out of a job and make his family go hungry . . ." (Villa-Vicencio 1986: 1).

The problem with white liberals was not so much their lack of sympathy for blacks but their reluctance to relinquish their entrenched positions. White liberals have been keen to be the spokespeople of blacks as long as such utterances did not undermine their vested interests or power.

TUTU'S POLITICAL OUTLOOK

One cannot speak of Tutu's political outlook without understanding his theological outlook. Prayer is so important to him that one cannot but wonder whether he would not have done well in a monastery. He reads the Bible with relentless avidity. The biblical theme which has most captured his attention is the transfiguration. Some of his other key theological foci also need to be examined.

THE NOTION OF *IMAGO DEI*

Tutu believes that all human beings, irrespective of their social position, status, gender, colour or creed are created in the image of God. He believes that biological factors have nothing to do with the quintessence of humanity. Tutu's view has always been that a person who discriminates against others and treats them as less than God intended them to be insults not only that person but also the Supreme Being Him/Herself.

Even though Clayton sincerely believed in the infinite worth of each person as God's image, he adopted a very condescending attitude towards blacks. Many white liberals at the time believed that "Blacks had [not] reached the requisite levels of maturity" and needed to be

64

given time to develop under the guardianship of whites (Hulley 1993: 143, 146). Whilst Tutu was an inclusivist, Clayton was an exclusivist. Tutu's demand for the emancipation of blacks from the fetters of apartheid has been dubbed as meddling in mundane affairs, whereas Clayton's understanding of the church was that its primary duty was not to serve society but to worship God (Paton 1973: 121).

Tutu's call for the liberation of the oppressed blacks was based on his understanding of the Bible and he identified very closely with those who worked for liberation. It was this identification that led him to leave his pastoral duties in Lesotho to attend the funeral of Steve Biko in King William's Town. As if this was not enough, Tutu preached at the funeral of Chris Hani, a convinced Communist. At Hani's funeral he made remarks that must have left a bad taste in the mouths of those who wanted to hold onto power. He told the mourners that Mandela was "the president in waiting". He also said: "We want freedom now!" Clayton, by way of contrast, was convinced that the onus was upon the individual to rock the boat but he did not "think the Church ought to take a more active part" in protests (Clayton 1950).

Tutu's understanding of the *imago Dei* also moved him to oppose discrimination against women on the basis of their gender. In the Provincial Synod of the CPSA which took place in Swaziland in September 1992, he told the delegates that as a person who had fought against the discrimination of blacks on the basis of something about which they could not do anything, which was their colour, he also took it upon himself to fight for women who were discriminated against on the basis of something they could not do anything about, which was their gender. There is no doubt that Tutu's remarks influenced the debate on the issue of the ordination of women. Clayton despised women. When the Diocese of Johannesburg passed a motion in favour of admitting women to provincial and diocesan synods, Clayton "abstained from both comment and vote" (*The Watchman* 1942; see Paton 1973: 116).

TUTU'S PERCEPTIONS OF THE CHURCH AND THE STATE

Both Clayton and Tutu were followers of Augustine. Clayton followed Augustine uncritically, whereas Tutu was more prudent and analytical in using Augustine's views. Throughout his episcopacy Clayton enjoined his flock to obey earthly rulers. In his charge to the Diocesan

Synod of 1939 he told the synod delegates that "one must obey [the rulers], unless one believed that such confidence was disloyalty to God" (Clayton 1939). Clayton never went beyond Romans 13 as the basis of one's unquestionable submission to the state, whereas Tutu was adamant that in some cases Romans 13 should be pitted against Revelation 13. Tutu implied that the South African government had either become or was fast becoming "a beast" in the symbolic language of the Book of Revelation.

Tutu's letter of April 1988 to the State President, Mr P. W. Botha, shows that he was not prepared to backtrack on anything he had previously discussed with the State President. Tutu did not flinch from pointing out to Botha that apartheid was not only heretical but unbiblical, unchristian and evil. He did this although he had a profound conviction that the South African government at the time was illegitimate, whereas Clayton had "felt the Church, in the South Africa of the 1940s and 1950s, was living under a legitimate government" (Worsnip 1991: 36).

Tutu's opposition to apartheid was not only confined to verbal protests, but he translated these into action. On Monday, 29 February 1988, he led a peaceful march from St George's Cathedral to the Houses of Parliament to present a petition calling on the South African government to end the State of Emergency, unban political organisations and enter into negotiations with authentic black leaders (Tutu and Allen 1994: 81). This was not an isolated incident. Tutu was unflinching in his opposition to apartheid and yet he did all this as a man of peace. Time and again he assured the whites that it was never the intention of the blacks to drive them into the sea.

The Government of National Unity could not have found a more ideal person to head the Truth and Reconciliation Commission than Tutu. Tutu as a man of peace perceives the role of this commission to be a mechanism of opening "wounds so they can be cleansed and prevented from festering" (*Sowetan* 1995). He is now in a position to continue Christ's work of reconciliation. I can only conclude that Tutu does not stand firmly in the tradition of Clayton, but has a larger vision of the role of the church.

BIBLIOGRAPHY

Beinart, W. (1994), *Twentieth-century South Africa*, Oxford University Press, p. 141.

Bush, T. N.W., "Anglicans and apartheid", in *Africa South in exile*, Vol. 5, No. 4, July-September 1961, Cape Town: Africa South Publications.

Church Times, 2 January 1981.

Clayton, G.H. (1934), "Charge to the Johannesburg Diocesan Synod of 1934", in CPSA Archive, AB 191.

Clayton, G.H. (1939), "Charge to the Johannesburg Diocesan Synod of 1939", in CPSA Archive, AB 191.

Clayton, G.H. (1950), "Letter to the South African bishops", 30 January 1950, in CPSA Archive, AB 191, T/S.

Fisher Papers, Vol. 58 (1949), Lambeth Palace Library, London.

Hastings, A. (1979), *A history of African Christianity*, 1950-1975, Cambridge: Cambridge University Press.

Huddleston, T. (1956), *Naught for your comfort*, London: Collins.

Hulley, L.D., "The churches and political rights for blacks in Africa", *Studia Historiae Ecclesiasticae*, June 1993 Volume XIX, No. 1, University of South Africa.

Johannesburg Minute Book (1936-1961), Agendum 38(i) of Diocesan Synod of 21 October 1941 in CPSA Archive, AB 2013/D1 CPSA, Diocese of Johannesburg.

La Guma, A. (ed.) (1972), *Apartheid: A collection of writings on South African racism by South Africans*, London: Lawrence & Wishart Ltd.

Optatus of Mileve, *De schismate donatistarum*, C. Ziwsa (ed.), CSEL 26, Vienna, 1893. Quoted by H. Jedin and J. Dolan (eds.), *History of the Church*, Vol. ii, London: Burns & Oats.

Paton, A. (1973), *Apartheid and the Archbishop: The life and times of Geoffrey Clayton Archbishop of Cape Town*, Cape Town: David Philip.

Reeves, A. (1962), *South Africa – yesterday and tomorrow: The challenge to Christians*, London: Victor Gollancz, Ltd.

Sowetan, 1 December 1995.

Tutu, D. and J. Allen (eds.), (1994), *The rainbow people of God: The ministry of Desmond Tutu as Anglican Archbishop of Cape Town*. p. 70. All references to this work have been quoted from the manuscript rather than the published version.

Villa-Vicencio, C., "Archbishop Desmond Tutu: From Oslo to Cape Town", in B. Tlhagale and I. Mosala (1986), *Hammering swords into ploughshares*, Grand Rapids, Michigan: William B Eerdmans Publishing Company.

Walshe, P. (1983), *Church versus the State: The case of the Christian Institute*, London: C. Hurst & Co.

The Watchman, December 1934.

The Watchman, November 1942.

Worsnip, M.E. (1991), *Between the two fires: The Anglican Church and apartheid 1948 to 1957*, Pietermaritzburg: University of Natal Press.

Life and faith in an
African context

UTutu: Ngumntu lowo[1]

In the history of the struggle for liberation in South Africa, God has raised various leaders who have made their distinctive contributions. One such leader is Archbishop Desmond Tutu, who came into prominence during one of the darkest moments in the history of South Africa. The period 1970-1990 saw the implementation of the most draconian legislation of the apartheid era. Various measures that were designed to silence opposition to the policy of apartheid were taken. During this period, many people died under very suspicious circumstances, some of them while in police custody. This period of intensive repression ended with the release of Nelson Mandela, an event which triggered a process of transformation that led to the first democratic elections in South Africa in April 1994. The winds of change that had been blowing down the continent of Africa since the sixties had now finally reached its southernmost tip. It was in this milieu that Desmond Tutu emerged as a voice of the voiceless, proclaiming the imperative of God's justice, and thereby becoming God's messenger of hope in an environment of despair and despondency. He gave himself selflessly to the struggle for liberation as a sign of his deep sense of caring for the wellbeing of humanity. He also saw in the dawn of a new South Africa the truth that God reigns and that evil will not have the last word in his world, but that goodness prevails in the end.

One of the most significant contributions of Desmond Tutu has been the restoration of the dignity of the African person. The meteoric rise of this small man from Soweto, often described as "Um-

---

1. *UTutu: Ngumntu lowo* means "Tutu, the one in whom full personhood is manifested"; see also section dealing with Ubuntu at the end of this chapter.

dengentonga",[2] to the stature of a world statesman and Nobel Peace laureate has been a source of pride and inspiration to many Africans. Not only did it disprove the lie that Africans are inferior to other human beings, but it also affirmed that Africans have a destiny and a contribution to make in world affairs. Colonisation and oppression have had a negative and dehumanising effect on the African person. The wars of conquest of the nineteenth century led to the subjugation of Africans. For three centuries they were denied fundamental human rights. In the last four decades their oppression was intensified by the government's apartheid policy, which deliberately placed them in a position of permanent servitude through educational, social, economic and political programmes. Even the written history of this country has to a certain degree confirmed this position of servitude.

AFRICA – THE CRADLE OF HUMANITY

There is a saying that "history is written by the winner". That is why many history books have portrayed Africans as being somehow inferior to other human beings. Africans have been made to appear somewhat accidentally without any definite position in the course of history. They are sometimes perceived as "peripheral actors outside the main theatre of South African history, appearing rarely on the central stage, and even then only as hindrances, obstructing the progress of European civilization".[3] Yet Africans have a significant place in the history of humanity. Some hundred years ago, Charles Darwin speculated that evidence would come to light that the cradle of humanity was in Africa. Darwin's forecast has been confirmed by archaeologists who discovered fossil bones some thirty years ago in Olduvai, Tanzania, and in other sites in East Africa. Similar discoveries were made in Taung. As Basil Davidson puts it: "These signals from the past indicate that Africa was indeed the birthplace of the earliest type of [man], and the scene of some of [man's] first and most crucial stages of evolution."[4]

2. *Umdengentonga* means "Though small in stature and from humble beginnings, yet has greatness and tremendous abilities well beyond his appearance".
3. Maylam, P., A *history of the African people of South Africa from the early Iron Age to the 1970s;* St Martins Press: New York, 1986, p. 2.
4. Davidson, B., *Discovering Africa's past*, Longman: Hong Kong, 1978, p. 5.

Furthermore, archaeological evidence has revealed that Africans participated in the stone-age civilisation of some two million years ago. South African blacks are descendants of that great African heritage. Their presence in South Africa is attributed to a process of migration that took place throughout the continent of Africa. Archaeological evidence is available which shows that there were nomadic people in South Africa, whose major means of livelihood was hunting, for a period of about eight millennia to about 2 000 years ago. However, evidence for settled communities can be traced as far back as the third century.

Paul Maylam says that recent discoveries by archaeologists suggest that the earliest iron-age settlements existed in the area that stretches from as far north as Klein Africa in the Soutpansberg, to as far east as Mzonjani near Durban, and as far south as Tsholomnqa near East London. New sites in Mbashe Valley, Transkei, have recently been uncovered reflecting iron-age culture. Tim Maggs says that "by A.D. 600 if not earlier the lower lying areas of the Tugela Basin, below an altitude of about 1 000 m, were dotted with early iron age settlements. These were quite large villages, separated from one another by several kilometers and situated on the best arable land".[5]

And that was not all. There is evidence also of the existence of what are termed "late iron age" sites south of the Limpopo River which are dated at between 900 and 1400 AD. These settlements were found on higher ground in the South African regions previously known as Natal, Zululand, Transvaal and the Orange Free State. There is evidence of intensive exploitation of mineral resources during this period. For instance, in a place called Lolwe there were vast copper and iron deposits. "Lolwe . . . was the site of mineshafts, galleries and adits, which were uncovered in the course of blasting. A rough estimate by mining engineers indicates that well over 10,000 tons of rock containing secondary copper ore deposits . . . had been removed from the hill before the start of recent mining activities . . . Low grass covered mounds of slag and the occasional remains of a smelting furnace are scattered in the surrounding plain and attest to an iron and copper industry which is now only dimly remembered by the oldest members of the Phalaborwa tribe."[6]

There has also been further archaeological evidence which shows that there was a stone-age iron-melting industry at Dithakong, near

5. Maylam, P., p. 3.
6. Maylam, P., p. 12.

Kuruman. This indicates that there was some mining activity, albeit very rudimentary, several centuries prior to the arrival of the white people in South Africa. There is also evidence of the existence of an export trade between the sixteenth and the eighteenth centuries. Copper and tin from Messina and Phalaborwa were exported to world markets through Delagoa Bay.

All this information demonstrates in a convincing way that at least some 1 400 years before the arrival of white people in 1652 there was a vibrant African culture and civilisation in South Africa. Some of the African people were stock farmers and agriculturists, while others were involved in the mining industry. The technology that existed at the time was simple, but sufficient for the production of foodstuffs, clothing and farming implements, as well as the necessary equipment for the mining industry. Their past achievements indicate that Africans have a destiny and a future. Perhaps it was considerations such as those which prompted Mangaliso Sobukwe to say: "World civilization will not be complete until the African has made his full contribution. And even as the dying so-called Roman civilization received new life from the barbarians, so also will the decaying so-called Western civilization find a new and purer life from Africa."[7]

HUMAN DIGNITY

Fundamental to Desmond Tutu's affirmation of the dignity of human beings is his understanding of the doctrine of creation. He believes firmly that human beings are created in God's image. Creation in God's image is generally held to entail three elements:

● that each person is valuable in the sight of God and, therefore, has intrinsic worth and dignity;
● that human beings share a common identity. Humanity that
  is created in the likeness of the Godhead shares that quality of unity, which is a unity in diversity;
● that human beings have been given a task to be God's stew-
  ards on earth. As such, they have a responsibility to care for
  God's creation, and that entails accountability.

7. Pogrund, B., *How can man die better: Sobukwe and apartheid*, Peter Halbran, 1990.

Because of his understanding of humanity as a creation in God's image, Desmond Tutu saw apartheid as evil and an affront to the dignity of human beings. In his own words he said that apartheid was founded on a "biological irrelevance", which is the colour of a person's skin. In his usual flamboyant, charismatic and humorous style, with his typical wit and extraordinary gift of stating profound theological truths in simple language, Desmond helped people to deal with the complex issue of racial segregation. In the days of apartheid he suggested that in place of colour we could have had segregation based on the size of one's nose. Hence there would have been a government department of "small noses affairs". People with big noses would then be discriminated against. When people laughed, they realized how ridiculous it was to use colour as a basis of discrimination.

He also made even the most marginalised people feel that they matter before God. In one of his visits in the Diocese of Kimberley and Kuruman, during his sermons Desmond made people repeat after him: "I am a V.S.P.: A Very Special Person". This was a tremendous boost to people's self-esteem. He has often stressed that human beings should genuflect before each other, as each person is a creation in the image of God.

In his theology Desmond has always emphasised the centrality of God. Human beings are co-creators with God. As such they have a responsibility to co-operate with God in the realisation of God's purpose for the world. In the words that are inscribed in the pavement in the Anglican Cathedral in Pietermaritzburg that are attributed to Archbishop Desmond: "We are to labour with God to help God's children become ever more fully human which is a glorious destiny." Desmond has always sought to transcribe doctrine into duty. This is evidenced in the educational and development programmes he founded in order to help the poor and the marginalised. In the same way, it is imperative that as we engage ourselves in the process of nation building, positive measures that are aimed at the restoration of the dignity of the African person are undertaken. As a society which has been bruised and brutalised by the events of the past, we need to embark on practical and concrete steps that are directed towards a future where there is greater equality of opportunity and economic integration. Such measures should entail, inter alia:

- short-, medium- and long-term plans to bridge the gap in the educational, economic and social spheres;

- the imparting of skills and technological know-how in order to meet the demands of industry for the 21st century and beyond;
- accessibility to wealth-generating institutions in order to eliminate poverty, increase the standard of living, and enable Africans to make a meaningful contribution to the economy of the country;
- awareness programmes that are aimed at liberating enslaved minds and encouraging positive thinking as we move from protest to participation.

AFRICAN CULTURE AND SPIRITUALITY

Another significant contribution made by Desmond Tutu has been his emphasis on the necessity to relate Christianity to African culture. This is because of his conviction that for the Gospel to be relevant and meaningful, it has to be incarnated into the culture of people. "The Gospel is the same always and everywhere. Its manner of presentation changes in accordance with the culture within which it is proclaimed."[8]

A failure to recognise this will mean that Christianity for many Africans will remain "a strange religion", there being some part of their very selves and lives that are outside the gospel. Pope John Paul II has said that "a faith that does not affect a person's culture, is a faith not fully embraced, not entirely thought out and not fully lived".[9] We need, therefore, to incarnate the Gospel of Jesus Christ into the very lives and beings of Africans. St Irenaus once said: "The glory of God is the living human person, which here means believers fully alive, enabled to praise God with their cultural values".[10]

Related to this is the need for an affirmation of an African spirituality, which has sadly been neglected. Desmond Tutu in himself brought to the church in southern Africa a gift of freedom, laughter and joy in the richness of the diversity of cultures. His famous phrase "the rainbow people of God" encapsulates this. In his style of worship in danc-

8. This statement has been attributed to William Temple.
9. John Paul II, "Address to the Pontifical Council for Culture", 20 May 1982, *L'Osseratore Romano: Weekly Edition in English*, 28 June 1982, p. 7.
10. Quoted from *Instrumentum laborn*, Vatican Press, 1993, p. 47.

ing, music and preaching he has given us a glimpse of African spirituality. What is needed is an exploration of this diversity in a way that will enrich not only the church in southern Africa but also the universal church. God has placed us in a unique position in southern Africa. We have an incredible inheritance of spirituality that has been handed down to us through the ages. We have a church membership that has a background of European and African culture. We have people who have experienced renewal through the charismatic movement. There are people who are steeped in an Anglo-Catholic spirituality that has largely been influenced by the Anglican divines. What is required is an integration of these brands of spirituality into an authentic spirituality for southern Africa. This will bring about a new vitality, something distinctively African which we can call our own.

There are three aspects of the African world view that have a bearing on the exploration of an authentic spirituality for southern Africa. Firstly, God who is referred to as *Umvelinqangi, umdali wezulu nomhlaba*, is the source of all life and the creator of heaven and earth. Another word for God is *Nkulunkulu*, which means the greatest of the greatest. God is unknowable, above all things, and has no human profile. In African thought there is no separation between the spiritual and the secular. They are all an integral part of one reality. In Zulu cosmology, the primary creative principle is embodied in *Nomkhubulwane*, the creative force who is sometimes referred to as the daughter of God and goddess of balance. This creative force is not to be thought of in personal terms. It is a conception, a manifestation of the quality of God that has female powers of creativity, such as generosity, sensitivity, intelligence and concern for children. Mazisi Kunene says: "Nowhere is this more dramatically expressed than in the illuminatory symbol of the rainbow which signifies the emergence of a new order after the destructive tropical storms. The rainbow is considered the highest representation of her qualities" (*Uthingo lwe nkosazana*) [11]

The second aspect of the African world view is the understanding of life as one unit with different phases. The relationship between the living and the dead is expressed in many ways. For instance, on the occasion of the death of the head of a household, a feast to accompany him on his journey to the world of ancestors is held. This is known as *ukukhapha*. It takes the form of the slaughtering of a beast and some kind of ceremony presided over by a designated senior member of the

---

11. Kunene, M., *Anthem of the decades*, Fletcher & Son: Warwick, 1981.

family. After a period of a year, another ceremony takes place. This is known as the feast of return – *ukubuyisa* – whereby the deceased is integrated into the community of all guardian spirits.

Abaphantsi, i.e. the living dead, are understood as having some form of heightened existence. "The Ancestors, though living a heightened existence, are still the same people they were on earth."[12] There is here an emphasis on the continuity of life after death. Paradise, according to African thought, is not somewhere in the sky, it is in the underworld of the ancestors – *Kwabaphantsi*. Death is not something to be feared, as it is only a change from one form of existence to another. As Mazisi Kunene puts it: "Man must aspire to a spiritual state that shall re-unite him ultimately with his ancestors."[13] Hence, land in the African world view is not simply regarded as a piece of real estate; it has a very deep religious significance. Land is perceived as an organism that sustains the bond between the unborn, the living and the dead.

In African thought, therefore, all the forms of dualism that have plagued Western theology do not exist. Religion is not regarded as a separate compartment. It encompasses all of life. There is a symphony of life between this world and the next. That is why Archbishop Desmond Tutu has repeatedly stressed that one cannot talk about political life as if it exists in isolation. All life is one in the realm of God. Africans have a holistic view of life and a very high doctrine of humanity. An example of this can be seen in the way people greet each other. The question is always: "How is full life with you?" If a child is sick, or there are problems with livestock, or there is a drought, the response would be: "There is no life in us." The statement that Jesus made: "I have come that you might have life in its fullness," finds much resonance with Africans. The Good News for Africans is not so much about saving souls; it is about the restoration of humanity to its fullness.

The third aspect of the African world view is *Ubuntu* – humaneness. It has significant implications for human relationships, such as engendering a spirit of community and caring for one another. In African thought there is emphasis on the fact that an individual exists in community. John Pobee says: "It is often said that where Descartes said, 'I think, therefore I am', the African would say, 'I am related, therefore we are."[14]

12. Kunene, M., p. XVI.
13. Kunene, M., p. XVIII.
14. Pobee, J.S., *African theology*, Abingdon: Nashville, Tennessee, 1979, p. 49.

Tiyo Soga says: "*Thina ma Afrika singumzi wobuhlobo nobuzalwana obunzulu ngokudalwa*",[15] which means that we Africans have a deep-rooted sense of relationship and friendship. This aspect of African culture underscores an inherent, deep community awareness, and a care or concern for the wellbeing of the other. There is a well-known phrase, *Umntu Ngumntu Ngabantu* – a person, is a person through others. When someone is well disposed towards others, people say "Ngumntu Lowo", a phrase denoting the wholeness of personhood. Another interesting word, *Ubulali*, denotes the art of dealing with the other which affirms a person's humanity and which has the quality of appropriateness in human relationships.

This understanding of humanity also creates an enormous capacity for forgiveness. Once an African detects that a person means well, and that there is a readiness to move away from the wrong of the past, there is a willingness to move forward to a future that seeks to enhance the wellbeing of humanity. Nelson Mandela's willingness to forgive his jailers and his readiness to join hands with them in the transformation of South Africa is an apt illustration. As we salute Desmond and hail him for the significant contribution he has made to the restoration of the dignity of the African person, we need to affirm the following in African spirituality:

- A spirituality that is God-centred and that is rooted in the unshakeable truth that God is in control of all life.
- A spirituality that is rooted in a deep sense of community, as Africans by their very nature have a deep sense of belonging.
- A spirituality that has been purified by the experience of pain and suffering that is rooted in the cross of Jesus Christ which exhibits forgiveness, compassion, tenderness and a loving and a caring disposition towards the other. For Africans are a people whose identity is founded on Ubuntu.

15. Soga, T.B., *Intlalo ka Xhosa*, N.P: The Lovedale Press, 1974, p. 102.

Culture and ethnic diversity as sources of curse and blessing in the promotion of democratic change

INTRODUCTORY REMARKS

The importance of African culture is something that we, as black South African theologians, have been shy to talk about. This is understandable, given the fact that we went through many centuries of attempted suppression of African culture and religion by our white colonisers. For the most part, we were made to feel ashamed of our Africanness which, under white denomination, only reminded us of the collective helplessness and uselessness of African cultures, religion and gods in their failure to protect us against European military assault and our eventual subjugation and domination. In consequence, black theologians became suspicious of the "inculturation" approach to the construction of African theology – an attempt which tried to marry the essential core of the Christian message with the African world view, so that Christianity could at last speak with an African idiom and accent. As Edward W. Fashole-Luke (1976: 164) has eloquently put it: "in essence, the nature of the quest for African Christian theologies is to translate the one faith of Jesus Christ to suit the tongue, style, genius, character and culture of African peoples". Against this approach, black theologians devoted much energy to the construction of a black theology of liberation which was characterised by its emphasis on the struggle for socio-economic and political liberation from white racial oppression.

APPROPRIATION OF AFRICAN CULTURE BY SOUTH AFRICAN THEOLOGIANS

The appreciation of African culture by South African black theologians has come rather slowly, largely mediated by the Ecumenical Association of Third World Theologians (EATWOT) which provided a forum where African theologians of different persuasions could meet and be exposed to one another, and to other forms of liberation theologies, especially the Asian theology of liberation which emphasises cultural, religious and the socio-economic liberation. This exposure helped black South African theologians to realise more and more that while it is true that they suffered socio-economic and political injustice under white domination for over three hundred years, it does not follow that they have completely ceased being Africans. Because black South Africans were not and could not be fully Europeanised, it is not surprising that during times of crises in their lives many of them often resort to their African cultural and religious beliefs and practices. It is one of the ironies of history that the apartheid political system, which was designed to humiliate black people and trample upon their dignity, became the instrument that ensured that Africans would not succeed in rejecting their cultural and religious roots. The white protagonists of the apartheid regime constantly reminded them that they were Africans and not Europeans (regardless of their educational achievements or economic status), by legally forcing them to live in African townships.

We are not trying to praise the apartheid regime. The point that is being made here is that many South African blacks, for better or worse, are still steeped in their African cultural and religious milieu. Apartheid made them increasingly appreciative of their African culture and religious heritage. This, above all, has created a meeting point between themselves and other Africans in the rest of independent Africa.

As black South Africans came to appreciate the value of their African heritage, they began to re-examine their culture in order to discover resources with which they could reassert their African identity. They did this while at the same time acknowledging that, having lived under several colonial regimes since the arrival of white settlers in 1652, they knew little about their past, because white colonialism tried its best to uproot African culture and religions which were perceived as nothing but heathenism, indeed the work of the devil.

The colonialists' attack on African culture, however, did not succeed in uprooting the Africanness of black South Africans. For they realised that they had survived colonial onslaught and domination over the centuries precisely because they had retained the substantive core of their African identity, indeed their African culture, in terms of which both their past, present and future experiences could be defined. This substantive core of African culture is characterised by the hope and determination to survive as people of African descent. Put somewhat differently, this African hope and resilience are at the core of the African culture which enabled their forebears as well as the present generation of Africans to struggle against white settlers and to survive against innumerable odds. Not surprisingly, when leaders like Nelson Mandela and others were incarcerated and brutalised for almost three decades, no amount of dehumanisation, humiliation and tribulation could succeed in destroying their hope and resilience always to begin afresh their struggle against white domination in order to reconstruct their shattered lives with dignity and often without bitterness. Indeed, the miracle of achieving a non-racial and non-sexist democratic South Africa under the leadership of President Nelson Mandela, without a vengeful spirit, is the clearest demonstration of African determination to survive with dignity while retaining their humanness.

To summarise: the African culture we are talking about here refers to that internal force and resilience which has helped Africans both in the African continent and the diaspora to survive despite the atrocities of slavery, colonialism and post-colonial brutality, dictatorships and oppression which still characterise most African countries. It is that force which enabled Africans to retain their humanity and, above all, enabled their forefathers and foremothers as well as the present generation of people of African descent to articulate their rejection of attempted white destruction and denial of black humanity.

USES AND MISUSES OF AFRICAN CULTURE

Having outlined the positive aspects of African culture, especially the African hope and determination to struggle in potentially destructive and oppressive societies, I need to point out that culture is a double-edged sword: it can be used for beneficial as well as for destructive ends. It is an open secret that African cultures have been and still are being used as instruments of oppression by those who are in power to legitimise their privileged position. I had a very interesting discussion recently with a female theological student who told me that she finds it most revealing that her male fellow theological students agree with her in almost everything in theological discourses provided that no reference is made to African culture. But when theological discussions begin to touch on the relationships between men and women in Africa, the problem of culture suddenly crops up. This is because it is convenient for males to use aspects of African culture in order to perpetuate their privileged status. Indeed, too often culture has been used and is used by African males in the family context, as husbands, fathers, sons, brothers, etc., to try to safeguard and perpetuate their dominant positions at the expense of females. Also, in the larger society, dominant groups use the cultural expressions of the powerless and dominated masses for the sole purpose of making victims of society accept their position of domination as well as the entrenched positions of dominant groups (Maimela 1991: 6).

A good example of how culture can be used as an instrument of oppression is best exemplified by the colonial period. As we all know, colonisers came to Africa as agents of the European empires to subjugate and dominate African people. In order to achieve their objective, they targeted the African culture for destruction, hoping thereby to destroy the African sense of history and identity. By replacing African culture and religion with European culture, the colonisers believed that decultured African men and women would be easy to dominate and control.

In some instances this Europeanisation process did succeed, as some Africans began to lose their religion after adopting the new Christian religion of the missionaries. For instance, there were Africans who lost their sense of identity to the point of identifying with the value system of the colonisers. Recently a friend of mine told me that, while he was in Europe, he met a French-speaking African. As their conversation progressed he asked the French-speaking African what nationality he was. The French-speaking African responded by saying that he was French. The upshot of this story is that oppressed Africans often internalise European culture so thoroughly that they begin to believe that they are really not Africans, but French or English. Such people even try to imitate the mannerisms of their French or English colonial masters. Some Africans have gone so far as to try to change the colour of their skins by using skin-lightening creams or stretching their hair. The result of such internalisation of the culture and religious values of their colonial masters has had a devastating effect on the African personality, leading to what Engelbert Mveng referred to as an African "anthropological poverty", by which he means:

> . . . the general impoverishment of the people. Colonialism brought about a loss of their identity and diminishment of their creativity. It indiscriminately disrupted their communal tribal life and organization and destroyed their indigenous values, religious beliefs, and traditional culture. This result of

the ravages of colonialism is now maintained by economic and cultural neo-colonialism (cited in Frostin 1988: 15, 205).

Most of us still suffer from the effects of the deculturation process that accompanied the colonisation of Africa.

Missionaries came out to Africa as agents of the dominant West to promote European culture and economic and religious imperialism. They went out of their way to suppress and condemn African religion and culture as the work of the devil (Maimela 1985: 64-65). Africans were terrified by hell-preaching sermons and were, in that state, called upon to embrace the new Christian religion. What is significant here is that the kind of Christianity that was preached was one which was designed to make the colonised Africans docile and perpetually infantilised and subservient to their European masters. Hence leadership positions were largely restricted to Europeans. Even when church leadership passed on to the indigenous people, little changed in respect to the European domination of the African churches because of the whole ecclesiastical structure of bishops, presidents and moderators which was designed to perpetuate the European domination of black churches. Using the power of money and theological training, European churches continue to exercise their influence through these structures. Because of the effective monolopy which Europeans had over the training of pastors and priests, most African church leaders tend to be theologically more conservative than their European counterparts, believing that such conservatism will win them applause from their European handlers. And those of us who happened to be under black leadership in those churches know from experience that African church leaders can be more oppressive than European missionaries. In both secular and ecclesiastical matters, we have a situation where Africans have merely substituted colonial or missionary oppressors, for African oppressors the difference in the latter case being only the ecclesiastical garb. Here again the mistake of those who fought against European domination and oppression lay in the fact that they did not destroy the thrones from which secular or religious oppressors exercised their power.

CULTURE AS A RESOURCE FOR RESISTANCE

It was against this background of cultural and religious domination that African resistance groups, during the struggle for independence, emerged to promote the philosophy of negritude, African culture and African socialism. In South Africa people began to talk about black consciousness and it was through the mediation of this self-affirming philosophy that people began to reclaim pride in themselves and particularly their African self-respect. One important characteristic of this self-affirmation is best expressed in the saying: "black is beautiful".

I wish to give a few examples of how African culture was used as a resource for resistance. In the nineteenth-century struggle between the Xhosa and the British, a prophetess by the name of Nongqawuse invoked African traditional religion by telling the oppressed blacks to carry out certain rituals so that the ancestors might help them to drive the white settler colonialists into the sea. Of course, the outcome was not as she had prophesied because the ancestors did not intervene. But the fact that Nongqawuse did not succeed does not obviate the fact that she was trying to use the African culture and religion as a resource for resistance against colonial domination and oppression. Her story, in my view, demonstrates the fact that there are certain aspects in African culture and religion which can be used by the oppressed. In so doing, oppressed groups reject various forms of cultural and religious expressions of the dominant group. Oppressed groups often adopt those aspects of their culture or religion which are deemed more useful for their cause and struggle to strengthen and reinforce their own resistance against class domination.

In the religious sphere, many Africans resisted conversion to Christianity. Even those who embraced the new Christian religion expressed their resistance to total conversion by continuing to carry out African traditional religious rites and rituals, a practice commonly known as syncretism (Maimela 1985: 71-73). Those of us who have served African congregations as ministers of religion can testify to the shock we often experience because of the strong emphasis on African traditional rites at funerals. For instance, when a person in the family has died, it is not uncommon that traditional rituals which are understood as helpful in the facilitation of the passage of the dead into the world of the spirits (ancestors) are conducted in tandem with Christian burial rites. In such situations, we often see relatives of the deceased throwing clothes, blankets or other articles in or on top of the grave, even while the Christian minister of religion conducts the Christian part of the burial. Similarly, when a child is born into a Christian family, the African parents do not hesitate to turn to the diviner or medicine man or woman to acquire charms or medicine that will help avert potential diseases or discourage witches or evil spirits from threatening the life of the child. At the same time, African parents will, however, proceed with the usual Christian rites such as baptism. Recently I was pleasantly surprised to learn that, if some of our young people have not had a good night's sleep or have a problem, they will go to the graveyard in the early hours to visit the graves of their parents or grandparents before going to church services.

Without entering into the debate as to whether syncretistic practices are right or wrong, let it suffice to say that the incidences I have referred to are, in my view, expressions of resistance to total conversion to a kind of Christianity that is utterly devoid of African cultural underpinnings. It is this kind of resistance to Western cultural and religious imperialism which led to the breakaway of the so-called African Independent Churches from the white denominations in the nineteenth century. These breakaways were nothing more than attempts by Africans to resist white cultural domination.

USES AND MISUSES OF CULTURE AND RELIGION IN THE BIBLE

Having briefly explained how African culture and religion have been used either as instruments of domination or as resources for resistance, let me now briefly refer to problems relating to the uses of Scripture, in order to demonstrate that the misuse of culture and religion is not peculiar to Africans. In the Old Testament we find an interesting story in the Book of Kings where there was a struggle over the land (1 Kings 21:1-28). Here the dominant group, represented by the king and his wife, wanted to use cultural and religious arguments as well as the power and prestige of their political position to legitimate their dispossession of a poor person, Naboth. In response, Naboth appealed to a certain interpretation of culture and religion which represented the core of Israelite social ethics and justice, namely, that a family's property could not be taken away or alienated from its owners, however lowly such owners might be. By appealing to this interpretation, the poor man, Naboth, managed to reinforce his resistance to King Ahaz's attempted possession of his land. The Scriptures tell us that Naboth won over the king, much to the displeasure of Jezebel, who refused to accept defeat. Instead she devised a vicious strategy in order to accomplish her wish to take away Naboth's land.

The struggle between Naboth and King Ahab seems to confirm the correctness of the warning of the Prophet Samuel against the creation of a monarchy in Israel. Samuel had warned Israel that the monarchy would have its own political economics, with far-reaching consequences for the nation, because it would lead to the creation of social classes. There would be the noble class, the king's counsellors, the army generals, the courtiers and so forth – all of whom would want to be rewarded. All these privileged classes would claim certain rights and favours from the king because of the special duties they believed they performed for the royal family and the nation. Indeed, there would be nothing unusual in such an arrangement because, as we all know, if a military coup is staged, the person who becomes the new ruler tends to surround himself with the military. His first act of appreciation is often expressed through dishing out better salaries and privileges for the military, thereby gaining favour with those who put him in power. In the light of the above, King Ahab was thus merely using his class position in his dispossession of Naboth.

There are many other examples which Old Testament scholars could cite to give their papers depth and content. One such example is the conflict between Jewish tribal exclusivism, which was used to sanction the dispossession of the Canaanites, as opposed to the universalism of God's love, which is forcefully expressed in the Book of Ruth and the Book of the Prophet Jonah.

With regard to the New Testament's uses of culture and religion, there are numerous examples which one could cite. Firstly, there is the story about Jesus' continuing debate with the Jewish ruling class. In these debates, we are told that Jesus would often quote a Jewish tradition such as: "You have heard that it was said that 'an eye for an eye' and 'a tooth for a tooth' but I tell you . . ." (Matthew 5:21ff).

Secondly, there were many discriminatory relationships between Jews and Samaritans, based on culture and religion, reflected in the story of Jesus' discussion with the Samaritan woman at the well. During this discussion Jesus ended up turning the Jewish traditional belief about Samaritans on its head. In addition, there are strands in the Gospel tradition which clearly express themselves against the use of religion and culture to oppress the so-called gentiles, women, slaves and other underdogs. The clearest expression is found in St Paul's letter to the Galatians where it is argued that for those who are baptised into Christ, there is "neither Jew nor Greek, slave nor free, male or female" because they are all one in Jesus Christ (Galations 3:26-28. See also Colossians 3:11, Ephesians 2:22-23).

Thirdly, other misuses of Jewish culture and religion to legitimate the oppression of outcasts in society, such as lepers, publicans, and so-called sinners or harlots, could be used with great benefit by New Testament scholars to demonstrate the twofold manner in which both culture and religion are often used to reinforce or resist domination.

Over against this, one could cite the Magnificat which expresses the liberating power of God. This could be used by the underdogs to resist their domination and oppression at the hands of the powerful. In a similar vein, liberation theology has appealed to Jesus' first sermon to construct a picture of a caring and liberating God who has taken the preferential option for the oppressed and downtrodden (Luke 4:16-21).

Fourthly, the story about Jesus' feeding of the multitudes gives a clear expression of the twofold uses of culture and religion in society. On the one hand, there is a suggestion by Jesus' disciples that the masses must be told to go away and purchase food for themselves since there were not sufficient loaves of bread and fish to feed the masses. The assumption here is that the masses must accept the logic of the existing unequal distribution of economic resources which benefits the capitalist few whose goods must be bought by the underprivileged masses. On the other hand, Jesus uses the Jewish cultural and religious argument to make an important ethical statement, namely, that sharing in situations of human need is the best solution because sharing makes it possible for everyone to have something to eat. After Jesus' death and resurrection, the Book of Acts tells us how this new social ethic was carried to its full expression by the early church (Acts 2:42-47, 4:32-5:10, 6:1-7).

The above examples, all taken from biblical material, demonstrate, I believe, the dialectic nature of both culture and religion as instruments of domination and resistance. By highlighting the twofold uses of culture and religion my aim was to demonstrate a very problematic dimension in the Judeo-Christian tradition, which stems from the historic alliance between religious authorities and the ruling classes in most societies. That alliance runs like a red thread through the pages of both the Old and New Testament and has continued throughout the history of the church.

Invariably, this relationship has often implied a co-option of religious authorities so that they might construct a theology to serve the state. This misuse of religion is made possible by the fact that the Bible itself is a problematic book, and one can find material to support almost any cause or point of view. Let it suffice here to mention but two main trends in the Hebrew Bible that lend themselves to the use of religion, either as an instrument of oppression or as resource for liberation. On the one hand, there is the so-called royal trend in which religion is systematically used to legitimate the Israelite ruling class, as opposed to the prophetic trend, which tends to appeal to the covenant tradition to promote the cause of the poor and the marginalised. On the other hand, there is the Mosaic trend which, taking its cue from the story of God's appointment of Moses to liberate the Hebrew slaves from Egypt, suggests that God is the God of the poor and downtrodden (Brueggemann 1983: 313).

Both traditions exist side by side in the Hebrew Bible. Therefore, as we read the Bible, we should not forget the fact that it does have more than one message. Consequently, we are called upon to make some choices between different biblical messages, because we simply cannot read the Bible as if it uniformly mediates the same message, representing one trend. Rather, because there are contradictory messages, representing different theological trends, we must make up our minds about which aspects of its traditions or messages we want to appeal to in order to justify our theological propositions. Put somewhat differently, while the Bible is there for us as Christians to use, we have to recognise the fact that the rich and powerful read messages from the Bible that are different from those that are read by and appealed to by oppressed groups. Put more crudely, different people read the Bible using different social lenses, depending on their locus in society. Therefore, it should not surprise us that dominant groups are most likely to find in the Bible messages that favour them, while the dominated groups emphasise different texts which support the cause of their own struggle for liberation.

USES AND MISUSES OF ETHNIC DIVERSITY

Tribal or ethnic conflicts, some of which have given rise to civil wars, floods of refugees and the destruction of some African societies, as illustrated by the destruction that has recently occurred in Rwanda, are indications that, like culture, ethnic diversity can be used by politicians for destructive ends. In South Africa, the political ideology of apartheid was designed precisely to exploit the reality of ethnic diversity to further the socio-economic and political interests of the dominant whites. Defenders of apartheid went so far as to justify the ideol-

89

ogy by misusing the Scriptures. A favourite text was the story of the tower of Babel which tells us of the confusion of tongues. It was deduced from the story that it is God's will that separate races and nations should be separated in order that they might live far from one another. As the will of God, this separation was not revoked in Christ's reconciliatory work. Hence the book of the Acts of the Apostles narrates the speaking of different tongues at Pentecost, the difference being only that the Spirit enabled different races to hear one another.

A recent example of the misuse of cultural diversity in South Africa is that of Chief Buthelezi and his Inkatha Freedom Party, who nearly pushed South Africa to the brink of disaster by arguing that a united South Africa would lead to the destruction of the so-called Zulu nation. This misuse of ethnic diversity in order to promote Zulu ethnic political life led to conflict, untold misery and the killing of over 4 000 people between 1991 and 1994. It remains a source of conflict which can be exploited for party political ends.

Yet God's gift of racial and cultural diversity should be seen as a source of strength and enrichment. Indeed, life would be dull and poor if different ethnic groups were to be reduced to sameness or one common denominator. In the South African situation, it was precisely the acceptance of diversity which forced politicians to seek a compromise by a creating a federal constitution which promotes the devolution of power to the nine regions. Therefore, diversity which has resulted in a federal constitution has provided a check on the central government and should be seen as supportive of democratic change in South Africa. The "miracle" of the transformation of South Africa into a non-racial democracy in April 1994 has resulted in the creation of a country whose citizens proudly refer to themselves as "the rainbow people of God" – a vision that Archbishop Desmond Tutu spared no energy to promote. It is a vision that may yet help us to embrace and perceive our cultural diversity as a blessing rather than a curse – a blessing which could be tapped to provide our young democratic nation with a firmer and enduring foundation.

CONCLUSION

In conclusion, it should be pointed out that the struggle for human rights for African people has been going on for a long time. Africans in South Africa and elsewhere have fought gallantly over the years for their political rights ever since these rights were usurped by European colonialists. Indeed, the struggle against colonialism during the 1950s and 1960s was nothing short of a struggle for human rights and the democratisation of political institutions in Africa. For Africans decided to take their lives into their own hands in order to shape their destiny through their participation in the democratisation process. Unfortunately, our detractors often miss this because of their tendency to want to disconnect the struggle against colonialism from the African struggle for the democratisation of their social institutions. Yet they should be seen as two sides of the same coin.

It is an open secret that Africans have a long record of struggle for democratisation, both on the African continent and the diaspora. In South Africa, the African people campaigned tirelessly and made representations to Britain for their freedom and the democratisation of society. When Britain failed to accede to their demands, the African National Congress (ANC) was formed in 1912 precisely to continue the struggle for democratisation. The Pan African Congress (PAC), which was formed in 1959, was another social movement which mediated and transmitted African culture, encouraging Africans to think positively about themselves. The PAC went so far as to reject the notion of different races, arguing that there is only one human race. Finally, the Black Consciousness Movement that arose in 1968 under the auspices of the South African Student Organisation was another cultural and spiritual movement that promulgated African culture and encouraged black people to take pride in their blackness, thereby challenging them to become subjects of their own history. So strong was the influence of the Black Consciousness Movement (BC) that Africans decided to confront one of the mightiest military machines on the African continent, namely the South African regime, in 1976. Once they regained their pride, Africans were fearless to the point of rendering the South African military and police brutality useless. In so doing, they laid the foundation for the collapse of the white regime which finally surrendered power to the majority during 1994. This majority victory came about because Africans were prepared to die for their beliefs and democratic rights and, in their fearless sacrifices, they destroyed the will of the white minority to govern over the black majority.

Indeed, what inspired African leaders like Nelson Mandela, Walter Sisulu, Oliver Tambo (ANC), Robert Sobukwe (PAC) and Steve Biko (BC) to endure many years of harassment, dehumanisation and oppression was the African yearning for justice, human rights and democratisation of society. This yearning for democracy was shared by other African leaders such as Kwame Nkruma (Ghana), Jomo Kenyatta (Kenya), Julius Nyerere (Tanzania), Kenneth Kaunda (Zambia) and Robert Mugabe (Zimbabwe), just to mention a few. All these leaders made enormous sacrifices, because they were driven by their determination to bring about human rights and democratic change in their countries.

Finally, we need to remind ourselves that the African people have a long tradition of struggle for democratic change. It is fitting that we should reflect on effective ways of bringing about more democratic changes in the other African countries so that all women and men can at last have a place in the sun, as subjects of the creation of both their history and destiny. In order to achieve this objective, the primary role of the church is to teach people to be dissatisfied with the oppressive and often undemocratic societies in which they live. Above all, people must be taught to believe in themselves and in their capacity to transform both themselves and their social environment. They have to be reminded that no social institution has been directly created by the hand of God. Rather, all social institutions are human creations and, therefore, are amenable to change by human intervention and creativity so that they might better serve the needs of human beings.

BIBLIOGRAPHY

Brueggermann, W. (1983), "Trajectories in Old Testament literature and the sociology of ancient Israel", in *The Bible and liberation: Politica and social hermeneutics*, Maryknoll: Orbis.

Fashole-Luke, E.W. (1976), "The quest for African Christian theologies", in *Scottish Journal of Theology*, 29:2.

Frotsin, P. (1985), *Liberation theology in Tanzania and South Africa*, Lund: Lund University Press.

Maimela, S.S. (1985), "Salvation in African traditional religions", in *Missionalia*, 13: 2, August.

Maimela, S.S. (1991), "Religion and culture: Blessings or curses" in *Journal of Black Theology*, 5: 1, May 1991.

The Ubuntu theology of Desmond Tutu

I seek to determine how a definition of Archbishop Tutu's theology, in light of his ecclesiology and the South African context, seeks a remedy to the following situation: how "History has still to produce an example of people giving up power voluntarily without external coercion".[1] Instead of assuming narratives of the will to power as expressed through racial discourse, Tutu's theology, derived from his culture and ecclesiology, is best described through an Ubuntu theology which is about the achievement of absolute dependence on God and neighbour in such a way that the eventuality of human identity is discovered therein. In short, Tutu's view of the *imago Dei* as human interdependence develops into this theology of Ubuntu.[2] Tutu states:

1. Tutu, "The options which face South Africa: Real political power-sharing or a bloodbath," in *Divided or united power: Views on the new constitutional dispensation by prominent South African political leaders*, J.A. du Pisani (ed.), Johannesburg: Lex Patria Publishers, 1986, p. 314.
2. This is true also on an ecumenical level for Tutu. He creates a common discourse for world religions on the basis of the Divine exalting humanity to the level of the divine in order to engage in conversation and relationship. In this conterminous way, the divine and human world religions champion the cause of the oppressed since: "They have no one to champion their cause except the adherents of the different religions . . . If they fail to do so then their faiths deserve to be consigned to the limbo of utterly irrelevant and uselessness." Tutu refers mainly to Islam's alms giving, Hinduism's incarnations in the form of avatars, and Gandhi's use of satyagraha. Tutu concludes: "And so we behold with awe and pride as a Mother Theresa and her nuns together with Hindu and Muslim ladies serving so gently and lovingly the derelicts picked off the streets of Calcutta so that they may die with some dignity. They pour oil on the sickmaking sores, sometimes which speaks of the divine balm of love and compassion." See Tutu, handwritten address, "World religions for human dignity and world peace", Nairobi, 1984.

They [white people] laugh, they love, they cuddle babies, they weep, they eat, they sleep – they are human. But if they are human, why, oh why can't they see that we laugh too, we love too, we weep too, we cuddle babies too, we eat, we sleep – why can't they see that it is impossible for things to go on like this?[3]

Being cuddled and kissed by our mothers and fathers we learn to grow in the atmosphere of security and love that all that handling engenders and that is how we learn to communicate our love and caring in subsequent times – holding hands, squeezing each other and kissing as lovers do.[4]

The definition of Ubuntu and how Tutu's theological interpretation of it counters the theological narrative of apartheid have to do with how the *imago Dei* is made intelligible in South Africa. Tutu summarises the problem this way: "It is absolutely necessary for us to share certain values otherwise discourse between us would be impossible for we would be without common points of reference."[5] I stress the intelligibility of the concept of Ubuntu because the environment in which Tutu seeks to explain its meaning has been corrupted by ideologies of power totally contrary to the concept of Ubuntu. Tutu's Ubuntu theology seeks to understand these tendencies of power: "And as Gustavo Gutierrez declares, 'We can't love our enemies, if we don't have them.'"[6]

Tutu explains further:

In their 35 years of rule the Nationalists have found their own solution to the vexed question of political power and white-black coexistence in this part of the continent. They have decided that they will keep power firmly in their grasp, and that coexistence will only be on terms dictated by them.[7]

3. Tutu, address to the South African Institute of Race Relations, quoted in David Winner, *Desmond Tutu: The brave and eloquent Archbishop struggling against apartheid in South Africa*, Dublin: Wolfhound Press, 1989, p. 26
4. Tutu, handwritten address, "Continuing education seminar", Diocese of East Oregon, Ascension School, Cove, Oregon, 15-18 August 1983.
5. Tutu, handwritten address, "Apartheid and confession", Pretoria University, undated.
6. Tutu, "Where is now thy God?", Trinity Institute, New York, 8 January 1989.
7. Tutu, "The plight of the resettled and other rural poor: The stand of the

Underlying Tutu's examination of power is the presupposition that Ubuntu,[8] as an African concept, provides the basis for a particular theology in which Tutu is able to conclude:

> We will grow in the knowledge that they [white people] too are God's children, even though they may be our oppressors, though they may be our enemies. Paradoxically, and more truly, they are really our sisters and our brothers, because we have dared, and have the privilege to call God "Abba", Our Father. Therefore, they belong together with us in the family of God, and their humanity is caught up in our humanity, as ours is caught up in theirs.[9]

Tutu's view of the spiritual life means that Ubuntu is more than humanism – Tutu presents a new kind of liberational spirituality. His conscious movement toward contemplative spirituality has been a defining feature of his episcopate. Therefore, any work on Tutu needs to take into account the correct interaction of spirituality, unfortunately perceived in the Western world through individualistic schemes of psychoanalysis, with effective social impact on structural forms of oppression. Tutu thinks:

> We are each a God-carrier, a tabernacle of the Holy Spirit, indwelt by God the holy and most blessed Trinity. To treat one such as less than this is not just wrong . . . It is veritably blasphemous and sacrilegious. It is to spit in the face of God. Consequently injustice, racism, exploitation, oppression are to be opposed not as a political task but as a response to a religious, a spiritual imperative. Not to oppose these manifestations of evil would be tantamount to disobeying God. God has created us for interdependence as God has created us in his image – the image of a divine fellowship of the holy

Church", in *Up against the fences: Poverty, passes and privilege in South Africa*, Hermann Giliomee and Lawrence Schlemmer, (eds.), Cape Town: David Philip, 1985.
8. For other references to Ubuntu see Tutu's article, "Persecution of Christians under apartheid", in *Christianity & Apartheid* folder; and Tutu, "Referendum, apartheid and Mogopa", 1984-1985.
9. Tutu, "Where is now thy God?"

and blessed Trinity. The self-sufficient human being is a contradiction in terms, is subhuman. God has created us to be different in order that we can realize our need of one another. There is an African idiom: "A person is a person through other persons." I learn how to be human through association with other human beings.[10]

WHAT IS NOT UBUNTU?

Before addressing the explicit question of what constitutes Ubuntu, in order to distinguish Ubuntu from other schemes of humanism, it is advantageous to recognise its antithesis commonly found in the Western world. Ubuntu is not humanism in the Western sense of favouring enlightenment notions that truth claims are located in the rational capacities of individuals. The African conceptualisation of being human is antithetical to enlightenment notions, because Western humanism tends more toward materialism than toward an African balance between material and spiritual realities.[11] Phillip Sherrard facilitates my contrast between African and Western accounts of anthropology through his account of the Western demise of the concept of being human, that in fact being human in the Western world is more equivalent to material being. Sherrard explains:

> There is, however, a price to be paid for fabricating around us a society which is as artificial and as mechanized as our own, and this is that we can exist in it only on condition that we adapt ourselves to it. This is our punishment. The social form which we have adopted cuts our consciousness to fit its needs, its imperatives tailor our experience. The inorganic technological world that we have invented lays

10. Tutu, "My credo", *Living philosophies: The reflections of some eminent men and women of our time*, Clifton Fadiman (ed.), New York: Doubleday, 1990, p. 235.
11. Some European historians counter this claim by painting a picture of southern Africa characterised by tribal wars and famine. However, African scholars such as Gabriel Setiloane state that such accounts leave out three elements which may have contributed to such war and famine 150 years (1652) before missionaries arrived in South Africa, i.e., "White man, the horse and the gun and ammunition". See the discussion in Setiloane, *The image of God among the Sotho-Tswana*, p. 123.

hold on our interior being and seeks to reduce it to a blind inorganic mechanical thing. It seeks to eliminate whole emotional areas of our life, demanding that we be a new type of being, a type that is not human as this has been understood in both the religious and humanist ages – one that has no heart, no affections, no spontaneity and is as impersonal as the metals and processes of calculation in which it is involved. And it is not only our emotional world that is deadened. The world of our creative imagination and intelligence is also impoverished.[12]

A fabricated society of competition is the sign of the fall of creation and it is the opposite of Ubuntu. For Tutu something is clearly disparate about a system of people whose *telos* (goal) is to achieve "autonomy of market-forces" despite the concomitant result of atheism and dehumanisation. This is clear because personhood is defined through the value of the product a person produces.

> So you say to that old lady walking the dusty streets of Soweto, whose African name her employer doesn't know because she says it's too difficult, so I'll call you by a name, even if it is not yours. You are Jane, Jane Annie. You say to her, Mummy, mummy as you walk the streets and they say who's that and you say, I am God's viceroy. You are someone very special to God and the divine image did not say it will indwell clever people. Whether you are clever or not so clever, whether you are beautiful or when people see you, they cover their faces, oh yes; whether you are tall or short, whether you are substantial or not so substantial [you are God's viceroys].[13]

This means that, as a Christian and as a person who is a member of the church, processes of dehumanisation cannot be tolerated. In this

12. Phillip Sherrard, "Science and the dehuminization of man", quoted in Maulana Faried Esack, *The second Desmond Tutu peace lecture*, published by the South African Chapter of the World Conference on Religion and Peace, 13 September 1986.
13. Tutu, transcript of Tutu's sermon in Birmingham Cathedral, 21 April 1988. Published by the Committee for Black Affairs, Birmingham, Diocesan Office, p. 3, hereafter, "Birmingham Cathedral Address".

light Tutu reasons: "Is it not revealing how when we meet people for the first time we soon ask, 'by the way, what do you do?' meaning what gives you value?"[14]

From Tutu's perspective of Ubuntu the reader learns that it is not human systems which encourage a high degree of competitiveness and selfishness. Such systems demonstrate the greatest discrepancy to God's creation of interdependence, i.e., incommensurate difference.[15] Tutu shows this discrepancy as he recounts the creation narrative in which Adam needs Eve as a sign of our interdependency.[16]

> Apartheid says people are created for separation, people are created for apartheid, people are created for alienation and division, disharmony and disunity and we say, the scripture says, people are made for togetherness, people are made for fellowship.
>
> You know that lovely story in the Bible. Adam is placed in the Garden of Eden and everything is hunky-dory in the garden. Everything is very nice, they are all very friendly with each other. Did I say everybody was happy? No, actually Adam was not entirely happy and God is solicitous for Adam and He looks on and says, "No, it is not good for man to be alone." So God says, "Adam, how about choosing a partner?"
>
> So God makes the animals pass one by one in front of Adam. And God says to Adam, "What about this one?" Adam says, "Not on your life." "What about this one?" "No." God says, "Ah, I've got it." So God puts Adam to sleep and out of his rib he produces this delectable creature Eve and when Adam awakes, he says "wow", this is just what the doctor ordered. But that is to say, you and I are made for interdependency.[17]

Tutu's interpretation of the creation narrative illustrates the profound truth, that instead of being made for disproportionate differences,

14. Tutu, "Grace upon grace", in *Journal for Preachers*, Vol. xv, No. 1, Decatur, Georgia, *Journal for Preachers*, Advent 1991, p. 20.
15. Tutu, sermon, printed after 7 October 1989.
16. Tutu provides this humorous account of Adam's search for Eve in "Birmingham Cathedral Address", and Tutu, undated handwritten address, "Why we must oppose apartheid", Grahamstown.
17. Tutu, "Birmingham Cathedral Address", p. 3.

God's creation continually informs people that identity and relationships go hand in hand. The obsession with individualism and self-achievement is countered for Tutu in Jesus' claims of discipling individuals to move outside of competitive cosmologies. Tutu states:

> Now the radical point about Jesus' question [re: the Good Samaritan] is: Who proved a neighbour to the man in need? You, gathered here, are in fact not meant to discover who your neighbour is (whom you are supposed to love as yourself as the second great commandment). No, you are meant to be asking, "To whom am I going to be a neighbour – Who is in need and whose need must I meet as a neighbour with this privilege and this responsibility?" You and I are the ones who are to be judged for failing to be neighbour to those in need.[18]

It is with this evidence of proving to be neighbour that I now turn to constructive definitions of Ubuntu.

WHAT IS UBUNTU?

To answer this question requires a turning away from Western definitions of personhood, i.e., of persons as consumers. Tutu's more specific connotation of the term Ubuntu derives from the expression *Umuntu ngumuntu ngabanye bantu*.[19] Not an easily translatable Xhosa concept, generally this proverbial expression means that each individual's humanity is ideally expressed in relationship with others and, in turn, individuality is truly expressed. Or "a person depends on other

---

18. Tutu, address, "Love reveals my neighbour, my responsibility", 16 December 1981.
19. "Almost all the peoples occupying the southern third of the African continent, from the Cameroon-Nigerian seaboard in the west to the Somalia-Kenyan coastline in the east and southwards as far as Port Elizabeth, speak a closely related group of languages known as the Bantu languages." *General history of Africa III: Africa from the seventh to the eleventh century.* I. Hrbek (ed.), Berkeley: The University of California Press, 1992, p. 75. Because the term "Bantu" was used in a divisive and derogatory manner by the apartheid government, it is not commonly used in English except in a technical sense, for example, in anthropology and linguistics.

persons to be a person".[20] Muendanyi Mahamba describes someone with Ubuntu, as for example, "Mpho has Ubuntu," or that Mpho is someone who cares about the deepest needs of others and who adheres faithfully to all social obligations. Mpho is conscious not only of her personal rights, but also of her duties to her neighbour. On the other hand, to say" *"Neo ga se motho"* (i.e., Neo lacks *botho*), implies that Neo is unfaithful in her social obligations, and is in fact a self-centred person.[21] One of Tutu's first references to Ubuntu is in his description of the African world view. Tutu states:

> In the African *Weltanschauung*, a person is not basically an independent solitary entity. A person is human precisely in being enveloped in the community of other human beings, in being caught up in the bundle of life. To be is to participate. The summum bonum here is not independence but sharing, interdependence. And what is true of the human person is surely true of human aggregations. Even in modern day Africa this understanding of human nature determines some government policies. After all, the Arusha Declaration is counterbalanced by the concept of "ujamaa" in Tanzania and "harambee" in Kenya. This is the reason I have spoken of a proper ambivalence towards [economic] viability – acknowledged its positive aspects while rejecting its negative ones and this in an explicit way. A dialectical tension exists here which must not be too easily resolved by opting for one or other of the alternatives.[22]

20. Augustine Shutte, "Philosophy for Africa", paper at the University of Cape Town, South Africa, p. 5.
21. Muendanyi Mahamba, "Ubuntu and democracy", in *Challenge*, June/July, No. 16, 1993, p. 7.
22. Tutu, "Viability", in *Relevant theology for Africa*: Report on a Consultation of the Missiological Institute at Lutheran Theological College, Mapumulo, Natal, 12-21 September 1972, Hans-Jurgen Becken (ed.), Durban: Lutheran Publishing House, 1973, p. 38. In my research, I notice the development of Tutu's first explicit reference to Ubuntu is in Tutu, "My search for God", St Mary's Jubilee Lenten Talks, St Alban's, Ferreirarstown, 5 April 1979. Ubuntu has remained a constant theme even until Tutu's most recent work, *The rainbow people of God*, October 1994.

From this African *Weltanschauung*, Ubuntu shapes Tutu's subsequent work to disallow false dichotomies of black and white people so as to allow Ubuntu to be an African source by which to make racial reconciliation intelligible on a cultural level. Tutu needs to communicate on this level of discourse because African scholars agree that the African *Weltanschauung* is the interdependence of persons for the exercise, development and fulfilment of their potential to be both individuals and community.[23] If this is the case, attention must also be given to how persons are interdependent among racial classifications. Ubuntu provides this, and becomes an invaluable concept for Tutu's theological model.

In light of Tutu's complex task of addressing both a white community notoriously known for abusive measures towards blacks and a black community equally caught up in the severe measures of condemning "collaborators" to gruesome deaths, the reader may question my display of Ubuntu theology as providing insufficient constitution to make personhood intelligible in incommensurate, racial discourse. Nevertheless, it is a risk I am willing to take. As I relate Tutu's spirituality to Anglican figures such as Trevor Huddleston, I calculate my risk and am reassured that Tutu's Ubuntu theology becomes even more vital to his South African context through his integration of moral, ascetical and political dynamics, which all demand the formation of personhood in community. For most of South African history, however, the opposite force, the disintegration of relationships between black and white people, has occurred. Trevor Huddleston explains this tragic situation with his encounter with a white English-speaking police officer who says to him:

> "But anyway, Father, you know yourself that seventy per cent of the people in this place are criminals." [Huddleston responds] I suggested that if that was the official attitude of the police, they were not very likely to win the trust and

23. A similar conceptualisation of Ubuntu may found in the doctrines of African socialism, especially expounded by Julius K. Nyerere's *ujumaa*. See J.K. Nyerere, *Ujamaa: Essays on socialism*, London: Oxford University Press, 1968; *Freedom and development*, Oxford: Oxford University Press, 1973; and "The rational choice", in A. Coulson (ed.), *African socialism in practice: The Tanzanian experience*, Nottingham: Spokesman Publishers, 1979, pp. 19-26. Masolo provides a critique of Nyerere's socialism as providing a poor sociological assessment of the causes and effects of communalistic attitudes in *Some aspects and prospectives of African philosophy today*, Institutio Italo-Africano, Rome, 1981.

confidence of Sophiatown. It was, to me at least, an interesting comment on the whole, sad situation. Just one more
indication of the same basic mental attitude. The native is
a problem: he is never a person.[24]

For Tutu, people must always be seen as ends in themselves in order to
understand Ubuntu, because to counter extremely antagonistic and
individualistic language, Tutu thinks that persons are ends in themselves only through the discovery of who they are in others.[25] For example, a person does not know that she is beautiful unless there is another person who can make beauty intelligible to her. In short, the *telos* of
persons must always remain a mystery, otherwise constricting definitions of people in terms of race inevitably lead to dehumanising forces.

These forces often run rampant and unchecked in the South African
context. In the following quotation, Tutu illustrates this as he refers to
bureaucrats who carry out inhuman and dehumanising legislation in
which personhood is lost in the shuffle of paper and power:

> It is difficult to see that bewildered man cowering before
> you, hardly understanding the shouted order that merely
> adds to his confusion as he is shunted from one queue to
> the other, from one office to the next to get the prized
> stamp which will allow him to work. It is difficult to recog-
> nise him as perhaps the head of his family, as the husband
> of some loved wife, as the doting father of pampered chil-
> dren, as himself a child of God.[26]

For most of South African history, certain persons were condemned
by law to stunted physical, emotional and intellectual growth,
for they were victims of a deliberately inferior education designed to
prepare them for perpetual serfdom. However, such a system turns
on itself, as Tutu explains: ". . . when I dehumanise you I inexorably
dehumanise myself".[27] Black people were casualties of an apartheid

24. Trevor Huddleston, *Naught for your comfort*, London: Collins, 1956, p. 87.
25. See Tutu, address, "Apartheid and Christianity", 24 September 1982, for a dis-
    cussion of this paradox.
26. Tutu, address, "A black view of the law", Pretoria Attorneys, 25 March 1983.
27. Tutu, "Oxford Union Address – South Africa: Why I am hopeful", 23 February
    1994.

system that determined to make them aliens through allowing the "spurious citizenship of unviable homelands whose independence is recognised only by South Africa and her satellites".[28] Tutu's view of people appeals beyond a system that only perpetuates casualties of a racial war.

Tutu believes that humans are especially born as potentiality; if human beings grew up individually among wolves they would not know how to communicate as human beings. There would be no human posture or human ways of eating, sitting and walking. Therefore human beings become persons only by living in an environment conducive to the interaction of diverse personalities and cultures. If there is no such environment, personhood does not survive. Tutu illustrates this with the following allegory:

> There was once a light bulb which shone and shone like no light bulb had shone before. It captured all the limelight and began to strut about arrogantly quite unmindful of how it was that it could shine so brilliantly, thinking that it was all due to its own merit and skill. Then one day someone disconnected the famous light bulb from the light socket and placed it on the table and try as hard as it could, the light bulb could bring forth no light and brilliance. It lay there looking so disconsolate and dark and cold – and useless. Yes, it had never known that its light came from the power station and that it had been connected to the dynamo by little wires and flexes that lay hidden and unseen and totally unsung.[29]

This means for Tutu that Ubuntu is the environment of vulnerability, i.e., a set of relationships in which people are able to recognise that their humanity is bound up in the other's humanity.

Central to my thesis is the fact that Tutu's life and thought appeal to his society to move beyond racial distinctions as determinative of

28. Tutu, handwritten address, United Nations, May 1988.
29. Tutu, address, "Response at Graduation of Columbia University's Honorary Doctorate", presented by Columbia's president at the University of the Witwatersrand, 2 August 1982. The president and trustees came to South Africa because Tutu was prevented by the South African government from flying to New York.

human identity. Through Tutu's emphasis upon the church's life of worship, in which human identity is elevated as people find communion with others and God, Ubuntu makes sense of how South Africans should then proceed to operate on the basis of more than racial identity. In other words, people need not kill each other because they are black or white, but should instead rejoice in how God has created them differently so that new meanings and identities are always possible.

Unlike many Western forces which seek to "establish" who a person or community is, Tutu's Ubuntu excludes Western tendencies of grasping competitiveness.[30] The beauty of Ubuntu is that instead of there being warring factions, instead of being manipulative and self-seeking, that person who lives in Ubuntu is "more willing to make excuses for others"[31] and even discover new meaning in other persons. Therefore Ubuntu is an attribute that distinguishes humans from mere animals; as Tutu concludes: "If you throw a bone to a group of dogs you won't hear them say: 'After you!' "[32]

UBUNTU PROVIDES A WAY AHEAD

Most explicit for Tutu's context, the beatitude of Ubuntu is that it provides an alternative to vengeance. Tutu states: "I saw it in Zimbabwe yet again last week. It is what has allowed Mr Smith to survive in a post-independent Zimbabwe."[33] South Africa – black and white – can be human together, and will define tyranny only by first living together.[34] Again, perspective determines actions and Ubuntu provides an invaluable perspective in which white and black people may see themselves as more than racial rivals. "When you look at someone with eyes of love," Tutu believes, "you see a reality differently from that of some-

30. Tutu, "A Christian vision of the future of South Africa". Essay submitted to be published in *Christianity in South Africa* to Prof Martin Prozesky, University of Natal, 31 July 1989.
31. Tutu, address, "The nature and value of theology", undated.
32. Tutu, "Human rights in South Africa", in Monitor, SACC Library Resource Centre, undated.
33. Ibid.
34. Ibid.

one who looks at the same person without love, with hatred or even just indifference.[35]

Instead of perpetuating the system of apartheid, Tutu believes that Ubuntu means that personhood develops through the church as the church witnesses to the world that God is the one who loves human identities into being, even before individuals conceived of rights or perspectives of tyranny. In other words, God's love is prevenient – it is there before everything else and calls all justifications for control into account. As a Christian, no-one can claim control of life. To gain the vision to negotiate how to be in the world is to access the life of grace in God. Any claim of control or power is delusory and foolish, as Tutu explains: "Jesus gave a new, very important responsibility to Peter. He said, 'Feed my sheep.' It's almost like asking a thief to become your treasurer."[36]

Through a theological Ubuntu the Christian concedes to the need to be transformed into a new identity, a new perspective which fully encompasses the truth which Tutu states: "God does not love us because we are lovable, but we are lovable precisely because God loves us. God's love is what gives us our worth . . . So we are liberated from the desire to achieve, to impress. We are the children of the divine love and nothing can change that fundamental fact about us."[37] As Tutu's Ubuntu theology unfolds it gives access to a new identity for South Africans, it also appeals to ancient African concepts of the harmony between individual and community which John Mbiti concludes as: "I am because we are, and since we are, therefore I am."[38]

35. Tutu, quoted in *Prayers for peace*, an anthology of readings and prayers select-ed by Archbishop Robert Runcie and Cardinal Basil Hume, London: SPCK, 1987, p. 41.
36. Tutu, handwritten sermon, Sunday School Teacher's Eucharist, St George's Cathedral, 2 February 1987.
37. Tutu, handwritten sermons, at St Philip's Washington DC, Christmas III, 1984.
38. John Mbiti, *African religions and philosophies*, New York: Doubleday and Company, 1970, p. 141.

African and Anglican

I am indebted to the United Society for the Propagation of the Gospel for allowing me to publish an edited and expanded version of this paper, which first appeared in *USPG Thinking Mission*, Issue 24, London, October 1995.

A LITTLE TOUCH OF PURPLE

"I believe that there are as yet untapped riches in African culture waiting to be used for the glory of God." So said Archbishop George Carey after his visit to Kenya to celebrate the centenary of the Church of the Province of Kenya in 1994. While there he took every opportunity to encourage the inclusion of African songs in Anglican worship. But Anglicanism is an ecclesiastical culture and the concern to maintain Anglican identity as defined by the symbolic structure and historic traditions of the Mother Church dies hard. One only had to see the roaring trade done by Wippels ecclesiastical outfitters in equipping African bishops with the trappings of their office at the 1988 Lambeth Conference. This even where there is an explicit Africanisation in the mode of leadership.

Until quite recently unity in the Anglican Communion was synonymous with liturgical unity, the Book of Common Prayer providing the symbolic focus. This was the liturgical baggage which Anglican missionaries brought with them to Africa. In an era which equated Christianity with Western ideas of progress and civilisation, denigrated indigenous values and culture, and supported the symbiotic association of cross and crown, the first black Anglicans invariably found their new identity as clones of their mentors within the colonial establishment. The colonisation of consciousness was complete. The only significant Anglican variation was in church tradition ranging from conservative Evangelical to high Anglo-Catholic. The ideology of the imperialistic era still seems to pervade African Anglicanism, even where the received tradition has been appropriated into indigenous cultures over more than a hundred years to serve quite different strategies and needs arising from an African context.[1]

Anglicanism was clothed in patriarchal middle-class Victorian dress and typically associated with upward social mobility and African aristocracy, sons of African rulers being a prime target for elitist education. Generations later it is not surprising that a male-dominated black Anglican leadership has been slow to respond to the prompting of the Lambeth fathers for indigenous liturgical revisions. In some regions, conservatism in upholding the received tradition may well be reinforced by class factors. The burgeoning Pentecostal and African-initiated churches tend to represent the marginalised working and peasant classes, catering for their needs with exuberant worship, healing services, communal support and shared leadership with women. How would middle-class Anglicans maintain their identity if their church followed suit? How would this affect their identity within the Anglican Communion? Fear of losing one's identity is particularly acute in times of rapid social change.

Some Anglicans in Kenya have complained that the African-style antiphonal prayers in the Kenyan Holy Communion Service are pentecostal and charismatic, "definitely non-Anglican". In South Africa, the introduction of marimbas (African xylophones) into worship in the 1980s was strenuously resisted as being "un-Anglican", until Archbishop Tutu gave them the seal of approval at his consecration service. Liturgical change also generates confusion. When a Ghanaian woman, initiated into a highly disciplined Anglo-Catholic missionary tradition, was told that fasting was now limited to a few hours before Holy Communion, she asked: "Since when has God changed his

1. See for example the discussion at the recent EDICESA (Ecumenical Documentation and Information Centre for Eastern and Southern Africa) conference in Harare. Dr Aynos Masotcha Moya, of the University of Zimbabwe, referred to the "constipation which was caused by swallowing the message of the Gospel together with the cultural plastic that came wrapping the Good News". He noted that although most Zimbabwean churches are now led by Africans, "they seem to perpetuate even negative missionary attitudes and practices".

mind?" Problematic for some too is the reluctance of women, the backbone of the African church, to find their voice and challenge the ecclesiastical status quo.

Obviously African Anglicanism has taken on significant regional variations in response to quite different historical experiences. Kevin Ward notes that when in the 1890s "Protestants" (Anglicans) in Uganda achieved power over Muslims and Catholics, they became identified as the Church of the Kabaka and an aristocracy. But, ipso facto, it also became a church of the peasants because of the long-held Kiganda tradition of *bakopi* (peasants) following their *omukama* (lord/chief). Thus, even though the predominant ethos of the Anglican church may appear to be middle class, and the church has even served to encourage a "bourgeoisification" of its members by providing education which opened the way for employment outside peasant subsistence cultivation, African theology may well be a bourgeois enterprise led by teachers and clergy searching for their alienated African (peasant) roots. Resistance to change in village churches, by holding on to traditional Anglicanism, may be an attempt to preserve local community values over against the more modern, mobile and individualistic culture of the town.[2]

The liturgical liberation of the historic mission churches may also be threatening where the churches have enjoyed power and privilege in supporting the political status quo. Transformation challenges the African church to free the gospel from its captivity to post-colonial or post-apartheid power structures, and to identify with the poor and the oppressed.[3] Significantly, at the height of the political struggle in South Africa in the 1980s, it was alternative liturgies, Bible studies and worship resources, "which linked the social needs and political aspirations of people to worship that were confiscated by the security police. The more learned texts written by academics and scholars on liberation and black theology were ignored".[4]

2. Personal communication from the Revd Dr Kevin Ward of the Department of Theology and Religious Studies, Leeds University, and formerly of Bishop Tucker College, Uganda, 29 November 1995.
3. Jean-Marc Ela, *African cry* Maryknoll, 1980, p. 52.
4. C. Villa-Vicencio, "To be servant of the people", *Sojourners*, December 1992, p. 28.

"WOULD GOD RECOGNISE YOU IN AFRICAN DRESS?"

This is the question Archbishop Tutu has long been asking in urging "the rehabilitation of the African's rich cultural heritage and religious consciousness".[5] Writing in 1973, he confronted the assumption that "you had to be as it were circumcised into a Westerner, if you were an African, before God could hear you".

> The missionaries were bringing the light of the Gospel to the dark continent. These poor native pagans had to be clothed in Western clothes so that they could speak to the white man's God, the only God, who was obviously unable to recognise them unless they were decently clad. These poor creatures must be made to sing the white man's hymns hopelessly badly translated, they had to worship in the white man's unemotional and individualistic way, they had to think and speak to God and all the wonderful Gospel truths in the white man's well-proven terms.

Archbishop Tutu challenged African theology to recover its prophetic calling, beginning with "radical spiritual decolonization":

> We have had our own way of communion with deity, ways which meant that we were able to speak authentically as ourselves and not as pale imitations of others . . . Why should we feel that something is amiss if our theology is too dramatic for verbalization but can be expressed only adequately in the joyous song and the scintillating movement of Africa's dance in the liturgy?

Liturgists in the Church of the Province of Southern Africa (CPSA) have supported Archbishop Tutu in calling for the freeing of their liturgical tradition from "ideological captivity". But they stress that liturgy cannot simply be dressed up in new language if its theological basis has not been thoroughly investigated. "The most archaic liturgi-

---

5. This and the following quotations from Desmond Tutu, "Whither African theology?" in *Christianity in independent Africa*, edited by E. Fashole-Luke et al, London, 1978, pp. 365-369, and *Bishopscourt Update*, 20 August 1991, 7/91, p. 4.

cal forms can sometimes be celebrated with surprisingly modern understanding and results. Changing the ritual form by itself does not change the community's understanding of what it is doing." The formal liturgy of white congregations, enshrining and articulating a privatised spirituality, is contrasted unfavourably with the spontaneous living liturgy of many black congregations, reflecting "a corporate engagement between God and the community". Black congregations are in turn criticised because "the experience of God in worship is all too often not directly connected with Christian action in the world."[6]

Over the years Archbishop Tutu has continued to argue that only when African theology is true to itself will it speak relevantly to contemporary Africa, and that this will enrich our common Christian heritage. He suggests that the affinity of African religious insights with the Bible has much to teach the West about the corporateness of human existence and the sense of the numinous. Bishop Manas Buthelezi of the Evangelical Lutheran Church in Southern Africa has warned of the danger of romanticising "African spiritual concepts", but supports the quest to "recapture the wholeness of life" as found in an African heritage. Similarly, Presiding Bishop Stanley Mogoba has called on the Methodist Church to become an "authentic African Church" by engaging in dialogue between "African traditional religion and Western Christianity".[7]

Bishop Winston Njongonkulu Ndungane is another Anglican leader who focuses on this theme. In his enthronement charge to his diocese of Kimberley and Kuruman in 1991, he highlighted the fact that the CPSA is a church rooted in Africa, with 80 per cent of its membership having a background of African culture – "a culture that has been sadly neglected in the life of our church . . . While we uphold the content of the gospel which we have received as sacrosanct, nevertheless there is a need for an evaluation of the form, the language and the idiom in which it is to be communicated to us, which has largely been influenced by Western European culture."[8] Bishop Njongonkulu

6. T. Paterson, "A liturgy for liberation", in *Bounty in bondage. The Anglican Church in Southern Africa*, edited by F. England and T. Paterson, Johannesburg, 1989, p. 56.
7. Report from Yaounde, Cameroon, *Seek*, August 1989; Report from the Methodist Annual Conference, Umtata, 1994, *Challenge*, No. 29, April/May 1995.
8. *Church Times*, 27 September 1991.

instances a range of African concepts besides music and liturgy which might change church thinking:

> There is the way in which the poor were traditionally cared for: people would lend them a cow to milk, or leave something in the fields for them at harvest time. There's been a rich understanding of humanity in the African world view, with the concept of the living dead looking after us, interceding on our behalf with God. There has been no separation of the secular and the religious, which has been the Western European norm. African culture provides models in initiation rites involving comprehensive training for adulthood in areas such as ethics and marriage. It deals, for example, with how two families linked in marriage come into a relationship.[9]

But the freeing of Anglicanism from its Western forms is fraught with difficulties. Bishop Tilewa Johnson speaks of how Anglican converts in Gambia resisted missionary pressure to abandon indigenous thought-patterns and practices by holding on to them in secret. "On top we behaved as Christians," he confessed, "but deep down we had another God, a real African god, whom we went to when we were in trouble. We now have to find ways of engaging with that." According to Bishop Johnson, the people of Sierra Leone and Gambia are both African and Western in their ways, in contrast to Nigeria, where "indigenous tribes have owned the Christian faith". They have inherited a Victorian Christianity complete with robed choirs, incense and bells. Although some use is made of the new West African service book, "people prefer to use what is familiar, what Father taught them years ago. Also, because we don't use English every day we don't see the need for 'thees' and 'saiths' to change." [10]

Archbishop Tutu stresses the danger of "religious schizophrenia", where African Christians live in two different cultures, one of their religion and the other of their everyday life:

> With part of himself (the African Christian) has been compelled to pay lip service to Christianity as understood,

9. *Anglican Update*, Vol. 1: 4, May 1994.
10. Interview with Colin Moreton, *Church Times*, 21 January 1994, p. 7.

expressed and preached by the white man. But with an even greater part of himself, a part he has been often ashamed to acknowledge openly and which he has struggled to repress, he has felt that his Africanness was being violated. The white man's largely cerebral religion was hardly touching the depths of his African soul; he was being redeemed from sins he did not believe he had committed; he was being given answers to questions he had not asked.[11]

TO BE OR NOT TO BE . . .

The legacy of Western dependence is a fierce loyalty of many Africans to the received Anglican tradition. But while liturgies framed in alien conceptual categories may well contribute towards an Anglican identity, they may also fail to meet the existential needs of the worshipping community. Too often the historic mission churches in Africa have become service agencies for "Sunday Christians". They baptise, marry and bury members, while the Pentecostal and African-initiated churches provide for their spiritual and physical needs, sometimes in secret and, at least in the past, in fear of excommunication.

Nonetheless, there is resistance to change which may well relate to historic circumstances. People who have self-consciously put aside what they regard as their "tainted animist past", as in the Anglican Diocese of Antsiranana in Madagsacar, have fiercely opposed the introduction of indigenous music into church worship. They have inherited a high Catholic tradition of prayer book and incense, cottas and cassocks. For them a service said rather than sung would be like "a meal without salt". But the music must be Anglican chants and hymns, remembered by heart, sung with great gusto, and possibly accompanied by a harmonium. They have consciously resisted the Roman Catholic example of bringing in drums, indigenous dancing and Malagasy music.[12] In contrast, the neighbouring Diocese of Toamasina, led by a bishop from Canada, is experimenting with indigenous elements as in the centenary service to mark the arrival of the first Anglican missionaries, and in ordination services.

This raises the question of where the call for liturgical change is

11. Tutu, p. 366.
12. Interview with Bishop Keith Benzies, Oxford, 17 January 1994.

coming from. An African delegate to the Third International Anglican Liturgical Consultation in York in 1989 defined colonialism as "Europeans telling Africans how to be European", while neo-colonialism was said to be "Europeans telling Africans how to be African". In fact the Anglican primates and the Anglican Consultative Council, meeting in Cape Town in 1993, gave enthusiastic support to inculturation,[13] as did the Anglican Global Conference on Dynamic Evangelism Towards 2000, in Kanuga, North Carolina, in September 1995.

In South Africa, academics and theologians have retained a clear divide between African theology and black theology. Because of the political circumstances in the country, the ongoing need to explore the relationship of the gospel to the existential situation of black suffering and oppression meant that black theology remained the priority until 1993. Elsewhere in Africa, as countries gained their independence, the key issue was how to be both African and Christian. Now the tables have turned. Liberated from the apartheid era in South Africa, the dialogue between Christianity and African culture has come to the fore, spawning a proliferation of consultations on the subject. In other parts of Africa the worsening socio-political situation is demanding that questions like war and genocide, refugees, ethnicity, AIDS, national debt, corrupt leadership, oppression of women, brutalisation of children, reconciliation and restitution, set the theological agenda.

In 1995, the African Synod of the Roman Catholic Church, meeting in Rome, proposed a new vision of the church as "the Family of God". This image emphasises care for others, solidarity, warmth in human relationships, acceptance, dialogue and trust. Evangelisation will thus be aimed at avoiding ethnocentrism and excessive particularism, trying instead to encourage reconciliation and "true communion" between different groups.[14] This would mesh with the concern for reconciliation throughout southern Africa.

The Roman Catholic Church in Africa has previously taken the lead. Following the Second Vatican Council, it made a concerted move to explore indigenous ways of expressing Christian faith. In 1974, a group of black South African Catholics, lay and ordained, challenged fellow blacks to find indigenous forms of worship. They cited the

13. L. McGeary and J. Rosenthal (eds.), *A transforming vision. Suffering and glory in God's world*, Cape Town, 1993, London, 1993, pp. 97-8.
14. *FOCUS* (Newsletter of the National Missionary Council of England and Wales), November 1995: No. 79.

Xhosa adage that "it does not become you to dance in another man's [sic] garb".[15] The Lumko Missiological Institute in Lady Frere, Transkei, took the initiative in developing neo-African church compositions using marimbas (wooden xylophones) and African drums, and hosted two consultations on African anthropology.[16] The CPSA was slow to follow suit, although the Provincial Board of Mission did hold forums on "African Culture and Christianity" at different centres in 1983, culminating in a National Forum at Rhodes University in 1985[17]. The Department of Religious Studies at the University of the Transkei alone continued with this work in the late 1980s.[18]

Inculturation is now firmly on the CPSA agenda. In March 1994, the Bishops of the Province resolved on the constitution of a Standing Commission on Christianity and African Culture. Two months later, the CPSA Provincial Conference on Mission and Ministry at Modderpoort identified "inculturation of the church, including liturgy", as being integral to its Focus for Action. In April 1995, a consultation was held for lay and ordained black leaders in the CPSA, entitled "Call to Conversion: Black Anglicans in a Transforming Church for a New Society".[19] Dioceses have followed suit with clergy schools debating how the church could employ "traditional African" attitudes to ancestors, land, healing and worship.[20] These moves have been complemented by intensive ecumenical interaction.

What is often forgotten is that over the years lone African voices within the CPSA have tried to develop an African expression of Christianity against considerable odds. In fact the first black Anglican conference was held by an African elite at St Mark's Mission, Transkei, in November 1869! These sons of African leaders, former students of Zonnebloem College in Cape Town, wished to develop an indigenous church, albeit

15. Letter from Hammanskraal, 19 April 1974.
16. Heinz Kuckertz, CSSp (ed.), *Culture and morality*, Lumko Missiological Institute, 1979 and *Ancestor religion in Southern Africa*, Lumko, 1981. See also the extensive list of music publications and tapes compiled by Dave Dargie.
17. Plenary papers were published in *Journal of Theology for Southern Africa*, 51, June 1985.
18. Publications of their Religious Studies forums: L. Kretzschmar (ed.), *Christianity and African culture*, Unitra, March 1988, and L. Pato (ed.), *Towards an authentic African Christianity*, Unitra, March 1989.
19. *From hope to fulfillment*, Report of the CPSA Black Leaders Consultation, Kempton Park, April 1995.
20. e.g. Pretoria clergy school, *Anglican Update*, Vol. 2:3, April 1995.

within the colonial missionary framework. They suggested the establishment of a self-supporting mission station in which every member would work at a trade as well as being an evangelist. Incidentally, they were also keen cricketers, being commended for their "gentlemanly" behaviour in a match against Queenstown in 1870.[21] It was not until the 1940s that "indigenisation" became a political issue in the CPSA.

The African Catholic Church movement was the brainchild of the Revds James Calata and Mashite Maimane, Anglican priests in the Dioceses of Grahamstown and Pretoria and members of the Provincial Board of Mission. Calata was also active in the African National Congress at the time, being in turn Cape president, Secretary-General, and senior chaplain. The African Catholic movement was an attempt to establish a separate African branch within the Anglican Church, seeking "to enhance, and use to the full, the African spiritual gifts and powers, as well as African ability and intelligence where it may be found". The plan was speedily squashed by the Synod of Bishops as being schismatic and likely to reinforce the new Nationalist government's segregation policies.[22]

African theologians in the CPSA have also struggled to be recognised. In 1945, Father Austin Maboee, son of an Anglican priest, was so incensed at hearing a missionary at a Sunday School conference condemn Basotho customs, that he spent the next seven years collecting information from old Basotho men and women. But he could not persuade the church to use African music, nor the CPSA to publish his treatise, *Modimo: Christian theology in a Sotho context*. Not only does his theology engage with Basotho myth and religious concepts, but he offers a range of practical ways forward. It was only a chance meeting that led to the manuscript's publication shortly before Fr Maboee's death in 1982.[23] Bishop Sigqibo Dwane has also done pioneering studies in looking at "Christianity in relation to Xhosa religion".[24] What is encouraging is that renewed interest in this field is not being launched in a vacuum.

21. Janet Hodgson, "Kid gloves and cricket on the Kei", *Religion in Southern Africa*, Vol. 8:2, July 1987, pp. 61-91.
22. Richard Shorten, *The legion of Christ's witnesses*, Centre for African Studies, University of Cape Town, Communications No. 15, 1987, pp. 13-14.
23. Edited by Janet Hodgson and Bill Domeris, Lumko Institute, 1982.
24. This is the title of Dwane's doctoral thesis, University of London, 1979. For an excellent discussion on the issues, see Luke Pato, "Becoming an African church", in *Bounty in bondage*, pp. 159-176.

In contrast to the Roman Catholic Church, Anglican Provinces have the right to work out their own liturgies.[25] But despite prompting from the last two Lambeth Conferences, and much activity in liturgical revision, most experimental liturgies from the African Provinces have continued to be modelled after a succession of Church of England revisions.[26] Originality is mainly limited to the use of local languages. An exception is the new series of Kenyan services (1989 and 1991), which claim to be both "thoroughly biblical and authentically African".

Ideally, liturgical renewal should take place through community decision-making and action, growing from the grassroots rather than being created and imposed by liturgical committees. But the support of bishops and priests is essential. This has been encouraged by a consultation on African culture and Anglican liturgy convened by the Council of Anglican Provinces in Africa (CAPA) at Kanamai, Kenya, in June 1993. Delegates from Burundi, Central Africa, Kenya, Rwanda, Southern Africa, Sudan, Tanzania, West Africa, Uganda and Zaire, sought Pan-African co-operation in drafting alternative liturgies which would reclaim African culture as the truly authentic context for worship.[27]

But how to define African culture in a contemporary context? Culture is dynamic and constantly changing. Many old customs, traditions and rites of passage have either been lost or have become irrelevant in a

25. Roman Catholic leaders in Africa have had to struggle with unsympathetic structures of Catholic communion, with a Canon Law that embodies Western cultural presuppositions, and a hierarchy afraid of losing control: A. Shorter, *Towards a theology of inculturation*, London, 1988, chapters 15-18.
26. Resolution 22c on Christ and Culture, 1988 Lambeth Conference, "urges the Church everywhere to work at expressing the unchanging Gospel of Christ in words, actions, names, customs, liturgies, which communicate relevantly in each contemporary society". Resolution 47 on Liturgical Freedom resolved that "each Province should be free, subject to essential universal Anglican norms of worship, and to valuing of traditional liturgical materials, to seek that expression of worship which is appropriate to the Christian people in their cultural context", in Colin Buchanan (ed.), *Lambeth and liturgy* 1988, Grove Worship series No. 106, p. 24. The "essential Anglican norms", contained within the Lambeth Quadrilateral, are the Bible, creeds, sacraments of the gospel and episcopal ordination.
27. For a report on the Kanamai Consultation see *News of Liturgy* no. 223, July 1993. Nigeria and the Indian Ocean were unrepresented.

modern African city. Nonetheless, the Rev. Elisha Mbonigaba urged that

> The singing of traditional hymns has long been an authentic African way of passing on religious knowledge, as is dancing, rhythm, swaying, embracing, and other gesture-language. If the Christian church is to survive in Africa, the issue is not whether inculturation *should* be done, but *how* it is done . . . Rites may change but thinking does not change. We still think and feel like Africans. We do not need to continue to be enemies to ourselves.

Issues discussed at Kanamai included using staple foods such as cassava and banana juice as eucharistic elements,[28] dialogue rather than a sermon, vestments patterned on local ceremonial dress, buildings more amenable to African congregational worship, the naming of children at baptism, the incorporation of traditional birth and puberty rites and African rituals relating to betrothal and marriage, anointing the dead with oil, wailing during the funeral service and gender inclusiveness at every level of congregational worship.

Difficulties also arise from the diversity and shifting landscape of African spirituality. For instance, the twenty-two tribal groupings in Uganda each have their own cultural context and need space to express the uniqueness of their relationship with God. What helps one group today may well hinder another, or even be outdated, tomorrow. Age differences were a particular concern in Burundi, with youth criticising outdated liturgies and opting for extempore prayers and unstructured worship

A distinction is usually drawn between indigenisation and inculturation in the process of cultural and liturgical change.[29] Indigenisation involves the co-option of some customs or artifacts of a local culture into what remains a basically Eurocentric act of worship.[30] Thus non-essential indigenous cultural elements such as liturgical vestments, dances,

---

28. The Church of Uganda used banana juice and cassava or dried banana hosts for its communion services until the 1920s, when as the result of a decision at the Lambeth Conference of that year, Bishop Willis insisted on using bread and wine, upsetting some old missionaries: Ward, 29 October 1995.
29. "Adaptation" and "accommodation" are used by Roman Catholics in much the same way as "indigenisation" in Protestantism.
30. G.A. Arbuckle, *Earthing the gospel. An inculturation handbook for pastoral workers*, London, 1990, p. 17.

rhythmic movements, drumming, songs, art, sculpture, architecture, etc. are drawn upon quite independently of one another to clothe worship in an African dress as long as they are "uncontaminated" by any "heathen" religious associations. This may be little more than a concessionary crumb.

The fear is of supposed syncretism in which Christian meaning is betrayed by "an illegitimate symbiosis" of cultural expression.[31] The syncretism bogey, reinforced by a pervasive missionary legacy which sees all African culture as inherently evil, tends to paralyse creative liturgical dialogue. Theological colleges provide ideal settings for experimental worship as at the College of the Transfiguration in Grahamstown. At Pentecost a seminarian "sang the praises" of God, Christ and the Holy Spirit before the altar in the manner of a Xhosa praise-singer, including typical dress and dramatic movement. This was followed by prayers in remembrance of African heroes of the faith, and a chorus of seminarians (and the Rector!) in black cassocks with a song-and-movement routine in honour of the Holy Spirit.

Indigenisation in the Anglican Church has typically involved developing black leadership. But the criteria for selection and training remained resolutely Western, with few ordinations to the priesthood until this century, let alone bishops. The first African bishop in southern Africa, Alphaeus Zulu, was consecrated an assistant bishop in 1960 and only became a diocesan bishop six years later.

Indigenisation merges into inculturation, which is described variously as "the ongoing dialogue between faith and culture or cultures",[32] or "the actual 'taking flesh' of Christianity in a culture or milieu". For Bosch, inculturation is not so much a case of the church being expanded, but of the church "being born anew in each new context and culture". This implies a double movement in which the Christian message transforms a culture and Christianity is in turn transformed by culture.[33] Planned inculturation implies "a willingness to listen to culture, to incorporate what is good and to challenge what is alien to the truth of God". Implementation presupposes cultural decolonisation, in which an attachment to ways of worship which are required neither by the gospel itself, nor by the local culture, are critically examined, as well as concern

---

31. Shorter, p. 12.
32. Shorter, p. 11; Arbuckle, pp. 17-20.
33. Shorter, pp. 225, 14; D.J. Bosch, *Transforming mission. Paradigm shifts in theology of mission*, Maryknoll, 1991, pp. 453-5.

for ethnic or minority groups. Above all there is the need to be open to innovation and experimentation, and to encourage local creativity.[34]

In the Anglican context, language has been a transitional element in the inculturation process, with translations of the Book of Common Prayer or modern Church of England series marking the first move. Language is critical to a people's identity, and African languages are particularly rich in symbols, metaphors, idioms, proverbs and imagery. The problem is the multiplicity of languages in Africa. English or French are often the only common bond within one country, as is Afrikaans within parts of southern Africa. Even in English, the idiomatic use of the language may have significant regional variations, while translations from English into the vernacular must be sensitive to local idiom.

In Nigeria, the Eucharist has been translated into Yoruba, Ibo and Hausa, but there are 120 languages nationwide. Southern Africa celebrated the simultaneous publication of a new Prayer Book in 1989 in six languages, with more added since. In Mozambique, liturgical translations into numerous vernaculars help liberate Anglicans from their Portuguese colonial past, an expensive exercise in a poor country. Madagascar is fortunate in having only one language, Malagasy (of Indonesian origin). But the Lutheran, Roman Catholic and Anglican churches each devised their own vocabularies and have only recently acquired an ecumenical New Testament in modern Malagasy with the Old Testament still to follow. Kenyan Anglicans use Swahili as a liturgical language in the towns. But village services are almost entirely in local languages – Kikuyu, Luo, Nandi, etc.[35] In Tanzania, Swahili is used liturgically almost universally, but they have the problem of bringing two distinct Anglican traditions of churchmanship together in their provincial liturgies.

Art and architecture are other starting points for Africanisation, but the missionary legacy of Aryan images of Christ remains, whether this be in crucifixes, mass statues, stained glass, Mothers' Union banners or Christmas cribs. It is almost impossible to chart the development of genuine inculturation in liturgical art because missionary influence is again pervasive. Grace Dieu mission in the Transvaal is renowned for its African carvings, but Eurocentric imagery was originally used as the model, and the fund-raising needs of the mission determined the market in Europe. Was the gradual infiltration of African imagery also market-led or did the

34. David Holeton (ed.) "Down to earth worship", *Liturgical inculturation in the Anglican communion*, Alcuin/Grow Liturgical Study 15, 1990, pp. 8-13.
35. Ward, 29 November 1995.

imagery perhaps serve as gospel teaching for non-literate people? African artwork in local churches, including furniture and furnishings, is also invariably anonymous, making historical analysis problematic.

In St Alban's Church, Dar es Salaam, a local artist was forbidden by the middle-class black congregation to use African figures in depicting a modern Stations of the Cross. He sneaked in a self-portrait of Simon of Cyrene. On the other hand, John Muafangejo (1943-1987), an Anglican from Ovamboland in Namibia, became internationally famous as a black artist. His linocuts often portray religious and biblical themes in relation to his personal, social and political context. The mural paintings which cover the walls, inside and out, of the Cyrene school chapel near Bulawayo are another celebration of African Christian imagery. So too, Arabic motifs give Mombasa Cathedral, built around 1905, a strongly eastern flavour reflecting local culture, but brass wall plaques and a brass eagle reading desk retain a post-colonial presence. The colonial tradition of pseudo-Gothic churches abounds and is ill-adapted to African conditions. New churches built with breeze blocks, as with St Mark's Theological College chapel in Dar es Salaam, are light and airy and blend well with tropical surroundings.

Questions do arise as to how one can achieve a dialogue between faith and a plurality of cultures. Here inculturation might need to relate to a specific context such as suffering, poverty, homelessness, peace and reconciliation, caring for the earth, or a uniting subculture such as the youth, the elderly or the deaf.

TALKING DRUMS, GUITARS, AND RESHROUDING THE DEAD

The litany of musical woes suffered under missionary domination is endless. African drumming, dancing and singing were all outlawed as being associated with pagan rituals, but the hymnody replacing them often made no sense. African languages are tonal, so that the meaning of words can radically change when translations of hymns are sung to English tunes. Even so, the Victorian tradition of church music remains highly revered, with the Halleluiah Chorus still being the pinnacle of achievement.[36] Plainsong has worked well because it

36. J. Hodgson, "Western and African music in southern Africa", in Holeton, pp. 37-38.

is flexible enough to follow tonality and speech patterns as when sung in Swahili.

Mass settings, hymns and choruses have been indigenised with creative use of harmony, call-and-response antiphonal singing, ululating, rhythmic body movement, hand-clapping, foot-stamping, and African musical instruments. Throughout Africa choruses have become the people's music, being derived from translations of Western evangelical, charismatic and pentecostal music, as well as a wealth of indigenous compositions from a variety of sources including African-initiated churches. They follow the circular pattern of African songs rather than the linear form of Western hymns, and do not depend on either literacy or hymn books. Many Anglican churches allow choruses before or after the service, and at the offertory, but more rarely during the service. More typically they are sung at weddings, funerals, evangelistic and healing services, open-air celebrations, all-night revivals and money-raising events, pilgrimages, street evangelism and Mothers' Union meetings.

New compositions can be inspired by keenly contested choir competitions and acquire wide circulation through the ubiquitous tape recorder. Revival movements are another source of liturgical initiative "from below" as *Iviyo lofakazi bakaKristu* (The Legion of Christ's Witnesses) in South Africa and the East African Revival, both stemming from the 1940s. Paradoxically, both these movements make a clear distinction between "Christian" and "pagan" ("traditional" African religion).[37] Although there seems to be little formal borrowing between different denominations, music has penetrated Anglican worship from Catholic and Methodist sources, whether this be in marimba masses, revival songs, or neo-African church compositions.

In urban contexts, youth, whether they be school or college students, young professionals or the unemployed or semi-unemployed town dwellers, may spearhead the freeing of worship. However, their interest is in the catchy revivalist choruses stemming from America rather than "traditional" African forms of music and singing. But even though electronic organs and guitars prevail over African flutes and stringed instruments, they invest their music with an African rhythm akin to township jazz.[38]

37. Ward, 29 November 1995; Shorten, 1987.
38. Ward, 29 November 1995. See also Brian Castle, *Sing a new song to the Lord. The power and potential of hymns,* London, 1994, for hymn compositions by youths in Zambia.

Drums have been more adaptable in being baptised into the new. In Uganda drumming was used as a call to worship from the beginning: the different mibala (*tattoos*) immediately distinguished whether it was a Catholic or Anglican service. But Buganda drumming was not acceptable inside the church. In many African churches drums are now used regularly in Anglican worship together with percussive instruments. Brass bands have been a popular Anglican institution since the nineteenth century, providing a cultural replacement which accorded with missionary sensibilities. But a black priest described the brass band accompaniment to a processional hymn as "the death march of African spirituality".

Solemn Mass in Ghana makes use of local musical instruments, whether these be bells or talking drums calling people to worship, the bamboo flute to announce the Old Testament reading, percussion and drumming for the gospel procession, the gong or rattle to add solemnity to the sanctus and proclamation of the mysteries, or the horn at the dismissal. The text remains a translation of the 1662 Book of Common Prayer but they have made the celebration their own. White handkerchiefs waved to the accompaniment of the sanctuary bell during the sanctus taps into Ghanaian forms of celebration and thanksgiving, with white signifying purity and victory. Bowing and genuflecting also resonate with the Ghanaian practice of bowing to any prominent figure in society, while libations are yet another cultural link.[39]

Over the years, dancing has been incorporated into worship in many African Anglican Provinces, more especially in offertory processions led by women or young girls. At a special service in Ndola Cathedral, Zambia, in 1994, Mothers' Union members, dressed in long blue flowing robes, brought in the offertory dancing the dance of the paramount chiefs. The dance had been adapted in praise of Jesus Christ, the Great Chief. Drumming heralded their entrance and their leader carried the ceremonial axe as they came down the aisle singing, "We bring you gifts, O God. We also bring you ourselves."[40]

Respect needs to be given to the highly developed and local forms

39. Archbishop Robert Okine, "Liturgical report of the Church of the Province of West Africa", represented to the CAPA conference at Kanamai, June 1993; E. Acheampong, "The Eucharist", Mission Studies dissertation, Selly Oak, June 1993, pp. 45-50.
40. The Rev. Simon Farrer, *USPG Project News*, No. 297, Diocese of Central Zambia, July 1994.

of Anglicanism which have evolved over a considerable time through-out Africa. Where people have selectively made the BCP their own, innovative forces may be at work which connect the outward expression of new Christian symbols with a whole subset of symbolic meanings deeply rooted in Africa. Foot-washing on Maundy Thursday, veneration of the cross on Good Friday, bowing and genuflecting, regular confession, making the sign of the cross, the liberal use of holy water and incense, and anointing with oil, may have become outmoded elsewhere in the church but can be integral to the Christian spirituality of a community. An African person is also a feasting person. Wherever African people gather there must be "beer and meat",[41] so that the sacramental sharing of food following a formal church service is seen as being integral to the communal act of worship.

Authentic inculturation ultimately comes "from below", as epitomised in the songs of evangelical Dinka Christians in the Episcopal Church of Sudan. In an ongoing situation of terrible suffering, and with their old beliefs having failed to deliver them from the horrors of war, the Dinka have turned to the protective power of Christ for both physical and spiritual salvation. The compositions in their continuously evolving corpus of music express their determination to survive, merging "strands of traditional form and content with the subjective Christian faith imbibed from the Anglican missions".[42]

The liturgical commemoration of ancestors remains a sensitive issue, with missionary structures dying hard. The Southern African Prayer Book refers only to the "faithful departed" but does include a liturgy for the dedication and unveiling of a tombstone. Copious use of incense at funeral services is obligatory as a means of uniting the living with the dead.[43] The new Kenyan service of Holy Communion is much bolder in referring to "God of our ancestors" and "our faithful ancestors", this having replaced "Christian ancestors" in the first draft. And whereas a metaphor for Jesus as "our Brother" remains in the final draft, God "eter-

41. Interview with the Rev. Christian Kokoali, Cape Town, June 1985.
42. Marc Nikkel, "Aspects of contemporary religious change among the Dinka", *Journal of Religion in Africa XXII*, I (1992), p. 80.
43. Luke Pato, "Communication with the ancestors and the significance of the unveiling of tombstones", in Kretzschmar, 1988, p. 12-29; Nxumalo, "Christ and ancestors in the African world", *Journal of Theology for Southern Africa*, 32, September 1980; J. Vundla, "African ancestors" in Holeton, pp. 32-36; Max Lungu, "Xhosa ancestor veneration and the communion of saints", MTh, University of South Africa, 1982.

nal Father" has been substituted for "our great Elder". Inculturation is positively embraced in intercessions based on a Kikuyu litany, repeated clapping punctuating the singing of the Gloria, and the Turkana-based blessing accompanied by sweeping movements of the arms.[44]

Canon Ronald Wynne confronted a different challenge in devising an appropriate creed for communities of new Christians among the Mbukushu refugees from Angola who settled in northwestern Botswana in the 1960s. Each clause of the creed is repeated after the minister with appropriate actions, providing a dramatic affirmation of belief.[45]

All Souls Day is a major festival throughout Africa with the reading out of the names of departed relatives at an evening Eucharist, no matter how long this might take. In Antsiranana, a service for reshrouding the dead is influenced by the Malagasy people's ancient links with West Java. They wind white silk cloth around the corpses and then lay them on stone slabs in family tombs. Every 20 to 25 years the remains are brought out and reshrouded by Christians and animists alike. The Anglican church offers a service of prayer and rejoicing at the reinterment, led by a priest.[46]

THE "TAKING FLESH" OF ANGLICANISM

An All-African liturgy was attempted in the 1960s as a means of uniting Anglican Provinces, but it was bound to flop as it followed the Church of South India format, was devoid of African content, and was written in English by a Westerner.[47] This raises the question of imposing self-conscious liturgies "from above".

44. *A Kenyan service of Holy Communion*, Nairobi, 1990. For a discussion of the first draft see Philip Tovey, *Inculturation: The Eucharist in Africa*, Alcuin/GROW Liturgical Study 7, 1988, p. 39. Cf. the draft liturgy which allows Chinese Christians "to express their gratitude and reverence toward their ancestors" by the Anglican bishop of Taiwan: *Anglican world*, Lent 1995.
45. R. Wynne, *The pool that never dries up*, USPG, London, 1988, p. 84.
46. Interview with Bishop Keith Benzies, 17 January 1994.
47. E. Mbonigaba, "Indigenization of the Liturgy", in *A kingdom of priests*, edited by T. Talley, Alcuin/GROW Liturgical Study 5, p. 40. An All-African Roman Catholic Eucharist also failed as it brought together a patchwork of unconnected and sometimes conflicting African elements from across the continent without any coherent symbolic structure to unite them. Cf. the more authentic "R.C. liturgies in Tanzania, Cameroon and Zaire", Tovey, pp. 32-8.

Authentic liturgical reform required sensitivity to both the theological basis of liturgy and the cultural anthropology of ritual. But while liturgists hotly debate whether to start with the text or the community, what is often forgotten is that the history of Christianity is a history of inculturation, a transforming dialogue between the gospel and culture in an ongoing process of religious change ever since the apostolic ministry: this as much in the Western world as in Africa. And while Anglican Church leaders nervously inquire whether there are any limits to inculturation, they seem oblivious to the wealth of informal liturgies rich in indigenous material which have long been the people's expression of faith within the Africa-wide Anglican Church. Church hierarchies have typically been suspicious of such popular religion, either ignoring its existence or trying to suppress it.

Even so, the *via media* approach of Anglican tradition has encouraged African people to incarnate the gospel with a whole range of movements and organisations, formal and informal, structured and unstructured, within the church, giving them their own African identity. In the Church of the Province of Southern Africa, the Order of Ethiopia is a unique example of an indigenous church which was incorporated into the Anglican Church in 1900. It has continued to function independently within the mother body and has its own bishop, clergy and liturgical ritual drawing on African, Anglican and Methodist sources.[48]

Other Anglican organisations in the CPSA with distinctive African identities include the Mothers' Union, youth guilds, and men's evangelism groups. The Mothers' Union is predominantly black in membership and celebrates the middle-class values of order, right living and respectability. Although it is structured according to its parent body in England, it functions as an African expression of Christianity with uniforms; an emphasis on prayer, sharing and mutual support; vibrant singing; rhythmic movement and the beating of a hand cushion; a distinctive style of prayer; sacrificial giving rather than fund-raising; admission to membership with a blousing ceremony; all-night vigils; and much more.[49] Church organisations for girls include the Guild of

48. Dwane, *Issues*, pp. 83-101; E. Tuckey, "The Order of Ethiopia. A study in African Church independency", BA Honours, University of the Witwatersrand, 1977; T.D. Verryn, *A history of the Order of Ethiopia*, Transvaal, 1972.
49. Claire Nye, "The Mothers' Union. A case study of African branches in the Anglican Diocese of Cape Town", BA Honours, University of Cape Town, 1987.

St Agnes, the Girls' Friendly Society and the Wayfarer movement.

The Bernard Mizeki Guild was founded by Anglican migrant workers in the Western Cape in the early 1970s as an evangelistic organisation for men. Mizeki is an African martyr, killed while pioneering an Anglican mission in Mashonaland (Zimbabwe) during the war in 1896. Originally coming from Portuguese East Africa (Mozambique) to Cape Town, he has a special meaning for migrant workers. The movement has spread countrywide but remains strongest among Xhosa-speaking men, distinguished by their purple waistcoats, ties and badges. The Anglican Men's Fellowship has much the same aims but tends to function among other language groupings. *Amadodana* are another group of male evangelists, seemingly modelled on the Methodist Young Men's Guild.

Iviyo lofakazi babaKristu (The Legion of Christ's Witnesses) founded in 1948 by the Rev Alphaeus Zulu and the Rev Philip Mbatha in Zululand, is a renewal movement which is mainly identified with Zulu-speaking men and women. In addition to being both charismatic and evangelical, laying great stress on the gifts and power of the Holy Spirit, it has a Rule of Life modelled on the Anglo-Catholic tradition of the Community of the Resurrection. In the early years it had to overcome fears within the church of its "independent" leanings and "unAnglican" charismatic style. More recently, its supposed links with *Inkatha* have caused concern, but it has generated large numbers of religious vocations.[50]

There have been a number of black religious orders within the CPSA. Some of the women's orders are multiracial, being linked with communities in the Anglican Church in England, such as the Community of the Holy Name and the Society of the Precious Blood (SPB). Others retained greater independence under their African founders, like the Community of St John the Baptist at St Cuthbert's, Tsolo, in Transkei,[51] and the Daughters of Mary in Sekhukhuneland. The Sisters of St Paul are a comparatively new order in Mozambique. Father Patrick Maekane, MBK, was trained by the Society of the Sacred Mission at Modderpoort and then founded the Community of the Servants of Christ in Lesotho. But his attempts to have his Basotho women's order, Handmaids of Mary Mother of Mercy, recognised by

50. Shorter, 1987.
51. See *An African foundress, Sister Alberta*, CSJB, published by the Wantage Sisters, n.d.

the church were foiled, and the SPB community was established at Masite instead.[52] Brother Josiah was another one-man community at Tsolo. Racism, identified as a lack of higher education, seems to have been significant in excluding black men from English orders.

Less formally structured movements with Anglican roots include News of Salvation (iiNdaba zoSindiso), a healing movement based on prayer founded by the late Mrs Paul in 1950 in Transkei. Although her movement remained independent of the church, Mrs Paul was licensed by the Bishop of St John in 1961. She died three years later but News of Salvation has continued, albeit in schismatic form, the symbolic focus of belonging being annual commemoration festivals at Tsolo.[53] Other healing and prayer movements, led by Anglicans amongst others, continue to arise, and their popularity is a reminder of the immediate needs of African people which are not being met by the church. In the early 1980s, Mrs Flora Ludlolo, known as MaRhadebo, of Cancele, Transkei, claimed to have inherited the mantle of Mrs Paul, using blessed water mixed with certain substances and offering money, power and health. Her claims to raise people from the dead had people flocking by the busload from far afield. However, a church investigation found no evidence of healing in the name of Christ and branded it a money-making venture.[54]

Annual pilgrimages which honour black heroic figures of the faith like Bernard Mizeki of Mashonaland, the virgin martyr Manche Masemola of Sekhukhuneland and the Sotho prophetess Mantsopa of Modderpoort, attract large followings of Anglicans together with other Christians to their regional eucharistic celebrations. Regarded by many as African saints, these figures have become significant symbols of black spirituality, being seen as a direct link to God. Cultic practices have grown up around the holy places associated with them, such as graves, groves of trees, caves and healing waters, not always to the church's satisfaction. But again manifest spiritual needs cannot be ignored.

52. Sister Theresia Mary, SPB, *Father Patrick Maekane*, M.B.K., CPSA: 1987.
53. Robert Tushana, *U-Elizabeth Paul*, Umtata, 1977; B.A. Pauw, *Christianity and Xhosa tradition*, Cape Town, 1975, pp. 261-291. Cf. the House to House Prayer movement (*Nyumba kwa Nyumba*) in the Anglican Diocese of Dar es Salaam, as an example of another evangelistic movement which incorporates healing and exorcism.
54. Janet Hodgson, "The faith-healer of Cancele: Some problems in analysing religious experience among black people", *Religion in South Africa*, vol. 4 (1), pp. 13-29, January 1983.

The *umgalelo* (*stokvel*) voluntary associations exemplify African religious initiative within urban parish life. These are mutual aid societies, such as burial and saving societies, which have taken on a church orientation, business proceedings being sandwiched between worship. They could be regarded as a new category of African-initiated church, but because of the flexibility of the Anglican Church are contained within its functioning.[55]

What is significant is that all these movements *within* the CPSA have developed a rich body of ritual which is rooted in African experience, in town and country. Their meetings, services and celebrations will invariably include some form of Anglican liturgy in their worship. At the same time, they give vivid expression to an enfleshment of Christianity through special dress or uniforms, all-night revival meetings, African-style singing, choruses, rhythmic movement, dancing, extempore prayer, witnessing and testimony, preaching, the exposition of the Word by laity, processing in the streets, the laying on of hands, healing and exorcism. They have indeed "translated the message of Jesus Christ into the living realities of the African soil".[56] But too often the church seems to overlook a viable African-initiated inculturation, which has taken form over many years right in its very midst.

The Anglican Church in Africa needs to be sensitive to the spiritual vitality of popular religion if it wants to take inculturation seriously and become the church of Africa. The twelve Anglican Provinces can only experience self-renewal by sharing in the African church's struggle to reclaim her indigenous liturgical genius.

---

55. C. Kokoali and J. Hodgson, "Mutual aid societies, another kind of independency", *Religion alive*, edited by G.C. Oosthuizen, Cape Town, 1986, pp. 138-150.
56. Interview with Bishop Njongonkulu Winston Ndungane, Diocese of Kimberley and Kuruman (CPSA), *The door*, July 1994, p. 5.

Why Christian ethics needs Africa

The time is ripe for Africa to make a rich contribution to Christian ethics. The time is long overdue, of course, for Africa to be taken seriously – for its traditions and thought patterns to be approached with respect by Christian theology in general and, as will be argued here, by Christian ethics in particular.

The motivation for such a claim could be that of etiquette – that it would simply be good manners for Christianty as a relative newcomer to Africa to bow to its host, just as a visitor owes it to a host to respect the domestic arrangements rather than to begin rearranging them on arrival. Indeed, if Christianity were to have taken African manners seriously from the time of its arrival here, it would have averted its eyes and waited to be spoken to by Africa before launching on its missionary offensive. Etiquette, however, important though it is, is not the motivation for this paper. Rather it is the sense that the Christian understanding of ethics and the moral life, which has been shaped almost entirely by Western culture, has seriously impoverished itself by not appreciating and learning from the customs, concepts and time-honoured wisdom of Africa.

IS THERE AN "AFRICAN ETHIC"?

A preliminary question will be whether it makes sense to speak of an "African ethic". Note will then be taken of the present state of African moral traditions, and will include a critical consideration of the impact of Christian mission and of modern urban life on African ethics. The main point will then be to indicate why Christian ethics, currently in a condition of weakness and need, should look to the vital remedies and nourishment Africa has to offer.

Is there such a thing as an African ethic? The instinctive answer is in the negative, because African life defies compartmentalisation. It is experienced holistically, therefore there is no separate category of life which may be labelled "ethics". Furthermore, this sounds like an impertinent question. It could be taken to imply that, while other cultures are ethical, African culture is not. That implication is certainly not intended, nor is it considered valid. What is valid is a question as to whether the term "ethics" can be used of the moral values held by the inhabitants of any country or population group as a whole, let alone of an entire continent – especially one as huge (22 per cent of the world's land area) and diverse as Africa.

Yet there are ethical themes and emphases which may be characterised as African, and an author can validly set out to write a book entitled *African Christian morality*. The valid assumption underlying this work of Benezet Bujo is of "the relevance of the Christian message for a black African ethic" and also of the possibility of setting down "some basic guidelines for a morality that is essentially African" (1990: 11).

I would strongly endorse Bujo's project and his basic proposition that the Christian message has a vital relevance for a black African ethic. I would also agree with him that it is indeed possible to identify and lay down guidelines for a morality that is essentially African. I would, however, go further and add the converse claim that an ethic that is "essentially African" is also of great relevance for Christian ethics today. Christianity has much to learn from the ancient wisdom of Africa, not least in the recovery of vital forgotten aspects of its own heritage.

AN OBSERVATION ON THE PRESENT STATE OF AFRICAN MORAL TRADITIONS

A complicating factor which would probably have come to Africa sooner or later even without the intervention of the European colonists is the secularisation process. A byproduct of modern science and technology, and of life in the urban-industrial complex, has been the eclipse of the old ways of acting and understanding the world. Together with and underlying that eclipse is a fading of the sense of religious dimension and depth. Long-standing traditions are being forgotten or, at least, have moved from the place of centrality and authority they once held in the community. In some cases, even when they are observed, their earlier significance is lost – people no longer remember precisely why a particular ritual or practice is followed.

A case in point is *ilobolo* – the Zulu tradition that the groom presents cattle to the family of his bride in order to seal the marriage of a Zulu man. Such a practice is at home in the pattern of life and the economic structure of rural kraals. It is sustained with difficulty in the urban townships, where the economy is no longer cattle-based and where families are fragmented both by the physical living arrangement of rows of small houses and by the labour system which imposes a new mobility on the men in particular. The obvious solution would seem to be the offering of money instead of cattle. A cash amount, however, simply does not convey the rich significance of the transfer of cattle. It is impersonal and, once the transfer is made, it disappears into a bank account and is easily forgotten, whereas the cattle were a visible, living reminder of new social ties and mutual obligations. It is easy to see that for the younger generations of urban Zulus the old *ilobolo* system should seem difficult, even pointless, to observe. There is great pressure to discard the old system entirely, but what is to take its place? What is to be the new social institution emerging as a substitute for the old? Where are sexual relationships now to be "housed"? There can be little doubt that the current widespread sexual promiscuity, the high rate of illegitimate births and of single parenthood in the townships stem largely from the loss of the old marriage system, and of the whole way of life of which it was part.

This is one instance of the profound and far-reaching changes that have overtaken the people of Africa in the past century. Clearly, such changes have brought with them enormous, ongoing social problems which present the churches with daunting moral and pastoral challenges.

CHURCH AND MISSION IN RESPECT OF AFRICAN MORAL TRADITION

What have the mainline churches[1] done to address such profound

1. By "mainline churches" is meant the denominations that came to South Africa from Europe and established both "mission" and "settler" operations. Among such churches are the Church of the Province of South Africa, the Methodist Church of Southern Africa, the United Congregational Church of South Africa, and the Presbyterian churches. The Lutheran, Dutch Reformed and the Roman Catholic churches might also be taken as belonging to this category.

changes in the lives of the people of Africa, changes in which church and mission have themselves been instrumental? Sadly, they seem to have done very little. The uncreative and unimaginative alternative offered by the churches and their pastoral and moral theology seems to be that the African practice should simply give way to the European. In the case of marriage, for instance, there seems at church institutional level to be little thought other than that African Christians should now marry in the Western way.

What is seldom recognised is that a change in practice and ritual carries with it the loss of the whole world of meaning. Have the churches and their theologians made serious attempts to take account of the richness of the traditional African understanding of marriage as a binding together of families, including the members who have died? The fact that such attempts have not been made is, sadly, indicative of an assumption that the African traditions do not matter or, worse, that they are heathen customs and therefore to be actively rejected. These, of course, have been characteristic attitudes of the mainline churches towards African culture and morality. The claim of this paper is that African and Christian traditions have great potential for mutual enrichment.

Further, the churches have an obligation to deal more respectfully with the time-honoured traditions and customs of those whom they would evangelise. Some of the reasons for such an obligation are as follows. First, it should be clearly understood that many of the practices endorsed and propagated by the churches are themselves cultural forms which are no more exempt from the critical scrutiny of the gospel than are the African forms. There is no inherent reason why the churches should follow Western rather than African customs and conventions. After all, Jesus and his early Middle Eastern disciples would have found both to be unusual and foreign!

Secondly, is there not more of a prima facie New Testament justification for respecting the ways of those different from ourselves than for condemning them? Even Paul, with his sharp eye for any practice out of keeping with the nature and will of God, and his passionate conviction regarding people's need for salvation, affirmed the natural sense of right and wrong among "the heathen" (Romans 2:14-15). Paul, like Jesus, seems not to have had any inclination to condemn out of hand any practice and institution not officially declared "Christian". For instance, while advising Christians not to take their disputes to civil courts (1 Corinthians 6:1-8), Paul nowhere suggests that those courts are evil and fit only to be closed down. Unfortunately their latter-day followers seem to be far more negatively disposed towards the institutions and practices of cultures other than their own. It seems that much missionary endeavour has been for the sake of the culture of Western Christendom rather than for the sake of a gospel which engages and judges all cultures.

The third reason concerns the practical matter of effective communication. Here again, the apostle Paul is a helpful role model. He seems to have adopted quite readily the concepts and methods of Stoics, Cynics and the mystery religions (but always "in Christ") in order to facilitate the effective communication and "marketing" of the gospel. The first Anglican bishop of Natal, John William Colenso, seems to have taken a leaf out of Paul's book in this regard. On the emotive subject of African marriage, for instance, Colenso held a view which was remarkably open and non-judgemental for his day. For instance, while acknowledging that polygamy was not in agreement with Christian teaching, he believed that the doors of the church should not be closed to people in polygamous marriages. "The price of conversion to Christianity should never be the dissolution of the family and perhaps the destitution of wives and children" (Guy 1983: 74). The enlightened and farsighted nature of Colenso's view expressed around the middle of the nineteenth century is confirmed in the guidelines for Christian marriage published by the All-Africa Council of Churches about a hundred years later (1963). That twentieth-century African statement could be taken as an endorsement and development of Colenso's views.

How different Christian ethics in Africa would have been if the generous, creative and imaginative approach of Colenso and those like him had prevailed. How very different and more positive the contribution of Christianity to human community in Africa would have been; how different relations between the races might have been. Given the highly influential role of the churches in South Africa, one might even be permitted to entertain the idea that the entire sad history of South Africa during the past century might have been transformed into one far happier and healthier. This approach by Christian missions would surely have benefited African people richly and have brought them ". . . a garland instead of ashes, the oil of gladness instead of mourning . . ." (Isaiah 61:3).

Perhaps the single most distinguishing feature of Colenso's view of mission in his day was his clear understanding that the gospel would have to find new vehicles of expression, and that the Christian life would have to develop new forms, if it was to be authentic in Africa. This is a hard lesson, which many white Christians here probably still find difficult to learn. For them the cultural forms of Europe are still somehow integral to Christianity itself. This European captivity of Christianity in Africa stands in need of determined challenge. People of vision, energy and courage are as much needed in Africa now, at the end of the twentieth century, as they were in the mid-nineteenth century when Colenso was bishop of Natal.[2]

Since the recent momentous changes in South Africa's political dispensation, there are opportunities for the development and implementation of a new expression of Christianity such as Colenso himself did not have and which has not existed since, as the cloud of white supremacy and apartheid spread over the land.

THE WEAKNESS OF MODERN CHRISTIAN ETHICS

During the past two centuries ethics in the Western world has tended to become a self-contained discipline. It has taken on a scientific aspect and has sought to rank itself alongside other modern academic disciplines. This modern tendency may have brought a scientific clarity and precision to the study of ethics, but it has also brought a clinical isolation. Along with the entire theological enterprise, desperate to be accepted as academically respectable, the relatively new discipline of Christian ethics has bound itself closely to dominant methods and approaches in ethics, those springing from the Enlightenment of eighteenth-century Europe. This binding has indeed become a bondage.

I have dealt elsewhere in some detail with the unfortunate effects of the ethics of the Enlightenment on Christian ethics and will not repeat that recent discussion here. I shall merely quote the concluding summary:

> In sum, the ethics of the Enlightenment is characterised by universalism, individualism, an understanding of society as

2. The same, of course, can be said of all the religious traditions imported into South Africa, but the dangers of arrogance, self-righteousness and closed-mindedness face Christianity more sharply as the dominant religion.

a rational contract, a punctiliar understanding of human experience, effectiveness as a moral factor, actions above persons, the priority of right over good, and a floating free from religious bases into secularism. It goes without saying that such an ethic is profoundly at odds with the ethics of Africa. (Richardson, forthcoming)

Two of the points mentioned above should be emphasised, and a third added, as key sources of the weakness of modern Christian ethics.

Individualism

The individualism that characterises modern Western life and thought is perhaps the most significant and far-reaching factor where the weakening of Christian ethics and moral life are concerned. How, in an individualist frame of thought, is altruism to be justified? Why should I feel any obligation to be my brother's (and sister's) keeper, except through the apparently arbitrary imposition of some impersonal rule? What structure is there for character formation and moral development, and in terms of what criteria is that formation and development to be evaluated? Where are moral role models to be found, except within myself and my own whimsical, subjective tastes and preferences? The chief social manifestation of individualism, of course, is the widespread modern malaise of loneliness and lack of belonging which is well described in Robert Nisbet's observation on urban life:

> The urban mode of life tends to create solitary souls, to uproot the individual from his [sic] customs, to confront him with a social void, and to weaken traditional restraints on personal conduct . . . Personal existence and social solidarity in the urban community appear to hang by a slender thread (quoted in Nisbet 1953: 16).

It is not surprising that this century has witnessed a longing for a sense of community and that, in sociology, "attentiveness to the theme of community appeared with the fear of its disappearance" (Moran 1974: 115). Christian theology has followed this quest for community but, with the loss of the experience of Christian community, theological treatments of the theme generally remain shrill and polemical.[3] Sound ecclesiology requires a solid communal foundation. That Christian ehtics needs such a communal base is well expressed by Edward Long:

> Christian ethics will be likely to be robust in the future only if there are vibrant communities of Christian faith all over the world and viable Christian institutions in the places where Christian ethicists try to work (Long 1984: 76).

Secularism

Another of the characteristics of modern Western ethics is its "floating free from religious bases into secularism", and Christian ethics is also seriously weakened by this development. Not only has the moral status and function of the Bible been reduced to that of "motivational stories" (see Braithwaite 1966), but the vitalising link between worship and the moral life is at best clouded and at worst vanished. Of course, this is yet another effect of individualism. If we "attend worship" only as individuals, we have little sense of the formative nature of the worship on the worshippers as a community, and it is precisely at the communal level that worship has its primary moral effect. C.F. D. Moule says (emphasising each of his five words in turn) that the key locus of Christian moral guidance is ". . . the Christian worshipping congregation listening critically" (1963: 372). That claim is surely correct and important, yet it is barely reflected in most accounts of Christian ethics today.

Dualism

The third point concerns dualism. There is in the Western thought that shapes Christian ethics an apparently inescapable separation of the spiritual and the material. The origins of this dualism in Greek and even Persian thinking are well known, but the seriousness of the effects on Christian thought and practice are not always realised. Perhaps it will suffice there to ask if Christian theology and ethics have

---

3. A major exception here is the work of Stanley Hauerwas who has both roundly criticised individualism and given powerful expression to an ecclesial Christian ethic.

any effective counter to the materialism that so dominates the values of modern consumer society. The power of socio-economic factors over the church in South Africa has been shown by Cochrane in his account of the churches as "servants of power" (1987).

Christianity in its moral expression has come to rely too heavily on the Constantinian arrangement which gives it the ethical pride of place in society. The church has come to expect its voice to be heard and heeded merely because it is the voice of the church. With the demise of Christendom, however, and the weakening of Western cultural and economic power, who is listening to that voice today? Do the church and its theologians have anything ethically distinctive and important to say, especially in a pluralistic society like present-day South Africa? How and where is Christian ethics to find the resources to counter the apparently irresisitible power of individualism and materialism?

WHAT AFRICA HAS TO OFFER CHRISTIAN ETHICS

As noted above, it is difficult to frame a general African ethic, yet there are moral themes and emphases that are emphatically African. It is from among these that Christian ethics in South Africa should profitably look for many needed resources today. Just three points will be selected here to contrast the weaknesses of Christian ethics mentioned above, but they cannot begin to capture the powerful spirit of Africa which defies analysis and dissection.

Communality

It is well known that communality is at the heart of African life. Mbiti's African counter to the Cartesian "I think, therefore I am" is by now very familiar.

> Whatever happens to the individual happens to the whole group, and whatever happens to the whole group happens to the individual. The individual can only say: "I am because we are: and since we are, therefore I am". This is a cardinal point in the understanding of the African view of man (Mbiti 1969: 108-109).

The effect of such an understanding on ethics can hardly be overestimated. Mbiti states: "Only in terms of other people does the individual become conscious of his own being, his own duties, his privileges and responsibilities towards himself and towards other people . . ." (1969: 118-119). Clearly, it is only in each particular community that character formation and moral development can possibly take place. Ethics is community-relative and community-specific. Role models are those held up within the present experience and the history of the community.

There is in this understanding and experience of the moral life a richness that modern Christian ethics, and indeed modern Christian life, longs for but cannot find.[4] Occasionally the desperately needed ecclesiological focus is recognised and aspired to, as in Werpehowski's observation in respect the church's role in the ethics of Karl Barth:

> As a community of belief, it is the place where normative reasons are forged through reflection on God's activity on behalf of persons. And as a community of witness and service, it is the place where character is deepened, where self-understanding is enhanced through self-denial. So my remarks lead naturally to a Christian ethical focus on the community of belief (Werpehowski 1981: 317).

Would that an ecclesiological focus in theology and the enterprise of Christian ethics could find each other within the experience of belonging in the communal life of the church in South Africa. Christian ethicists would discover a new, rich source of nourishment. They would also recover deep roots in Christianity's own heritage – the "corporate personality" of the people of God in the Old Testament,[5] the intense unity which Jesus prayed his disciples might know (John 17:11), and life in "the body" as envisioned by Paul (Romans 12:4-5; 1 Corinthians 12:12-27).[6]

---

4. Representative exceptions to this rule are the work of Stanley Hauerwas, already noted, and also that of John Howard Yoder.
5. H. Wheeler Robinson (1913: 87-91) did much to bring this biblical concept to the attention of biblical scholars in the English-speaking world.
6. Jonathan Draper attacks individualistic interpretations of Paul's metaphor, "the temple of the Holy Spirit", which are currently prevalent in popular religiosity and personal morality. He argues convincingly that this metaphor must be understood communally (Draper 1987: 57-65).

Religious rituals

The erosion of African traditional life by modern secularisation has been noted above. It has also been noted that the weakening of the link between worship and ethics is an effect of individualism. African communalism, by contrast, holds together the moral life and its religious rituals. Mbiti explains, quoting Maquet:

> The people define good and evil by saying that "that is good [or evil] which tradition has defined as good [or evil]". According to this definition, evil and good are relative values attributed and categorised by society, with regard to certain events, actions, and practices (Mbiti 1970: 248-249).

Those "events, actions, and practices" are mostly, if not entirely, classifiable as religious rituals. It is through its rituals that the community confers on its people their place, status and role. It is in its rituals that the community remembers its past, honours its ancestors, holds up its values, and understands its corporate identity. The rituals are therefore the source and inspiration of all coherence, not least regarding personal identity and moral life. Traditional morality in Africa is inconceivable, as well as unattainable, without reference to the rituals of its communities. If Christian ethics were to learn from this, it would discover a new (but old) ground for coherence and clarity in its moral concepts, and new inspiration and energy for the Christian moral life.

Ubuntu

It goes without saying that African communality includes mutual caring and sharing – altruism is almost a redundant word! This aspect of the moral life of Africa is best summed up in the term Ubuntu. English translations are inadequate, because of the very lack of the social reality out of which the term springs, but close approximations are "humaneness", "compassion", "fellow-feeling". Herein lies a powerful counter to the acquisitiveness and greed so evident in Western lifestyles. Moyo puts it well:

> The Church in Africa can build on the traditional understanding of the good life. For Christians, all that one owns

has been received from God and every member is, individually, a steward of what in the ultimate analysis belongs to God. Traditionalists believed they received whatever they had from or through the ancestor who expected them to share with others and to look after one another. The Christian community ought to be a community of sharing since it owes its existence to a God who shared his life with humanity in Jesus Christ. It is a community in which all members ought to be keepers of one another. Christians are more than an extended family; they are a universal family of God through Christ (Moyo 1992: 57).

Underlying Ubuntu is a holism that is foreign to dualistic Western thinking. Moyo is clear that there is no distinction in African tradition between the material and the spiritual. This is why the African notion of goodness necessarily involves sharing. Ownership of material things can never be exclusive – "for my use only". There is in the possession of material goods an obligation to see that others who lack such goods are cared for. Do we not have here the sounding board for a new resonance in the frail, hollow Christian cry "love one another"?

Again, African tradition reminds us of Christian essentials. There are loud echoes here of the community of the Acts of the Apostles and of the communities to which Paul wrote his moral injunctions. Moyo's further point that in African tradition caring and sharing were not exclusive to one's own group only but inclusive of the stranger (Moyo 1992), is a particularly sharp challenge to the church and individual Christians in the "rainbow" pluralism of South Africa's still-fragmented society.

In conclusion, the opening claim of this paper was that Africa has a rich contribution to make to Christian ethics. I have indicated why I think Christian ethics is currently in urgent need of precisely the kind of help African tradition has to offer. Just in case this may be taken to be the irredeemably colonial West seeking to drain the resources of Africa yet again, I would like to make two closing points. First, unlike the case of a colonial power growing fat off its ill-gotten gains from the colonies, we are not dealing here in commodities. We are dealing in the kind of gift that enriches the giver at least as much as it does the recipient. Africa will receive blessing and honour to the extent that others are blessed by African tradition and wisdom. Secondly, if Christian ethics looks to Africa for guidance and inspiration, as this paper has suggested, a new, fruitful relationship may arise between African moral tradition and Christian ethics. That relationship will not be without its differences and debates,[7] but it may well hold a unique double potential – both to revitalise Christian ethics and to save African traditions from erosion by the secularisation process.

BIBLIOGRAPHY

All-Africa Council of Churches and World Council of Churces, (1963), *The Christian home and family life*.

Braithwaite, R.B. (1966), "An empiricist's view of the nature of religious belief", pp. 53-73 in I.T. Ramsey (ed.), *Christian ethics and contemporary philosophy*, London: SCM.

Bujo, B. (1990), *African Christian morality at the age of inculturation*, Nairobi: St Paul Publications.

Cochrane, J.R. (1987), *Servants of power: The role of English-speaking churches 1903-1930*, Johannesburg: Ravan Press.

Draper, J.A. (1978), "The tip of an iceberg: The temple of the Holy Spirit", *Journal of Theology for Southern Africa*, 59 (July): 57-65.

Guy, J. (1983), *The heretic: A study of the life of John William Colenso 1814-1883*, Johannesburg: Ravan Press and Pietermaritzburg: University of Natal Press.

Kasenene, P. (1994), "Ethics in African theology", pp. 138-147 in C. Villa-Vicencio and J. de Gruchy (eds.), *Doing ethics in context: South African perspectives (Theology and praxis: Volume two)*, Cape Town: David Philip and New York: Orbis Books.

Long, E.L. (1984), *Academic bonding and social concern: The society of Christian ethics 1959-1983*, USA: Religious Ethics, Incorporated.

Mbiti, J.S. (1969), *African religions and philosophy*, London: Heinemann.

Mbiti, J.S. (1970), *Concepts of God in Africa*, London: SPCK.

Moran, G. (1974), *Religious body: Design for a new reformation*, New York: The Seabury Press.

7. Some of the differences will be unavoidable and, perhaps, irresolvable, due to the incompatible world views. There are also shortcomings in African ethics which should be challenged, such as the two pointed out by Peter Kasenene, 1994: 143 – sexism, and the tendency to disregard individual freedom.

Moule, C.F. D. (1963), "Important moral issues – prolegomena: The New Testament and moral decisions", *The Expository Times*, 74/12 (September), 370-373.

Moyo, A. (1992), "Material things in African society: Implications for African ethics", pp. 49-57 in J.N.K. Mugambi and A. Nasimiyu-Wasike (eds.), *Moral and ethical issues in African Christianity*, Nairobi: Initiatives Publishers.

Nisbet, R.A. (1953), *The quest for community*, New York: Oxford University Press.

Richardson, R.N., "Can Christian ethics find its way, and itself, in Africa?" *Journal of Theology for Southern Africa*, Forthcoming.

Robinson, H.W. (1913), *The religious ideas of the Old Testament*, London: Duckworth.

Werpehowski, W. (1981), "Command and history in the ethics of Karl Barth", *The Journal of Religious Ethics*, 9/2 (Fall): 298-320.

Morality, religion

and society

"For such a thing is not done in Israel": Violence against women

INTRODUCTION

Violence is an endemic reality in our society.

The very fabric of our communities is fracturing as fear invades South African homes and lurks at stop streets. Our hope for a democratic and peaceful future based on a culture of human rights is at risk, as evidenced by calls for a return of the death penalty and heavier sentences for criminals. The physically less powerful members of society such as the elderly, women and children are particularly vulnerable to acts of violence. Old people are murdered for the price of a cinema ticket. Women are raped and battered in their homes, on the streets and in the veld. Children are abused by those they trust. Feminist ethicist Christine Gudorf writes that violence is a narcotic. She describes a violent society in terms that are close to the South African bone: "A public caught up in violence cannot feel its own pain. It does not know that it is hungry, or tired, or wounded. It has no consciousness to spare for feeling, it only acts until the acting is done, until the public falls apart into its discrete individual persons" (Gudorf 1922: 15).

Reactions to this ubiquitous violence vary. Many South Africans are growing numb, other are increasingly angry and yet others are meeting violence with violence. Violence is a theological problem, for it calls into question the very nature of humanity and it raises doubts about God's presence in and care for this world. It has ethical, doctrinal and pastoral dimensions. The victims of violence cry out for healing. My Archbishop is world famous as a man whose life has been devoted to the promotion of peace. As a tribute to his commitment, I wish to examine the nature of violence and then proceed to examine violence against women, using rape as a specific and contextually problematic manifestation of such violence. Finally, a response to violence is sought in the community of faith.

THE POLITICS OF VIOLENCE

Not surprisingly, violence is one of the most debated social issues in our country today. The context and ways in which this topic is debated vary, depending on people's race, gender, class and social location. Our political ideologies, our social theories and our personal histories shape our perceptions of violence as well as our desire to engage with it.

In a penetrating study on violence, Susanne Kappeler (1995: 1)[1] points out that violence is named after its victims: violence against children, violence against animals, hatred of foreigners and violence against women. She observes that it is striking that when violence is spoken about it is commonly about the violence committed by someone else: the violence of the structures, the violence of the criminals, the violence of Bosnia or Rwanda. Projection onto others serves to blanket the common human propensity to violence. When violence is owned, it is not condemned but condoned. The violence perpetrated over decades to prop up the white minority government in this country was justified in terms of the "total onslaught". All wars are justified by the participants as just wars.

According to Kappeler (1995: 1), violence is recognised by its visible effects such as bloodied bodies and the material destruction of objects. The invisible forms of violence, such as threats, insults or humiliation are seldom matters for general concern. These kinds of violence are recognised by the victims and defined from their perspective. Violence against women and against children are prime examples of invisible forms of violence. Rape, incest and wife-battering are usually hidden acts of violence, whose victims often connive in blanketing them with silence for a number of reasons. Wives protect battering husbands because of their fear of further retaliation and because of ingrained relationships of dependency. Raped women remain silent because of feelings of shame and societal prejudice. Children who are victims of incest are too often subject to threats or simply not believed.

In the light of South Africa's racist history there are compelling reasons for concluding that the roots of our continuing violence lie in the system of apartheid. The uprooting and destruction of communities of people, unemployment, poverty and overcrowding all contribute to the present climate of violence. Feminists also, in analysing the preconditions of vio-

1. I acknowledge my indebtedness to Susanne Kappeler's work for the first section of this article.

lence based on women's experience, have found that unequal power relations create conditions for violence. There is much validity in these arguments. Yet both contain a dangerous assumption. In essence these arguments are behaviourist. Human actions are seen as the exclusive product of circumstance and human agency in acts of violence is ignored.

This underlying assumption has further implications. The ostensible aim of arguments based only on political and social analysis is to draw attention to the pervasive structural violence of race and class oppression. Yet, as Kappeler (1995: 3) points out, such "explanations" "ignore the fact that not everyone experiencing the same oppression uses violence, that is, that these circumstances do not 'cause' violent behaviour. They overlook, in other words, that the perpetrator has *decided* to violate, even if this decision was made in circumstances of limited choice". Kappeler (1995: 3) continues:

> To overlook this decision, however, is itself a political decision, serving particular interests. In the first instance it serves to exonerate the perpetrators, whose responsibility is thus transferred to circumstances and a history for which other people (who remain beyond reach) are responsible. Moreover, it helps to stigmatize all those living in poverty and oppression: because they are obvious victims of violence and oppression, they are held to be potential perpetrators themselves. This slanders all the women who have experienced sexual violence, yet do not use violence against others, and libels those experiencing racist and class oppression, yet do not necessarily act out violence. Far from supporting those oppressed by classist, racist or sexist oppression, it sells out these entire groups in the interest of exonerating individual members.

All situations of injustice, in whatever guises they appear, must be abolished. But once violence is explained solely in terms of people's circumstances, the implication is that the solution lies wholly in changing the circumstances. The suggestion that people need to change is missing from this argument. "We turn the perpetrators of violence into the victims of circumstances, who as victims by definition cannot act sensibly . . ." (Kappeler 1995: 4). We find it easier to talk about changing circumstances than to address the equally fundamental need to change our attitudes and our behaviour. It is simpler to appeal to the might of the state for more stringent law enforcement and more punitive measures by the courts than to examine our own hearts and our own proclivities to violence. *The recognition that people make choices demands that one takes seriously both the will to violence as well as how we choose to respond to violence.* The question of agency, of choice, is extremely important in the search for an appropriate theological and pastoral response to violence.

RAPE – A CASE STUDY OF VIOLENCE AGAINST WOMEN IN SOUTH AFRICA

Violence against women (and children) is a universal phenomenon (Fiorenza 1991: vii-x) which is not limited by class, geographical area, ethnicity, culture or any other circumstances. The Reconstruction and Development Programme (RDP) acknowledges this state of affairs when it states the need to "focus on the reconstruction of family and community life by prioritising and responding to the needs of . . . women and children who have been victims of domestic and other forms of violence" (RDP, section 2.13.15).[2] As a theologian committed to the needs of the poor and marginalised in our society, I shall use rape as a case study of violence against women in South Africa, in the search for an appropriate response to violence in the community of faith.

The term "violence against women" refers broadly to domestic violence, rape and assault. Unlike domestic violence which cuts across all barriers,[3] recorded victims of rape are concentrated among the poor

2. At a conference of Violence against Women, held at the University of Cape Town, November 1995, Deputy President Thabo Mbeki described this phenomenon as "a terrible war, a campaign of repression that has been hidden away. The issue of violence against women must affect us all. It challenges the dignity of all men and women and we have to stand up against the perpetrators".

3. See Mmatshilo Motsei, *Detection of woman battering in health care settings: The case of Alexandra Health Clinic*, Women's Health Project, paper no. 30, January 1993, p. 5. He states that contrary to conventional wisdom, research has shown that "the perpetrators of violence against women include men who hold respectable jobs and positions in society . . . These include lawyers, doctors, psychologists, psychiatrists, priests and business executives." Furthermore, People Opposing Women Abuse (POWA) found in a study of inquest records that every six days at least one woman is killed by her partner and that more than half of all women murdered are killed by a partner or a male friend (*The Star*, 21 November 1995).

and disadvantaged women and the children of South Africa (Human Rights Watch/Africa, HRW/A, 1995: 52). While acknowledging that all women are potential rape victims, poor women in this country are more vulnerable to rape than are those coming from the privileged classes. This is not surprising, as poor women do not have private transportation, need to walk long distances and live in areas plagued by crime, gangsterism, overcrowding and poverty and, in order to work, are often required to leave and return home in the dark. Accurate statistics on rape are notoriously difficult to come by. Victims[4] are, for a variety of reasons, reluctant to report rape to the police and government legal and social services. These reasons often stem from negative perceptions or experiences of the police, fear of retaliation, shame and social stigma. Reported cases of rape show a clearly increasing trend over the last five years (see Schurink 1992: 339, HRW/A 1995: 50-59). In 1994 alone, 32 107 cases of rape were reported, an increase of 16 per cent on the previous year. This means, on average, eighty-eight rapes reported a day and a yearly rate of 149,5 rapes per hundred thousand people (HRW/A 1995: 51).[5] "The figure for the reported rapes of children rose by almost 60 per cent in 1994 – from 4 736 cases in 1993 to 7 559 cases in 1994" (HRW/A 1995: 51).[6] Rape Crisis in Cape Town in an interview with Human Rights Watch/Africa (1995: 55) noted that the majority of women they see are adolescent victims of gang rape or "jackrolling". According to the South African Police, rape is one of the most underreported crimes in South Africa. In 1994, the South African Police estimated that for every rape reported, thirty-five rapes go unreported, "that is, reported cases make up only 2,8 per cent of all rapes, giving a total figure of approximately one million rapes a year" (HRW/A 1995: 51). These figures remain estimates, but what is clear is that rape is rampant and of crucial concern to women, to men, to the state,[7] to the health sector and to the church.

4. As women are both victims and survivors, these terms are used interchangeably.
5. In the United States, the reported rape rate was 42 per hundred thousand in 1990 (HRW/A 1995: 51).
6. More than 13 000 rape cases involving children under the age of fourteen were reported between 1989 and 1993 to the South African Child Protection Unit (*Argus*, 6 May 1993).
7. The recent report by Human Rights Watch/Africa (November 1995) deals at length with the largely inadequate state response to violence against women.

RAPE – A THEOLOGICAL PROBLEM

Sexual violence is undeniably a pastoral concern. At its core it is also a theological problem. It is an issue of justice and an issue of the abuse of power. From a feminist perspective, justice is seen as the praxis which creates the common good, something women deserve. Justice, according to Beverly Harrison (1985: 90) is nothing less than "communal right-relationship". Whatever taints, distorts, corrupts or perverts relations between people is unjust. Victims of sexual violence are abused for the gratification of those more powerful than themselves. Rape is therefore the unjust, evil abuse of coercive power and as such it is a theological problem.

Rape, as a theological problem, is not limited to the act of rape itself. Feminist theologians have identified a number of ways in which Christian theories and Christian praxis themselves contribute to the problem of rape. Elizabeth Schüssler Fiorenza (1944: xiii-xvii) makes the following points in regard to four key traditional theological discourses: First, the socio-cultural politics of subordination have their roots in Greek philosophy and Roman law and are mediated to us through the scriptures. Patriarchal (or as she calls them "kyriarchal") patterns of the subordination of women, children, slaves and other marginal beings are doctrinally legitimated and experienced daily in the practices of the Christian church. Second, there is a link between the patriarchal teachings of submission and the teaching on the sinfulness of women. Women must be silent, women may not have authority over men because a woman, and not Adam, was deceived and became a transgressor (1 Timothy 2:11-15). Fiorenza (1992: xiv) writes: "Hence, the cultural pattern of making the victims of rape, incest or battering feel guilty and responsible for the victimization has its religious roots in the scriptural teaching that sin came into the world through Eve . . ." Third, scriptural texts themselves link suffering and victimisation to the suffering of Jesus. Slaves are enjoined to submit to patriarchal politics of domination by pointing to the example of Christ (1 Peter 2:18-23), and Christians are admonished to resist sin to the point of shedding their blood by pointing to Jesus "who for sake of the joy that was set before him endured the cross, disregarding its shame" (Hebrews 12:1-11). As Fiorenza (1992: xv) points out: "Feminist theology has underscored the perniciousness of such theological and christological discourses which stress that God sacrificed his son for our sins. If one extols the silent and freely chosen suffering of Christ, who was 'obedient to the point of death' (Philippians 2:8) as an example to be imitated by all those victimized by patriarchal oppression – especially those suffering from domestic and sexual abuse, one does not just legitimate but enable [sic] violence against women and children."[8] Fourth, the Christian values of love and forgiveness help to maintain relations of domination and the acceptance of abuse and victimisation. A Christian ethic which stresses an uncritical attitude of love which bears and endures "all things" (1 Corinthians 13:4-18) and forgiveness up to "seventy-seven times" (Matthew 18:21-22) merely serves to "construct a sacred canopy that compels victims to accept their sufferings without resistance" (Fiorenza 1992: xvi).

The silence in the Christian church on the subject of violence against women in its preaching, teaching and pastoring[9] raises questions about the nature of the church, its self-understanding of its pastoral role, its theological insights and the priorities of its leaders, clergy and theologians. Suffice it to say that "official" Christian praxis communicates at best an uncaring timidity about this shocking problem. It is not surprising that the majority of women of faith who have been raped prefer to seek succour from secular bodies such as Rape Crisis or POWA (People Opposing Women Abuse) rather than from their priests or ministers.

Violated women today are not primarily finding healing in their religious institutions. Questions such as "Why is this happening to me?" "Why has God allowed this to happen to me?" "Is it my fault?" constitute both theological and pastoral crises for the woman of faith. Feelings of guilt, shame, anger, abandonment by God and by your community and the need to break the silence around an experience of horror and abuse, cry out for adequate theological and pastoral responses. How can the victim become the survivor?

8. For an insightful discussion on the link between christologies which focus on the suffering Christ and the abuse of women, see Joanne Carlson Brown and Rebecca Parker (1990), "For God so loved the world?", in *Christianity, patriarchy and abuse: A feminist critique*, pp. 1-30.
9. As it is on the issues of battering and incest. In the course of an empirical study conducted by me in 1993 in which 86 people were questioned, only one person had actually heard a sermon on rape. See Denise M. Ackermann, "2 Samuel 13:1-22", in C.W. Burger, B.A. Müller and D.J. Smit (eds.), *Riglyne vir prediking oor regverdiging en reg. Woord teen die Lig* 111/3, pp. 89-98, Cape Town: Lux Verbi, 1993. This article can also be consulted for homiletical notes on this passage.

CHOICE AND SURVIVAL

1 Samuel 13:1-22 tells the tragic story of Tamar's rape by her half-brother Amnon.[10] It is a story of betrayal in a family, a story of the abuse of privilege and power in a world where men coerce and manipulate their power to achieve their ends. Tamar's cry: "No, my brother, do not force me; for such a thing is not done in Israel; do not do anything so vile!" (verse 13) is to no avail. "But he would not listen to her; and being stronger than she, he forced her and lay with her (verse 14). There is no restitution or justice for Tamar. Her life is ruined by events over which she has no control. "So Tamar remained, a desolate woman, in her brother Absalom's house" (verse 20). This story poignantly illustrates the victim's lack of choice, while at the same time the perpetrator's will to coercive violence is clear.

As members of the community of faith we make choices which can either assist or retard the path to survival and healing of believing women who have been raped. I do not mean to imply that the survival of these women lies solely in the hand of the church. Experience of working with victims of violence has given me great respect for the work of secular bodies in this regard. I am also filled with admiration for the heroic courage of the victims themselves. Some women find the will to resist the effects of being violated by understanding that this involuntary suffering is never justifiable, has no purpose, serves no greater good and is never legitimated by God. Others find resistance in the appropriate, valid and healthy response of anger. Righteous anger is a theologically imperative response to a situation of injustice. Anger in situations of abuse can, however, often be misdirected, either towards the victim's partner or family or, as often happens, towards herself in an inward, self-destructive manner which blocks the path to healing.[11] Once the victim has identified the source responsible for her abuse and directed her anger towards this source, she can begin to

10. See Phyllis Trible (1984), *Texts of terror: Literary feminist readings of biblical narratives*, pp. 1-8, 37-63 and Fokkelien van Dijk-Hemmes, "Tamar en de grenzen van het patriarchaat; tussen verkrachting en verleiding", in Mieke Bal e.a., *En Sara in haar tent lachte . . . Patriarchaat en verzet in Bijbelverhalen*, pp. 47-71, Utrecht: Hes Publishers, 1984. All biblical quotations are taken from the New Revised Standard Version, Oxford University Press, 1989.
11. See *Fortune* 1983, *Sexual violence*, pp. 204-208, for a discussion on anger as response to abuse.

find the will and the energy to resist. And sadly for others, like Tamar, there is only desolation.

What choices can the church make which will facilitate the healing of violated women? The first and fundamental step in a process of survival is to break the silence surrounding this deplorable and complex issue. A woman's experience of violation is a story which is not part of the dominant discourse, yet it is a story which shapes and explains her identity as an individual and as a member of a community. Just as the voices of oppressed groups must be heard, so must the stories of violation be told so that the full identity of a community can be known (Poling 1991: 189) and the individual ministered to. Such telling of experiences can take place in small selected groups where victims feel "safe"; they can also be "spoken" by raising the topic of rape in preaching, in teaching and in our liturgical actions. Our desire to care for one another is profoundly called into question if we are ambivalent or apathetic and therefore silent on this issue.

Second, we continue at our peril to propagate theologies which perpetuate male dominance bolstered by structures in which male power is not appropriately limited. Sexual violence is overwhelmingly a problem in which women are the victims. Inclusive theologies, in which women are valued equally with men and not as adjuncts to male purposes and in which women's dignity and liberty are upheld and underscored by church practices, are urgently needed to redress common notions of women's inferiority which underlie so much abuse of women. All theology stems from the depth of human experience. Our experiences differ and therefore critical reflection on difference and otherness is essential if we are to be sensitive to the stories of those on the margins: violated women, children, the poor.

We believe that Jesus Christ was alive to human suffering in all its manifestations. He could not have been oblivious to the harm done to women by acts of sexual violence. Yet, to a suffering humanity he promised life in abundance (John 10:10). Does this promise not spring from his knowledge that human beings, both individually and together, can choose to resist violence and can work together for healing from its terrible consequences? Can he not be saying: "I know about injustice and suffering. I have seen the universal will to violence. Nevertheless, I tell you there is a better way. Resist violence, resist its consequences. I am with you. Choose life."?

In summary, acts of violence such as rape are acts in which perpetrators choose to use coercive power over others. How we as the community of faith respond to such acts is also a matter of choice. Cultural, religious, social and political determinism work against the human capacity to choose to change situations. We are by our very nature beings who are created with the will to choose. Clearly we do not choose acts of violation. Clearly political and social circumstances give members of a certain class, race or gender more choices than are available to others. But equally clearly human beings have the capacity to choose: either to be crippled by violence, or to use the power of human agency to resist unto healing together as believing people. Indeed, such a thing as rape is not done in Israel. Neither is a life of unending brokenness, of eternal victimisation, inevitable for a citizen of the new Israel.

BIBLIOGRAPHY

Brown, Joanne Carlson and Carole R. Bohn (eds.), (1989), *Christianity, patriarchy and abuse: A feminist critique*, New York: The Pilgrim Press.

Fiorenza, Elizabeth Schüssler (1994), Introduction, in E.S. Fiorenza and M.S. Copeland (eds.), pp. vii-xxiv.

Fiorenza, Elizabeth Schüssler and Mary Shawn Copeland (eds.), *Violence against women*, London: SCM Press, Concilium 1994/1.

Fortune, Marie Marshall (1983), *Sexual violence: The unmentionable sin. An ethical and pastoral perspective*, Cleveland: The Pilgrim Press.

Gudorf, Christine E. (1992), *Victimization: Examining Christian complicity*, Philadelphia: Trinity Press International.

Harrison, Beverly Wildung (1985), *Making the connections: Essays in feminist social ethics*, Boston: Beacon Press.

Human Rights Watch/Africa (1995), *Violence against women in South Africa. A state response to domestic violence and rape*, New York: Human Rights Watch.

Kappeler, Susanne (1995), *The will of violence: The politics of personal behavior*, New York: Teachers College Press, Columbia University.

Poling, James Newton (1991), *The abuse of power: A theological problem*, Nashville: Abingdon Press.

Schurink, Evanthe (1992), "Rape victimization", in W.J. Schurink, W.F. Krugel, I. Snyman, pp. 337-356.

Schurink, W.J., Ina Snyman, W.F. Krugel, assisted by Laetitia Slabbert (eds) (1992), *Victimization: Nature and trends*, Pretoria: HSRC Publishers.

Vogelman, L. (1990), *The sexual face of violence: Rapists on rape*, Johannesburg: Ravan Press.

Children, sexism and the church

A rchbishop Desmond Tutu stands out clearly as a symbol of integrity and hope. In the midst of a church that compromised with apartheid he refused to conform. When the church showed an ambivalent response to liberation theology, he played a prophetic role and cried out against injustice and oppression. He embodied and kept alive the theology of resistance to injustice.

In the difficult years of the 1970s and 80s Desmond Tutu demonstrated that the church did stand for justice and was concerned about the poor and the oppressed. His example helped people keep the faith, rather than rejecting the church and Christianity as agents of apartheid and the Bible as a tool for oppression. Some rejected him, but time has vindicated his stance.

His witness against apartheid helped to affirm the inherent goodness and life-giving nature of Christianity. It gives assurance that there is a theology of liberation "which affirms the equality of all races which is neither silenced nor destroyed by the failings of the church. It is one which haunts them as a relentless and disruptive memory" (Villa-Vicencio 1988: 174).

When it comes to sexism little is said and still less is done with respect to equality in the church. Instead the church seems to be riddled with sexism. The patriarchal nature of Christianity can be found in the history of the church, in the present-day structures of the church and in the scriptures. The Old Testament authors assumed that patriarchy was the will of God for the social order.[1] For example, the laws of the Old Testament are addressed solely to the

---

1. Patriarchy is about the "patterned or institutional legitimations of male superiority" (Harrison 1985: 117).

male heads of families, and not to women, children or slaves.

This presumption prevails even in the New Testament, but there are exceptions. For example, Jesus in his actions and teachings was different and actively worked against patriarchy.[2] The records of the ministry of certain women in the early church and several prophetic flashes point towards the equality of all as envisioned by the gospel, but these are generally not affirmed by the church. Instead the patriarchal nature of Christianity is either never acknowledged or else seen as God-given.

Children are socialised into a sexist version of Christianity. As they mature they may come to question this as it conflicts with the dignity and equality of women. The fact that they unconsciously absorbed a sexist understanding of Christianity as children makes it difficult for them to examine their faith rationally and this may lead to a rejection of Christianity. In the following essay some of the sexist elements in the church and Sunday school programme are highlighted and suggestions for non-sexist Christian education are made.

A CRISIS OF FAITH

Socialisation is "the process by which individuals learn the ways of a society or group so that they can function within it" (Popenoe 1977: 109). Most socialisation takes place in the first few years of life. The old Jesuit saying that if you gave them a child until the age of seven they would have him forever confirms this perception. It is during these first years of life that the strongest impressions are formed, and these are difficult to change.

Many children enjoy Sunday school and do not analyse what they are taught. Certain traditions, norms, values and attitudes that are practised by the church are internalised. Without questioning, children accept a sexist understanding of Christianity, which embraces a hierarchical gender order with men over women. As children grow older their love of God and positive experience of church may be undermined by the sexist practices and structures of the church. They

2. See Dowell 1987: Jesus transgressed Jewish law (Luke 14:1-6). Talking to the Samaritan woman was breaking the rigid social barriers (John 4:7-26). The story of Mary and Martha affirms the ministry of women in a sphere other than the domestic (Luke 10:38-42).

may come to realise that sexism was present in the presentation and interpretation of Christianity from as early as they can remember. Many feminist principles such as the equality of men and women are undermined by church tradition which supports the subordinate position of women and upholds sexist practices. This may lead to a crisis of faith, as it is difficult to reconcile the positive memories and experiences of Sunday school with the hurt and disillusionment at the realisation of the androcentric nature of Christianity.[3] Either their experience as women reaching for equality is wrong or else the way women are socialised within the church is at fault. If the basic assumptions of the church on matters such as the inferiority of women are false, then there will be disharmony between the teaching of the church and the rest of a person's life. Yet, because of their high expectations and value placed on the church and in Christianity, the disillusionment is all the more painful and difficult to accept.

Children's faith and love of God depend greatly on their upbringing and early experiences of God and of the church. If church is solemn and children have to be quiet and do what they are told, participating only when invited to do so, then God will probably be seen as a patriarchal, authority figure. This view of God will be even stronger if God is always pictured as a man, probably an old white man, and always spoken of as "He" or "King".

These images may stay with people, leading them to a distorted notion of God. They may not be aware of it, but the hidden thoughts, memories and feelings from the subconscious influence them and their thinking and acting. For example, they may be going to church out of guilt or from fear of a tyrant God. There may be no real joy in their commitment to God and the church. Instead they act out of a sense of duty because they perceive God as a dictatorial, authoritarian figure who is watching them and judging them.

It is hard for adults to examine their beliefs critically and to adapt or change them in order to develop a more integrated, non-sexist faith. To do this may pose a threat to their whole belief system. This means that many women remain in the church and uncritically accept sexist teachings, or else they leave the church completely. A few stay in the church and critically question what is being taught and done, but this is not easy as such individuals may be labelled trouble-makers or even heretics for rejecting the values into which they have been socialised by the church.

3. Androcentric can be defined as "male-centred".

THE AGENTS OF SOCIALISATION

Socialisation into the church includes formal Christian education in Sunday schools, but most socialisation is unconscious and comes through being part of the faith community. Children absorb what happens around them: the language used, the symbols, people's roles, the patterns and atmosphere of worship as well as the attitudes and values of the church community.

The church's ministry to parents is vital, as initially they make the deepest impression on children's faith. Parents and teachers may not be aware of the patriarchal nature of their understanding of Christianity because that is how Christianity was presented to them. This means, however, that they will teach their children in a like manner. They will probably always refer to God in masculine terms. They may well endorse exclusively male leadership in the church, either consciously or unconsciously.

Worship

Worship can be used deliberately to educate, but it also influences people at a subconscious level. Often this is the case with children as they do not understand the symbolism and deeper meanings of the liturgy and ritual. Children subconsciously associate the most visible people who conduct the service as the leaders. These are usually men and so children, without rationalising it, come to expect that men will lead and women will follow.

The way God is usually described as Father, King, Lord and Almighty reinforces this perception. Children understand these terms literally. God is "He", God is big and powerful. They do not see these as mere metaphors for God, as inadequate human attempts to describe the indescribable. The exclusive male language and imagery for God tends to legitimate patterns of male domination and patriarchy both in the church and in society.

Jesus' use of the title "Father" needs to be seen in the context of the times. Jesus wanted to teach people that God cares for them and that people, in turn, can approach God. People can call God "Abba", an intimate family word for father, symbolising God's love. Today the term "father" tends to illustrate a patriarchal and oppressive authority, rather than the loving concern of God. Those who insist on calling God "Father" may affirm that God's fatherhood does not make

God male or literally a father. This distinction may be too difficult for children. If one continually refers to God as "Father" then God is a father.

The Bible

The Bible is read regularly in church without acknowledging that it was written largely by men and for men, and so tends to be sexist despite flashes of inspiration which speak to women's experience and rise above the patriarchal culture. The Bible can be used either to promote the full humanity of women or to hinder it. It can help to recover the liberating experiences and visions of the people of God, or it can be used in an authoritarian manner to silence all revivals and opposition to the status quo.

The attitudes of society affect the way the Bible is interpreted. The church's theology and the interpretation of scripture seem to be influenced by the patriarchal nature of South African society. Often, those things which are accepted in society are accepted by the church, while those things that are rejected by society are also rejected by the church. For example, male leadership, which is seen as the norm in society, is inherent in the theology of the church, while slavery, which is nowadays rejected by most societies, is not accepted by the church. The church condemns slavery as oppressive and unchristian, despite the fact that Paul gives instructions to slaves and slave masters. Patriarchy, on the other hand, which is accepted by society, is not condemned by the church. It would be consistent for the church to reject sexism, as well as class and racial oppression. Instead the church tends to cling to sexist, first-century practices that deny the thrust of the entire Bible toward personal and social wholeness and unity in Christ.

Children's Bibles

Children's Bibles are used by parents at home and at Sunday schools by teachers to help them tell Bible stories in a way that will be more easily understood by the children. Children's Bibles generally follow the Bible fairly closely. There is little overt sexism. Rather women are simply ignored or portrayed in traditional roles.

Most children's Bibles have far more stories about men than women. For example *My first Bible in pictures*, by Kenneth Taylor, consists of 120 stories out of which eighteen are about women or have an illustration of a woman. Considering the small number of women in the Bible this may not seem too bad, except that these women are portrayed primarily as mothers, wives and helpers.

The illustrations in many Bibles are mostly of men. For example, in the story "The rushing wind", only men are shown being given the Holy Spirit (Trafton 1989: 124).

A child's first Bible, by Sandol Stoddard, is refreshingly non-sexist. God is "God", not "He" or "She". For example, in the creation story it says: "Now God was pleased, seeing that all of this work was very, very good. But there were no people yet, and so God made man and woman, giving them both a likeness to the Being and the Spirit of their Maker" (Stoddard 1991: 15). Jesus calls his disciples to follow him as he will make them "fishers of human beings" (Stoddard 1991: 75).

Sunday school materials

Sunday school materials, such as the Scripture Union books, are of a high standard. They are basically non-sexist when it comes to stories in modern-day settings or when using modern stories to illustrate certain principles. Stories of boys and girls are used with the same kind of frequency to teach the same kinds of truths. There is some stereotyping of roles, but this is probably because it is what the children will identify with most readily. For example, Jesus is at home helping mother with the dishes and father with the garden.

There is less gender equality in the Bible stories as the Bible is a largely androcentric book, written from a male perspective and recording mainly the experiences of men. Sunday schools generally choose the most popular stories in the Bible rather than seeking out the overlooked stories about women. Paul is used as an example of a missionary, but if we are to teach that God calls both girls and boys as missionaries, then the example of Paul should be balanced with an example such as Priscilla (Acts 18; Romans 16:3).

God is always portrayed in masculine terms. There is no attempt to try to balance these images with feminine ones. A few impersonal images such as God as creator and comforter are used, but are immediately followed by a masculine pronoun that indicates that, in fact, God is male.

THE WAY FORWARD

To make the socialisation of children into the church less sexist, there is a need firstly to educate the community of faith so that sexism is seen as a problem, and secondly to provide non-sexist and non-oppressive teaching and practice in the church. Ideally these must be part of the child's upbringing in the church, and not issues that arise once beliefs are already established. This means that the church needs to discover "ways that honour the feminine element, as well as women, in other than compensatory fashion" (Morny 1990: 16). The Christian vision of "neither male nor female" (Galatians 3:28) must become a reality.

The use of the Bible

One of the ways forward is to recognise that theological thinking has been done almost entirely by men. This means that it is necessary to develop various norms or sets of criteria to critique traditional theology. Feminist theology is helpful here because it acknowledges that scripture is used selectively to support certain beliefs, and it exposes the sexist interpretations of scripture and develops guidelines for interpreting scripture.

If socialisation of children into the church is to become less sexist, the patriarchal nature of the Bible needs to be exposed. Androcentrism is basic and inherent in the biblical narratives. This means that scripture should be read with a hermeneutics of suspicion, recalling that scripture has been used to justify slavery, sexual oppression, nationalism and the like. This hermeneutics uncovers as much as possible of these distortions. If the Bible is read in this way it can be used by women as an instrument of liberation, rather than oppression, despite its limitations and patriarchal nature. One needs to take the particularity of God's actions through Israel and Christ seriously. The texts should be seen in their original context, rather than being imposed uncritically on the present modern situation. Instead of clinging to the sinful social order into which the gospel was first introduced, Christians should reach for the saving vision of a society regenerated by the power of the gospel.

The interpretation of scripture is not objective but influenced by one's interests and presuppositions that come from one's particular social and cultural milieu. Everyone selects certain texts, but not everyone is aware that they are doing so. Sunday school teachers could select stories about women in the Bible in order to present Christianity in a less sexist manner. If children are to have a non-sexist faith it is essential to emphasise stories about women and not just to tell stories of men. To help affirm and encourage women, the stories of women in the Bible should be remembered, even those stories of women which are very brief. The fact that they are recorded at all is significant, when one considers the patriarchal nature of biblical times.

The biblical writers were limited, fallible human beings. Particular passages do not necessarily reflect the will of God, but are distorted by the human writer and culture. They are a reflection of these, rather than the will of God. This is not to deny that the Bible is God-inspired, but rather that, "fully human words, marked by human particularity and limitations, disclose the divine word to us" (Johnson 1989: 100).

The Bible could be read with a hermeneutics of remembrance. The terrible incidents and mistakenly sinful religious understandings should not be denied and overlooked. In this way we may be able to see some of what the texts do not say. "We must remember with no whitewashing the struggles and suffering of our foremothers whose stories are hidden behind the texts" (Johnson 1989: 102). In this way, the God who worked through love, and not the God who rules through patriarchal power and domination, can be found.

Considering the fact that the Bible was written in a patriarchal context, by men, it is amazing that there is any record of women at all. Jesus' disciples were astonished that he should be talking to a woman, yet the story of the Samaritan woman is preserved. The stories of Mary and Martha (Luke 10:38-42), the woman who touched Jesus' cloak (Luke 8:40ff), and the women disciples (Luke 8:1-3) are also recorded. These are just a few examples of stories which overturn the patriarchal norm. Evidence of how radical Jesus' attitude to women was can be seen in the accusation that he mixed with "prostitutes" (Luke 7:39) and allowed women to sit at his feet as disciples and learn (Luke 10:38-42).

The Bible contains occasional details about women in leadership roles. These come through despite the patriarchal nature of the ministry of the church. It was not that there were so few women leaders, or that they did so little, but that their actions and stories were generally not recorded and preserved. However, women were not simply marginalised figures in the early church; they also exercised leadership as missionaries, founders of the Christian communities,

163

apostles, prophets and leaders of the church (Keane 1989: 5).

The church needs to emphasise rather than neglect the few stories and details about women. For example, if the lesson is about prophets, the examples of Elijah, Samuel and Amos can be used, but Huldah should also be mentioned (2 Kings 22; 2 Chronicles 34:14-28).

What can be done at Sunday school?

If the socialisation of children in the church is to be non-sexist more stories about women need to be included in the Sunday school teaching programme. Moreover, these stories need to be of women who are active people of God, leading God's people, speaking God's message and doing God's work. Women need to be seen in roles other than the traditional ones of mother and comforter. Often it is difficult for parents and teachers to find stories about women leaders in the Bible. One of the reasons for this is the way the Bible is translated. Fiorenza shows how the work of many New Testament women is overlooked because titles such as "*prostatis*" and "*diakonos*" are translated as helpers or servants when used for women and as deacons, apostles and leaders when applied to men. For example, in Romans 16:1-2 Phoebe is described as "diakonos". This is often translated as helper, servant or deaconess rather than deacon, missionary leader or minister.[4]

The women in the Old Testament should not be overlooked. Stories of the matriarchs as well as the patriarchs can be told. The lessons on prophets could be dealt with in a far more inclusive manner by mentioning some female prophets such as Deborah (Judges 4:4-16) and Huldah (2 Kings 22:14-20). Otherwise there is no acknowledgement that there were some women prophets. Other women who follow the tradition of Hebrew prophets and canticle singers are found in the Song of Miriam after the Exodus (Exodus 15:21) and in the Magnificat, the Song of Mary which is particularly interesting because of its theme of social reversal (Luke 1:46-55).[5]

There are women in the Psalms and Proverbs; for example, the woman who is described in Proverbs 31. She is certainly involved in many activities that have traditionally not been seen as part of a woman's role. There is also the woman in the Song of Solomon. This

4. See Fiorenza 1983: 170ff.
5. Wittenberg, in Ackermann, et al, 1991: 3ff.

song reflects a wonderful degree of equality in the relationship between the lovers. It overcomes the all too common patterns of dominance and subservience.

The gospels lend themselves to inclusive stories because Jesus was so radical and non-sexist in his actions and attitudes. There are stories in the gospels where God is portrayed as male and other stories where God is portrayed as female. For example, God is likened to a shepherd in the story of the lost sheep (Luke 15:1-7), and to a woman in the story of the lost coin (Luke 15:1-10). Jesus compares the kingdom of God to a mustard seed and to yeast. The mustard seed belongs to the male world of the farmer, but the yeast belongs to the female world of the woman making bread (Luke 13:18-21; Matthew 13:31-33).

The many healing stories are good ones to use in the Sunday school as they are inclusive of both men, women and children. Jesus heals the woman with the flow of blood, thus overturning the cultic stigma (Mark 5:25-34; Luke 8:43-49). Jesus reveals that the power of the traditional laws that had governed women's lives for centuries was broken as Jesus set them free, healed them and gave them wholeness.

In stories about the disciples or the friends of Jesus both men and women should be included. The female friends of Jesus may be less well known than the male disciples, but they were the ones who at the time of his death stayed close and remained faithful until the end (Mark 15:40). It was a woman who was the first to see Jesus alive after the resurrection and to be told by Jesus to go and tell the others (John 20). Mary sat at the feet of Jesus and learnt as any other disciple would (Luke 10:39-42). Susanna and Joanna can be mentioned alongside Peter, James and John (Luke 8:3). There are many other stories such as that of the Syro-Phoenician woman (Mark 7:20-30) that are significant in terms of their affirmation of women.

When teaching or talking about Acts and the missionary activity of the early church, stories of both men and women need to be included. The additional information from the Pauline literature shows that women mentioned in Acts were not exceptional, but representative of early Christian women. Acts concentrates on Peter and even more on Paul. The church tends to do the same and forget that there were others who were active and working to spread the gospel. There is Phoebe, a fellow worker with Paul, whom he mentions in Romans 16:1. Very little is known about her but the children could use their imaginations. What are the things she did? Where did she evangelise? Did she do similar things to Paul and have similar experiences? A lesson around Phoebe as well as Paul helps to balance the impression that men do the real work of mission and women are the assistants.

Euodia and Syntyche worked side by side with Paul. Paul considers the authority of these women so great that he fears their dissension could endanger the Christian community in Philippi (Philippians 4:2-3). Churches met in the houses of certain women such as Lydia (Acts 16:14), and Nympha (Colossians 4:15). Mary (Romans 16:6), and Tryphaena (Romans 16:12) are commended for having "laboured hard" in the Lord. There were the four daughters of Philip who prophesied and proclaimed God's message (Acts 21:9). These early workers in the church are often overlooked because the church has grown accustomed to male leadership. However, this was not always the case. The Council of Nicea in 325 saw deacons, including the female deacons, as clergy, and the Synod of Trullo in 692 ordained women deacons.[6]

To include these stories demands a new way of looking at biblical material. However, by including some stories about women whose names are mentioned in the Bible one is not moving away from the Bible. In fact, it is being more faithful to the Bible, as more of the Bible is used, rather than just a few favourite passages.

For older children it is helpful to explain that Paul is possessed by the need for order, so that the young churches will not be discredited and their growth hindered. Out of a concern for order, as he understands it with his rabbinical training, he restricts women's ministry in certain churches. He upholds the conventional behavioural codes of society for households, although he does soften them and expect slave masters and husbands to show fairness and love to a degree that the surrounding culture never expected. Love and order are seen as male provinces, while obedience and submission are the province of women, children and slaves (Dowell 1987: 33). Ephesians 5:21 speaks of mutual submission and gives hope of the recovery of the early Christian vision of a community of equals. Galatians 3:26-28 contains a creed which embodies an alternative world view of equality in Jesus.

Stories of men which reveal some of the traditionally feminine virtues should be told. The story of Jonathan can be told in the light of loyalty and compassion and not simply of friendship. Stories of the caring mother could be balanced with stories of caring fathers such as Eli (1 Samuel 2) or David's sorrow at the death of Absalom (2 Samuel 18).

6. Schmidt 1989, chapter 10.

An interesting trend regarding women can be detected in the Bible. Few women were mentioned in the Old Testament. In the New Testament more women are included. This trend could be a progressive revelation about the position of women. Much the same could be said of the Holy Spirit, as little is mentioned about the Holy Spirit in the Old Testament, and far more in the New. However, the Holy Spirit has always been a central person of the Trinity and today is given even more prominence. However, with regard to women, many interpreters remain tied to the cultural conditions of the first century, or worse still, to the Old Testament's culture.

Worship

The early church was characterised by charismatic, Spirit-led leadership in which sacramental power was located in the church rather than being the personal possession of a male cleric. The church could move nearer this kind of pattern with a recognition of the gifts of all people in the community. There should be greater mutuality of ministry with egalitarian rather than hierarchical structures.

Worship is very influential and needs to be made inclusive by the use of non-sexist language and by using both masculine and feminine images of God. God can be spoken of as "God" rather than as "He". If God is spoken of as "Father", there should also be times when God is described as "Mother". This would be biblical, as God is described as the mother eagle (Deuteronomy 32:11), the mother giving birth (Isaiah 42:14; Deuteronomy 32:18), the mother suckling (Isaiah 49:15), and the mother quieting (Psalm 131:2) (M. Walker 1989: 11). Some female imagery for the divine is a way of enhancing women's self-respect and giving them a sense of empowerment. "She" can stand for all that is meant by the word God, just as adequately as "He". Jesus' use of "Father" was intended to lead people to a greater intimacy with God. When it ceases to do this or is used to oppress women, it is contradictory and should be complemented by other images.

CONCLUSION

Socialisation within the church is not deliberately sexist. The teachers are committed to the children and to imparting the Christian faith to them. Sexist attitudes and a patriarchal religion are not consciously taught, but come across in the Sunday school material and programme. For example, sexism is subtly propagated by the way God is always referred to in masculine terms and through the fact that far more stories are of men than of women.

The challenge that is left to parents and teachers, as well as to the whole church, is to be faithful to the liberating gospel of Christ and to eradicate sexism from Sunday schools and churches. There needs to be a stand against sexism similar to Desmond Tutu's stand against racism. Non-sexist Christian education must be developed, so that children can be brought up in a non-sexist tradition and thus be less likely to face frustration and disenchantment with Christianity with reference to gender issues. In this way society may become less patriarchal, the church may become more balanced in its theology, more caring in its practice, and affirm and empower women. Such a church will more closely reflect what it truly means to be the female and male body of Christ.

BIBLIOGRAPHY

Books and Journals

Ackermann, D. et al. (1991), *Women hold up half the sky*, Pietermaritzburg: Cluster Publications.

Clanton, Jann Aldredge (1991), *In whose image? God and gender*, New York: Crossroad.

Dowell, S. and I. Hurcombe (1987), *Dispossessed daughters of Eve*, London: SPCK.

Fiorenza, Elizabeth Schüssler (1985), *Bread not stone*, Boston: Beacon Press.

Fiorenza, Elizabeth Schüssler (1983), *In memory of her*, London: SCM Press Ltd.

Harrison, Beverly Wildung (1985), *Making the connections*, Boston Press.

Hiesberger, Jean M. (1981), "The ultimate religious education challenge", in *Religious Education* 76(4), pp. 355-359.

Hughes, Gerard W. (1985), *God of surprises*, London: Darton, Longman & Todd.

Johnson, Susan (1989), *Christian spiritual formation in the Church*,

Nashville: Abingdon Press.

Keane, Marie Henry (1988), "Women in the theological anthropology of the early fathers", *Journal of Theology for Southern Africa*, 62, pp. 3-13.

Kimel, Alvin F. (1992), *Speaking the Christian God*, Grand Rapids Michigan: Eerdmans.

Kretzschmar, L. (1990), "Hermeneutics, culture and the Apostle Paul's view of women", *Women's Studies* 2/1, 37-51.

Loades, A. (ed.) (1990), *Feminist theology – A reader*, London: SPCK.

Longenecker, Richard N. (1984), *New Testament social ethics for today*, Michigan: Grand Rapids.

Mollenkott, V., "Women and the Bible: A challenge to male interpretations", *Mission Trends* 4: 221-233.

Morny, Joy (1990), "Equality or divinity: A false dichotomy?", *Journal of Feminist Studies in Religion* 6:16.

Popenoe, David (1977), *Sociology*, 3rd edition, Engelwood Cliffs, New Jersey: Prentice Hall Inc.

Procter-Smith, Marjorie (1990), *In her own rite – constructing feminist liturgical tradition*, Nashville: Abingdon Press.

Ruether, R. (1983), *Sexism and God-talk*, Boston: Beacon.

Russell, Letty M. (1987), *The household of freedom*, Philadelphia: Westminster Press.

Schmidt, Alvin John (1989), *Veiled and silenced*, Georgia: Mercer University Press.

Swartley, Willard M. (1983), *Slavery, sabbath, war and women*, New York: Herald Press.

Swart-Russell, Phoebe (1989), "Toward our liberation: A new vision of church and ministry", *Journal of Theology for Southern Africa*, 66.

Trible, Phyllis (1984), *Texts of terror: Liberating feminist readings of biblical narratives*, Philadephia: Fortress.

Villa-Vicencio, Charles (1988), *Trapped in apartheid*, Cape Town: David Philip.

Walker, Megan (1989), "The challenge of feminism to the Christian concept ofgod", *Journal of Theology for Southern Africa*, 66, pp. 4-20.

Children's Bibles

Batchelor, Mary (1988), *The children's Bible in 365 stories*, Cape Town: Struik Christian Books.

Dean, S. (1985), *Dean's gift book of Bible stories*, London: Ladgate Hill.

Stoddard, Sandol (1991), *A child's first Bible*, London: Hamlyn Children's Books.

Taylor, Kenneth N. (1989), *My first Bible in pictures*, Cape Town: Struik Christian Books.

Trafton, Debbie (1989), *My read and do Bible storybook*, Minneapolis: Augsburg Fortress.

Challenges facing women in South Africa

S outh Africa has moved a long way from where it was some three hundred years ago to where it is today. Therefore, given the nature of South African history, it is the responsibility of all its citizens to make sure that this country becomes friendly and caring to all.

It is an undisputed fact that women, especially black women, were disadvantaged in the old South Africa because of both their gender and the colour of their skin. They were denied the right to be full citizens of the country in which they were born and denied the right to make decisions for themselves. This explains why the majority of women are at the bottom of the socio-economic ladder and living in extreme poverty.

I believe that it is always important for us to live in the present and not to be imprisoned by the past, although I am not trying to suggest that women should forget their past for the sake of the present. My proposal is that the past should be one's history, that one should be aware of it but not let one's life be limited by it. If one dwells in the past he or she will not be able to live in the present. She or he will never be able to plan for the future. I suggest therefore that our history should be clearly written in our memories in order to be consulted when there is a need to do so. Women should now ask themselves what they should do for themselves and for the whole community to correct the wrongs of the past. The challenge for women is to be pro-active.

CHANGING A MIND SET

The challenge is for women to change their mind set. Women should move from always being told what to do to a position of also being able to tell others what to do, in conjunction with the rest of the society or community. Women should move from the dependence syndrome to having an independent mind, that is, a mind of their own. They should challenge the culture of silence in which they have been socialised. Women in general are not expected to have opinions of their own, let alone to disagree with men. From birth to death a girl child is meant to be seen and not heard. Mary Daly maintains that this silencing is used as a mechanism of social control and that women carry with them a general feeling of hopelessness, guilt and anxiety over social disapproval (Daly, 1973: 51).

In her book *Sister outsider*, Audre Lorde endorses the foregoing argument of the silence and the voicelessness of women when she says:

> I have come to believe over and over again that what is more important to me must be spoken, made verbal and shared, even at the risk of having it bruised or misunderstood . . . For we have been socialized to respect fear more than our own needs for language and definition, and while we wait in silence for that final luxury of fearlessness, the weight of that silence will choke us (Lorde 1984: 40-44).

This is a challenge to women to claim their voice and to let their thinking and their feelings be known.

It is also important to mention that a handful of women in South Africa have made their voices heard. We see them climbing the ladder and penetrating the glass ceiling which was constructed to hinder their progress. Women, both black and white, are now visible in politics. In parliament there are a number of women, some of whom are cabinet ministers; for example, the Ministers of Housing and Health. In addition to these, the Speaker is also a woman. Although there are so few, bearing in mind the population of women in the country, I do believe that everything has its beginning. It will be the responsibility of those who have already achieved some success to be inspiring role models for the younger generation. These women who are now in positions which were previously reserved for whites and for men should be engaged in the practical effort of trying to upgrade the standards of all the women in the country. In this regard, they will need support and motivation from the community at large, especially from other women.

The other challenge for women is that of restructuring or re-organising their families in such a way that each member of the family is valued equally as a person, and benefits equally from the wealth of that particular family. The roles that members of the family are engaged in should not be assigned according to gender but according to their own interests and abilities. It is obvious that there are some household chores that are not regarded as exciting by the young ones but, unfortunately, these still have to be done. In this case all members of the family should take turns in doing the housework.

The issue of the intimate relationship between husband and wife needs to be looked at as well. In the African set-up there is a lack of a close relationship between spouses, mainly because it is not encouraged. Often the lack of this close relationship is brought about by extended family members who are around all the time, expecting to be fed and nursed by their daughters-in-law.

I do not suggest in any way that we should do away with this part of our culture, namely that of giving service to one's in-laws, but we need to look at it critically. It is my feeling that the extended family system should not hinder other systems from blossoming and impacting upon members of the community in a positive way. It is not supposed to overshadow the significance of the intimate life of married people when they need to be by themselves. Women should not be forced to do things against their will. The spouses' interests should not be dominated by the interests of the group. There should be a balance between the two.

WOMEN'S WORK

We live in an era where both women and men work outside the home. This demands that even those who are full-time housewives should be given credit for what they do in the home. The time has passed where children were only the responsibility of the mother. Fathers have to be responsible as well. But if women are not able to articulate clearly what they want, there is no way that men and husbands will know what women expect of them. The true family is the family that respects all its members, regardless of their age or gender.

It is the unbalanced exercise of male power and authority within the family that leads to women and children being abused. Men who abuse their wives and children physically and emotionally do not

173

regard these members of their families as equal and as having the same rights as themselves. Unfortunately, women who are battered tend to blame themselves for the behaviour of their husbands. They think that they have "asked for it" in one way or another. They think that they are battered because they have angered their husbands. The end result of battering is the lowering of women's self-esteem and the killing of their confidence.

Susan Brooks Thistlethwaite believes that Christian women who are battered find it very difficult to accept the fact that battering or any kind of abuse of them is evil or wrong.

> They believe this because they have been taught that resistance to this injustice is unbiblical and unchristian. Christian women are supposed to be meek, and claiming rights for oneself is committing the sin of pride (Russell 1985: 99).

For many unfortunate women battering has led to their being killed by their spouses after a long period of abuse. Some women have committed suicide when they realised that no-one was going to offer to help them. This is a challenge to women to help each other to overcome the problem of abuse. No woman should boast and rejoice in being free and happy when many other women are enduring pain at the hands of their husbands. Abused women likewise should speak up; they should break the culture of silence in order to get help for themselves and others.

Among some church people in African communities it is sometimes believed that a woman who speaks about women's issues and women's oppression is a woman who is oppressed by her husband, or a divorcee, or a man-hater, or a woman who wants to be like men. This type of thinking prevents many women from standing up for their own emancipation. In this same society women are encouraged to keep all that happens to them secret. This, according to African culture, is a sign of a mature woman.

Economic justice is a concern for all women, black women in particular. One of the problems that black women face in the workplace is that they work very hard for long hours earning low wages that cannot sustain their families. Their wages do not usually compare with the type of work they do and what they produce. These jobs have no job security or certainty. Women's biological make-up is always used against them. They "are much more likely than men to experience social work intervention, because of their roles as mothers, wives, and carers of other dependents" (Langan 1992: 15).

There is a need to search for an economic model that will take humanity seriously, especially women. The one-sided model of the Western world does not seem to take black people seriously. The patriarchal model of almost all our countries does not respect women. We need to look for an economic model that will treat all people equally.

By equality here we mean that the economy should realize that although people are different in terms of race, ethnicity, gender, age and education, they nevertheless all have basic human needs and they are all valuable human beings. For women, equality in economic terms will mean the removal of the cultural, racial and gender biases that have encroached upon economic practices. I also advocate that women who are not employed outside their homes should be recognised and acknowledged by the economic structures as workers. According to Jodi L. Jacobson:

> The low evaluation of women's work begins with the fact that, in developing countries, most of women's activity takes place in the non-wage economy for the purpose of household consumption – producing food crops, collecting firewood, gathering fodder, and so on. "Income generation" of this type is critically important; indeed, the poorer the family, the more vital the contribution of women and girls in the essential goods that families are unable to buy with cash. But in the increasingly market orientated economies of the Third World, work that does not produce cash directly is heavily discounted (Jacobson 1992: 16-17).

The above quotation reiterates my earlier remarks on the need to value women's unpaid work. It is not true that women who are housewives do not work or are non-workers. For me the term "non-worker" referring to women is derogatory and it falsely classifies women. Women are always working and their work is never finished. In her book *If women were counted: A feminist economics* Marilyn Waring provides very interesting examples of four people who are doing different types of work. Two of them, according to economic standards, are non-workers.

Her first example is of a woman from Zimbabwe called Tendai. Her work starts at four in the morning: she fetches water eleven kilometres away from her home and she returns home at nine o'clock. She eats a little and goes out to fetch wood until twelve o'clock. When she comes back she washes dishes and prepares lunch for her family. She then goes out to search for wild vegetables for supper and then makes another evening trip for water. She prepares supper and her day ends at nine o'clock at night.

The second example is that of Cathy, a North American housewife. She prepares food, sets the table, serves the food, clears the table and washes the dishes. She dresses the children, drives them to school, does the laundry, irons the clothes, goes to the supermarket, fetches the children from school, keeps an eye on them and plays with them. The list goes on and on.

The third example is that of Ben, a highly trained member of the US military. "His regular duty is to descend to an underground facility where he waits with his colleague, for hours at a time, for an order to fire a nuclear missile."

The fourth example is that of Mario. He is a pimp and a drug addict in Rome. Mario's consumption of drugs and his services are illegal, but they are marketed. His activities are part of Italy's hidden economy. According to the international economic system, Tendai and Cathy are not working and they are therefore unproductive. The two men are productive (Waring 1988: 15, 16).

Marilyn Waring counters this evaluation by saying that Tendai and Cathy are the true productive workers and that their economic activity is of value. She accepts the fact that Ben and Mario do work, but their work is destructive, and their economic activity constitutes a major cost and threat to the planet.

Now the main question here is: how do we measure unpaid women's work in terms of payment? Who is to pay her if she has to be paid? In one of her suggestions, Carol Robb maintains that the solution to the degradation of a woman's work "would involve paying women for house work, though how to finance such payments with any measure of economic justice, . . . is as yet by no means that obvious" (Robb 1995: 4-5). Secondly, Robb suggests that "we might remove the association between women and housework by splitting all reproductive labour, including child care, between husband and wife or partner and partner" (Robb 1995: 5).

John B. Cobb, Jr., in his book *Sustaining the common good: A Christian perspective on the global economy*, agrees with Marilyn Waring, Jodi Jacobson and Carol Robb that value should be placed on women's unpaid work. But he believes that this will only happen when economists are willing to marry economics with the realities of the world. He maintains that at the moment economists work as if they are in the classroom studying economic theories – they do not take different contexts seriously.

This is a challenge to the people of South Africa to look for and uphold those economic theories that make sense and respect the people of this country. It is up to women to challenge the system and make it "women-friendly". Women will be able to challenge and change the system if they engage themselves with the on-going economic issues in the country. We also need to have women who are specialists in the field and who will be able to change the patriarchal theories that they have learnt in the classroom and come up with approaches that take the situation of women into account.

WOMEN AND THE CHURCH

The other institution that women need to challenge and change is the church and its interpretation of the Bible. The church, which claims to be the body of Christ, tends to resemble more closely a Jewish cultural institution than the body of those who live according to Christ's example of healing the sick, liberating the oppressed, giving sight to the blind, restoring dignity to the humiliated, and so on.

From the beginning of Christianity women have been denied the right to own it and even transform it. Christianity was and in some instances still is influenced by the ancient Jewish culture. In the ancient Jewish tradition women were regarded as perpetual minors. In Jewish religion women were segregated from men in the temple and synagogues. In the Jerusalem temple during the first century CE, women were permitted only in the "court of heathens" or "the women's court". The synagogue had two separate sections, the lecture hall and the worship room. Women were allowed to enter the lecture hall, but they could enter the worship area only if they remained behind a special screen. Both in the temple and in the synagogues women and men entered through separate entrances. Women were not allowed to participate in worship or read the Torah publicly.

The writings of the early church Fathers also distorted the image of women. Through the myth of Adam and Eve and their fall in the Garden of Eden women were made responsible for the sin of the entire world and they were seen as unredeemable beasts.

For a very long time women in some of our churches were denied the opportunity of taking leadership positions. Many of the modern arguments have been based on those used by the early church Fathers and their successors. I am convinced that even in those churches where women are allowed leadership positions there is a feeling among the majority of men that these women should be seen and not heard. There is not much space for them to operate, or even to achieve their goals. What is also frustrating is that women are expected to exercise their ministry in exactly the same way as men exercise theirs; any woman who does not do so is regarded as a failure. In order to satisfy the status quo some of these women have had to behave like men. They start to walk, talk and behave differently. In this way they disassociate themselves from other women.

It is the task of women in the ministry to find their own voice and to revolutionalise the patriarchal, hierarchical and Western theological training that they received mainly from the hands of men in order to empower other women. In her book, *Co-creating: A feminist vision of ministry*, Lynn N. Rhodes discovered that women in the ordained ministry that she interviewed see their roles, authority and power as different from that of men. Theirs is an authority and power with the people and not over the people. They maintain that women's theology is liberating for all people and that it is based on the experiences of the individual and the society.

WOMEN AND THE BIBLE

Another important task of women who are in the ministry is to re-interpret the Bible for themselves. The traditional interpretation of the Bible has killed women's self-confidence and self-esteem. It has blamed women for the sins of the world and presented them as unredeemable creatures. In Elizabeth Clark's words, for the early church Fathers:

> Women were God's creation, his [sic] good gift to men – and the curse of the world. They were weak in both mind and character and displayed dauntless courage, undertook prodigious feats of scholarship. Vain, deceitful, brimming with lust – they led men to Christ, fled sexual encounter,

178

wavered not at the executioner's threats, adorned themselves with sackcloth and ashes (Clark, 1983: 15).

The fact that in the second creation story a woman was created from
the rib which was taken from Adam when he was asleep is for the
church Fathers a clear indication that women were created inferior
and irrational.

What happened in the early church is happening in the contemporary churches as well. The Bible was and still is used in many situations as a tool to make black people good slaves, to justify the abuse
of women and to justify extramarital sexual activities. But it is amazing to see how some of these affected people were able and are still
able today to find liberation in the same Bible. Oppression of any kind
cannot be justified as having been ordained by God. God is a God of
liberation for all God's creatures. Women should try to develop an
authentic and inclusive interpretation of the Bible. Women's theology
is born and it will continue to be born when women's faith confronts
the injustices done to women by the church and society. Women's theology will be born when women's faith seeks to understand what is
happening around it; when that same faith tries to find a way in which
it can be involved.

Letty Russell suggests that women should always use the hermeneutic of suspicion when reading the Bible. She encourages them to
make use of the structure of tradition that has been presented to them
by biblical scholars, but they should raise "radical questions about the
oppressive ways that Scripture and tradition have been used and about
the unfaithfulness of church and synagogue as guardians of that tradition" (Russell 1985: 142).

The greatest task before women is to make the Bible relevant and
life-giving to themselves and to the whole community. Like men,
women are sinners who are striving for perfection, but they are not
unredeemable. As women we should struggle with the God who has
been presented to us as our enemy and be assisted by our God who is
our helper. Women "must defeat the Bible as patriarchal authority by
using the Bible as liberator" (Russell 1985: 140).

Our existing women's organisations in the church should not be
places of tears and pity all the time; they should also be places of
encouragement and gathering of strength. They should not only be
places of confession, but of forgiveness as well. These organisations
should not be places where there is authority from above (or authori-

ty as domination) but in these organisations authority should be exercised as a partnership of all its members.

THE FUTURE

I see great opportunities for women in our new South Africa. Education was one of the fields to which women, especially black women, were denied access mainly because of their economic status and cultural impediments. But education is now open to all, rich and poor, men and women alike. Women need to grab this opportunity for themselves and for their daughters. There is a need for women to gain knowledge for themselves and to build a better future. It is only when a person has armed herself or himself with an education that she or he is able to analyse the society in which she or he lives and be able to challenge effectively what needs to be changed. Effective education is the type of education that goes beyond theory to the practical action that promotes justice.

bell hooks [sic] believes that women's theology and struggles should incorporate a form of theory that will help women to deal with the issues which confront them. This theory should "provide a structure of analysis and thought that will synthesise that which is most visionary in women's thinking, talk, and discourse" (hooks [sic] 1989: 35).

In our institutions of learning, and in life in general, women's experiences, choices and reasoning or philosophy should be taken seriously. It is my experience in dealing with both male and female students, and my experience in women's organisations, that women tend to be more practical and experiential in their approach to things. It is also easy for women to speak from both the heart and the head, while the majority of men feel comfortable only when they speak from the head. I believe that both approaches are justifiable; the only problem is when one approach is elevated over and above the other.

Using the analogy of a basketball player, I would like to say to women: "the ball is in your hands". It is women's choice either to keep it or throw it to each other until it has been touched by all. It is the duty of those who have achieved something to make sure that others achieve as well. An educator's life becomes fulfilled when she or he sees her or his students prospering in all directions. South African women's motto should be "a good life for myself and a good life for others". Women should be their sisters' keepers. Only women are in a position to free themselves and make the world a happier and more enjoyable place in which to live.

BIBLIOGRAPHY

Clark, E. (1983), *Women in the early church*, Minnesota: Liturgical Press.

Cobb, J.B. Jr. (1994), *Sustaining the common good: A Christian perspective on the global economy*, Ohio: The Pilgrim Press.

Daly, M. (1973), *Beyond God the Father: Toward a philosophy of women's liberation*, Boston: Beacon Press.

hooks, b. (1989), *Talking back: Thinking feminist, thinking black*, Boston: South End Press.

Jacobson, J.L. (1992), *Worldwatch Paper 110, Gender bias: Roadblock to sustainable development*, Washington: Worldwatch Institute.

Langan, M. and L. Day (eds.) (1992), *Women's oppression and social work: Issues in anti-discriminatory practice*, London: Routledge.

Lorde, A. (1984), *Sister outsider: Essays and speeches*, California: The Crossing Press.

Rhodes, L.N. (1987), *Co-creating: A feminist vision of ministry*, Philadelphia: The Westminster Press.

Robb, C., From the seventh chapter of her forthcoming book, *Equal value*.

Russell, L.M. (ed) 1985), *Feminist interpretation of the Bible*, Philadelphia: The Westminster Press.

Siddons, P. (1980), *Speaking out for women: A biblical view*, Valley Forge, Pennsylvania: Judson Press.

Waring, M. (1988), *If women were counted: A new feminist economics*, San Francisco: Harper Collins.

Creating newness:
The spirituality of reconstruction

INTRODUCTION

For many years the predominant themes in Christian life and witness in South Africa were justice and reconciliation. Now the priority is becoming creative reconstruction and development. The older themes are being integrated in the new. Reconciliation with God and with one another is a never-ending process, motivating the effort to reach understanding and build community within the diversity of South African society. Vigilance for justice also never ends, but can now be expressed as a constructive watchfulness within the democratic system.

The new and dominant theme for South Africa and the subcontinent is reconstruction and development. To follow Christ today in this context entails developing a new spirituality of reconstruction, imbued with justice and reconciliation but focused on the vision of a new creation. It will entail the learning of new skills, and must bring together the advantaged and disadvantaged, rich and poor, black and white, in a spirituality of co-responsibility for the building of a new society.

"Spirituality" is a broad poetic word that can be defined in many ways. The authors of one book currently in wide use write that it is concerned with "the individual prayer and communion with God, both of the ordinary Christian and of those with special spiritual gifts, *and with the outer life which supports and flows from this devotion*" (Jones 1986: xxii, my italics). A recent definition from an evangelical source defines it succinctly, as allowing God to work in us while "doing everything possible on our part to ensure that the seed of the gospel takes root in our lives" (McGrath 1995: 8). A brief definition that may be found helpful is simply "life in-formed by prayer", or "life and personality in-formed by prayer", that is, human life guided and shaped from within by prayer and relationship with God.

The central Christian message revealed through the cross and res-

182

urrection is that the ultimate meaning of life is love. Christian spirituality rests on and springs from the centrality of God's love. God is love. To open ourselves to God's indwelling is to begin to see the world with the eyes of God the Creator and Redeemer, sharing at least in some remote way in God's delight and compassion for all that is made; and it is to know that one can trust God, and trust the possibilities for good in people, even in the midst of destructive evil.

The love revealed in Christ becomes our measure to test the worth of things; it is the goal that gives direction amid every expression of brokenness, deviousness and confusion. In God there is no darkness at all (1 John 1:5). God's light imparts a sensitivity that reveals what is true and untrue and gives birth to the prophet. Archbishop Tutu has exemplified this gift of insight, which will be needed as much in the age of development as ever in the past. The spirituality of reconstruction will take various forms, corresponding to the varied people and issues involved, but its common thread will be that it seeks to marry the inner dynamic of creative love springing from God with the outer need to engage in the reconstruction of people and society.

THE VISION OF RECONSTRUCTION

Reconstruction assumes both a need and a vision: it is a process of identifying needs and acting with determination, wisdom and compassion to turn the vision into reality. To take part in reconstruction in southern Africa is to make a specific concrete response to the universal call to act with God in redemption and re creation, building the Kingdom of God. Luke describes the dawning of the Kingdom when he opens his account of the teaching of Jesus, in a passage that echoes Isaiah and was often quoted in the days of the struggle:

> The Spirit of the Lord is upon me,
> because he has anointed me
> to bring good news to the poor.
> He has sent me to proclaim
> release to the captives
> and recovery of sight to the blind,
> to let the oppressed go free,
> to proclaim the year of the Lord's favour.
> (Luke 4:18-19 NRSV)

The shackles of past political oppression no longer bind the poor of southern Africa, but there remain shackles of social and economic deprivation and disadvantage on every level, of spirit, mind, and body. There is a need to work on all levels to heal, restore and create anew.

The Exodus provided the biblical paradigm for the liberation struggle. The paradigm for reconstruction is found in the visions of new creation in both Old and New Testaments. When the people of Israel are brought back to their devastated land after the Babylonian captivity, Deutero-Isaiah voices the divine vision of perfect restoration:

> For I am about to create new heavens
> and a new earth;
> The former things shall not be remembered
> or come to mind.
> But be glad and rejoice for ever
> in what I am creating;
> for I am about to create Jerusalem as a joy,
> and its people as a delight.
> I will rejoice in Jerusalem, and delight in my people;
> no more shall the sound of weeping be heard in it,
> or the cry of distress.
> No more shall there be in it an infant that lives a few days
> or an old person who does not live out a lifetime . . .
> They shall build houses and inhabit them;
> they shall plant vineyards and eat their fruit . . .
> They shall not labour in vain, or bear children for calamity;
> for they shall be offspring blessed by the Lord . . .
> The wolf and the lamb shall feed together,
> the lion shall eat straw like the ox.
> They shall not hurt or destroy
> on all my holy mountain, says the Lord.
> (Isaiah 65:17-25 NRSV)

In Isaiah's vision there is "shalom" that enfolds the whole of life, a state of material and spiritual peace and fulfilment: housing and health, employment, good crops, reconciliation between former enemies, the ending of violence. There is joy and rejoicing. The new creation, a gift of God, is more wonderful than all that went before.

The longing for a new creation is also expressed in the New Testament, and in part it is fulfilled. Jesus' life and resurrection usher in a new age in history, opening up new possibilities for humanity. In the apocalyptic passages and Revelation we find the theme of an entirely new creation, which is yet to be: "Then I saw a new heaven and a new earth: for the first heaven and the first earth had passed away . . . And the one who was seated on the throne said: 'See, I am making all things new' " (Revelation 21:1, 5). These verses suggest an act of radical discontinuity from what has been; but already as Christians we live in a time of promise, when the presence of the Kingdom of God has already been proclaimed and God's power to create anew breaks through and changes the patterns of human history. We are called to incarnate that promise in our own lives and, through our calling to be leaven in society, to incarnate the values of the Kingdom as far as possible in the life and structures of society around us. Our own activity meets God's activity in both individual and social spheres. Just as in our individual spiritual life our own efforts to become new people meet the transforming power of God's grace, so in our efforts to create new societies we discover that we are co-workers with God in realising God's vision for the world.

How to make the dream of *shalom* a reality in southern Africa today? The vision of God's Kingdom is transcendent, perfect, beyond complete attainment in this life but always calling us forward to greater fulfilment. As Charles Villa-Vicencio says, "the social demands of the gospel must never be reduced to the social realism of a given time and place". But its demands act as leaven within social reality to give shape and impetus to the work of reconstruction, "a task that will involve the theological wisdom of the ages and the discerning creativity of contextual decision making":

> It has to do with bridging the gap between the ideals of a people who have in their long exile (without and within the country) dreamed utopian dreams of a new South Africa, and the realities of a land torn apart by generations of race, gender and class division. It will at the same time need to be developed within a context marked by an apartheid-ravaged economy. Utopian visions created by prophets, preachers and poets are important ingredients in the process of reconstruction. Ultimately, however, these visions need to be translated into societal practice and laws operative in the here and now. This practice and these laws will necessarily fall short of the projected vision, but must pro-

vide the basis and vision for the long walk to social and economic freedom beyond political liberation (Villa-Vicencio 1992: 8).

The secular vision of the new society in South Africa is summed up in the Reconstruction and Development Programme, or RDP. This programme has been adopted as national policy by the multiparty Government of National Unity. It is devised by and for a multicultural, multifaith society, but has many points of contact with the biblical dream of a new creation and is a programme with which churches and Christian people can very positively relate. Although "the RDP" has become a national watchword, many do not know its principles and programmes, so it will be helpful to present them briefly here.

The Reconstruction and Development Programme rests on six basic principles. The first is that development activities must be *integrated and sustainable*: they must be holistic, avoid piecemeal planning and "harness all our resources in a coherent and purposeful effort that can be sustained into the future" (RDP 1994: 4). Second and vitally, the RDP is a *people-driven process*: "Our people, with their aspirations and collective determination, are our most important resource. The RDP is focused on our people's most immediate needs, and it relies, in turn, on their energies to drive the process of meeting these needs." Development "is not about the delivery of goods to a passive citizenry", but about the "active involvement and growing empowerment" of the people themselves (RDP 1994: 5).

Third, the RDP must promote *peace and security for all*, including the establishment of a police service and justice system that command respect and can combat crime and uphold human rights. Fourth, the RDP is itself a process of *nation-building*, creating a united society out of a South Africa that has historically been divided into "First" and "Third" worlds and enabling the nation to take its place in the subcontinent and the wider world. Fifth, the aim is to *link reconstruction and development*, that is, to enable developmental growth and reconstructive redistribution to happen simultaneously through rapid provision of modern infrastructure, education and training. Sixth and finally, the RDP should contribute to the *democratisation of South Africa* through the involvement of people in decision-making, in development planning and implementation.

For communities on the ground, the most immediately important of the five RDP programmes are the first two: *meeting basic needs* for jobs, land, housing, water, infrastructure, health and social welfare; and *developing our human resources* through education, training, and empowerment of all. The third programme, *building the economy*, aims at modernising and re-skilling South African industry. The fourth is *democratising the state and society*, through democratic government and the Bill of Rights, good policing and justice, an active role for civil society (of which the churches are a vital part), and the availability of information to enable socio-economic development. Finally, the fifth programme is *implementing the RDP*, focusing on the reorganisation of government and its finances so as to create a single development-oriented administrative structure equipped with appropriate legislation to facilitate development. At the same time, implementation demands the participation of people throughout society, hence the current movement to establish bodies such as Community Development Forums to empower and enable communities to take part in their own development, in tandem with local government.

NEED FOR RECONSTRUCTION

The word "reconstruction" reminds us that something has been seriously wrong and there is literally a need to reconstruct and develop something new. In many ways the new South Africa is a joyful and hopeful place. The transition period has afforded a glimpse of the joy of new creation, and the celebrations are being echoed on many further occasions, not least in sporting arenas! There is hunger for meaningful progress, and tremendous keenness to take part in the RDP, which means acquiring the knowledge and expertise to make it work. But the needs are very great: if a truly new life is to become reality for the vast majority, enormous barriers will have be surmounted.

Unemployment affects the whole population in South Africa and averages over 50 per cent among the black population. Population growth outstrips economic growth: in order to absorb all the new jobseekers each year, the South African economy would need to grow at double the 1995 rate of 3 per cent. A low base of education and skills makes South Africa an unattractive investment prospect, while lack of business skills and investment capital hampers the growth of the informal sector and the movement of new entrepreneurs and employers out of the informal sector into larger enterprises. There continues to be real suffering due to poverty. In the past Desmond Tutu often

187

told the story of the small girl he met in an Eastern Cape resettlement camp who said "when we have no food, we drink water to fill our bellies". Thousands of younger relatives of that small girl are still with us. The stress of poverty affects community development directly by making it difficult to mobilise voluntary effort.

It is estimated that about eight million people out of a population of around 40 million live in informal dwellings, so there is a backlog of about 2 million houses in the low-income sector. It is remarkable how homely a shack can be made to look, and there may be advantages like closeness to work, and a low or non-existent rent. But a shack settlement remains an uncomfortable and dangerous place, with little water and sanitation, prone to quick-spreading fires and too often situated on a flood plain. Funding is tight and housing policy has been slow to take shape, as has the demarcation of responsibilities between different departments and levels of government: so few houses have yet materialised.

Crime hampers development indirectly by preventing investment or diverting resources into security measures, and directly when land is illegally occupied, tools stolen, services vandalised. Statistics here can be puzzling. In December 1995 *The Star* reported that Gauteng alone accounted for 8 160 reported vehicle hijackings in the first 11 months of 1995, 75 per cent of the national total, giving an average of more than 24 hijackings per day with firearms involved in over 90 per cent of cases (*Star*, 20 December 1995). There was an immediate reaction from the Secretary of Safety and Security, Azhar Cachalia, the South African Police Services (SAPS) and insurance companies, who concurred that up to 75 per cent of reported hijackings turn out to be fraudulent claims made up for insurance purposes (*Saturday Star*, 23 December 1995: 1). That leaves 2 040 genuine hijackings in Gauteng, or about six per day – together with an almost incredible amount of fraud.

Education underpins all development – but it has been so poor that almost nothing can be assumed. Around 15 million adult South Africans are functionally illiterate (National Literacy Co-operation 1995: 1). The national matric pass rate in 1955 was 55 per cent. The results in terms of formal knowledge are frightening. A young person who had completed Standard 8, when asked where London is, pointed hopefully to Mozambique on the map, and when asked when Jesus was born, replied with great concentration: "Oh yes, in 18 . . . um, . . . 18 . . .!" Again the worst affected have been the black community. The churches do not seem to have filled even the biblical education gap. Ask members of a township congregation to explain the differ- ence between the Old and New Testaments, and one quickly realises that most are unaware that there is any difference. Many members of mainline churches are in fact functionally biblically illiterate. How can serious Christian formation take place unless this situation is radical- ly improved?

The manager of the Adult Basic Education and Training (ABET) Division at First National Bank (FNB), reports how he "researched the readability of several communications at the Bank and found that sometimes a gap of seven years existed between the reading level of the material staff were expected to read and their reading ability . . . 'We take so much for granted, students often have extensive knowl- edge about things familiar to them but lack basic knowledge that comes naturally to people with a formal education'" (CEP July 1995: 4). An ABET pilot course was launched within the FNB in 1994 and the need and enthusiasm are shown by the fact that 500 staff from the Gauteng region volunteered to join it in 1995.

In both urban and rural communities there is a serious and debili- tating lack of basic administrative skills such as writing minutes or keeping accounts. It is common to find people in small business or community-based organisations who have never written an invoice or receipt – and are inhibited from learning by an embarrassment that either tries to hide the deficiency or rejects such things as unnecessary or "not belonging to our culture". This confusion and lack of skills extend to a basic understanding of development, of project cycles and proposal writing – the essential life skills of a developing community. Most importantly, integrity and financial probity are often lacking or break down amid the temptations inherent in handling money in a poor community.

Deeper than lack of skill is a spiritual sickness that shows in a lack of compassion and foresight on behalf of others. South Africa has been an endemically violent land, where it has been a cliché that "human life is cheap". The World Health Organisation has South Africa top- ping the world's murder statistics with an average of 50 murders per 100 000 people per year, 800 per cent higher than the world average of 5,5 per 100 000 (*Star*, 15 December 1995) – an average of one mur- der every half hour in 1995. To add to this, careless – indeed, callous – driving causes around 10 000 deaths a year on South African roads. Industrial safety, in less formal industries as well as on the mines, is often a half-hearted affair.

At its worst other people are simply seen as rubbish, an attitude that was made official by apartheid: "to satisfy a racist obsession, people, God's children, have been uprooted and dumped as if they were rubbish or just things in a place where there was little work and even less food" (Tutu 1990: 233). The mentality is not however confined to the old government apparatus. One personal illustration may help to make this real.

One Sunday afternoon in 1993 I took a retreat in Soweto and then drove to Alexandra to get an update on the situation, which at that time was generally quiet. As I came into First Avenue a woman told me: "They've just killed someone – just up there." Further along the street stood a small crowd of young men from one of the hostels. As I drove closer I saw one of them lying on the ground. He was already lifeless, but others were still throwing stones at his head. I drew level with the stone-throwers and quietly asked one of them: "Why are you angry with him?" "They came here to shoot us," he replied, and he went on throwing stones at the victim's head, repeatedly calling him "rubbish". A few minutes later, while I was away looking for leaders and the police, they piled rubbish on him and set fire to the body.

Afterwards I established that two men from an East Rand hostel had had a personal quarrel with someone in the M2 hostel in Alexandra. They came to look for him, armed with a gun. Not finding him, one of them attempted to shoot a friend of his, and the two were then pursued up the hill by an angry posse. One was arrested and disarmed by a peace monitor, the other was killed by the crowd. Then his body was burned, for he was rubbish, to be expunged from the face of the earth.

Statistics were as muddled then as now, and I have little doubt that despite our best efforts with the local police this killing went down in national records as political and "unrest-related". But it was crime, fruit of the mind set that says people can be treated as rubbish.

Certainly the racism and politics of the past encouraged this attitude. Apartheid dragged human nature back towards its fallen state of alienation, division, separation, animosity and disharmony; while "the Bible declares unequivocally that we are created for fellowship, for togetherness, for community, for interdependence" (Tutu 1990: 236). Inhumanity was found at all extremes of the "struggle": the callousness of state security was answered by the necklacing of impimpis (informers) and "sell-outs". Acts of violence provoked acts of "self-defence" that were no more than indiscriminate retaliation. Hundreds of crime victims of all races in South Africa continue to be sacrificed to this same insensitivity to the value of each individual human life.

There is a counterbalancing perception: don't the poor of South Africa have a spirituality of humanity and community, of Ubuntu, that has African roots and has been refined by the pain and solidarity of the struggle? This perception is only part of the truth; indeed it can obscure the fact that sin is universal and there has been precious little space for personal or social development in the chaos of the "struggle". Many black leaders speak of a "loss of Ubuntu" and the need to recover it. On the one hand there is a longing for peace and unity, which has translated itself into a real commitment; on the other hand there is also a widespread culture of suspicion, fear, jealousy and insecurity; and threats and intimidation against persons and property are common. The African value of community itself can and does have its downside; it can manifest negatively as a communalism which scorns and punishes individual initiative – and thus effectively prevents progress. Development can be seriously hampered in the absence of a cohesive, tolerant and mutually supportive local community.

THE SPIRITUALITY OF RECONSTRUCTION

A spirituality of reconstruction is a way of becoming available through prayer and action to be a channel for God's work in the context of these immense needs. The work entails a co-operative effort to restore and develop persons and community; in which the disadvantaged and advantaged can work together with government, business, and funding and training organisations. The spirituality that underpins it must combine fundamental values with the practical skills of development.

The fundamental values that are needed are very much those listed in the New Testament as Christian virtues. These are qualities that can be at least partially acquired through some effort; and in their perfection they are gifts that show the presence of the Holy Spirit.

All Christian virtues are summed up in the divine love shown by Christ. God's love reaches out to all without exception, in an all-inclusive caring. It is friendship directed even to enemies in order to make them friends; all humanity is at least potentially included among the "friends" for whom Jesus died (John 15:13). The Holy Spirit gives "love, joy, peace, patience, kindness, generosity, faithfulness, gentleness, and self-control" (Galatians 5:22-3). St Paul urges those who are made new in Christ to abandon their former behaviour – anger, greed, lust, lying, abuse, slander, malicious gossip – and put on "the new self, which is being renewed according to the image of its creator", so that "there is no longer Greek and Jew, circumcised and uncircumcised, barbarian, Scythian, slave and free, but Christ is all in all" and in this new united community there are compassion, kindness, humility, patience, forgiveness, and "love, which binds everything together in perfect harmony" (Colossians 3:5-15). Love received and given makes us truly free: love is the final stage of liberation.

When the early Christians considered how to form Christian character, they added to the New Testament lists some of the central virtues of the ancient Greek and Roman world. St Ambrose christened four of these and called them the "cardinal" virtues: "justice" (which includes integrity, honesty and kindness); "courage" (including reliability and determination); "temperance" (balance and self-control) and "prudence" which means practical knowledge and wisdom about how things work and how to get things done. The Latin names are *justitia*, *fortitudo*, *temperantia* and *prudentia*. These qualities have a clear relevance to reconstruction; and St Augustine saw that they too are all aspects of love. They are facets of inner strength, developed humanity, true Ubuntu.

The great Christian virtues are faith, hope and love (1 Corinthians 13:15), which came to be called "theological" virtues because they relate us directly to God and cannot be acquired just by our own effort; they can only be established by God's own action, by grace. There are times during any effort to bring a new society into being when a person is thrown back on God with nothing else to trust in, nowhere else to place their hope, and no other cause to go on loving: and then the theological virtues are needed! They are always at the heart of all Christian spirituality, a well of peace and joy; and prayer is the way to receive them.

Reconstruction demands these kinds of qualities from all its participants. Love in reconstruction entails reaching out to others and bearing with one another as traumas are healed and gaps in knowledge and understanding filled. Patience and steadfastness are fundamental, for the process is likely to be agonisingly slow. Those working together could deepen their spirituality by "workshopping" their real difficulties and fears, praying, seeking answers in the Bible, going to try them out, and reflecting again on their experiences. In this way the spirituality of reconstruction can itself be developed. If we encounter God as active, challenging and transforming, we will be growing beyond a point where many people get stuck, seeing God simply as a protector and provider.

The disadvantaged who are in the process of moving away from a victim mentality need empowerment to believe in themselves and take on responsibilities. The advantaged might feel a primary need for courage to get involved and to go to places in or near townships that they have always regarded with fear, a fear that is now made worse by crime.

Fear, or anxiety which is fear spread out thin, remains probably the greatest inhibiting factor preventing a full sharing of human resources and skills between the advantaged and disadvantaged. The virtue of courage is needed; and in Christian understanding, it is born of love: "Perfect love casts out fear" (1 John 4:18). A decade ago Desmond Tutu told the UN General Assembly that "white South Africans are not demons: they are ordinary people, mostly scared" (1994: 102); and his own remedy was to tell all South Africans repeatedly and without exception that "God loves you!". Fear can inhibit development by preventing the skilled and unskilled from making lasting, fruitful contact with one another; but it can also inhibit development by perpetuating divisions, jealousy, and intimidation within poorer communities. To overcome these fears, Christians should be drawing on the love poured out from the heart of God; and that love is also the one legitimating and motivating factor to which they are beholden.

The Christian formation described above answers many of the fundamental needs for the reconstruction of human persons, which is as much needed as houses or jobs. Many commentators have noted that "most fundamental yet most neglected" need: "society needs better security and improved living conditions. But without moral values and discipline to underpin these, there will be no community left to enjoy the future" (*Sunday Times* editorial, 24 December 1995 quoting Judge Ismail Mahomed of the Constitutional Court). At present acts such as the abolition of the death penalty, or the gun-free campaign, send different messages to people at different levels of understanding. A whole new culture of human values, human rights and respect for the law is yet to be established, to permeate areas at all levels of South African society where it is still far from being understood or practised.

Formation for development also requires practical skills. There are courses becoming available, and the churches can and should be playing an immense role in practical empowerment, linking it with the formation of values. Communities need training in basic understanding of development, how to plan projects and organise co-operatively around development issues, how to relate to government through new structures and new development legislation.

The skills of conflict resolution and community development are basic to reconstruction and these skills are also important in the church: there is a considerable overlap between conflict resolution, development, and the skills needed pastorally to build community and make it possible for the church to be a paradigm of the new society. The church should be a reservoir of these skills, not only among the ordained but also among the laity.

There are new and exciting insights emerging in these fields. Ron Kraybill, a Mennonite who has worked on conflict resolution and the RDP, says "an important consensus has recently emerged between the fields of conflict resolution and development, offering valuable new insights on how to address social problems". The parties to "deep-rooted conflict" – in Ireland, the Middle East, former Yugoslavia, apartheid-era South Africa – perceive the conflicts to be about power and resources. If these are in fact the only issues, then the conflicts seem incapable of being resolved because power and resources are finite and there are never enough to satisfy everyone. At the same time, development is also inherently conflictual because it too concerns issues of power and distribution of resources. But a new understanding, that opens new doors, is emerging:

> Conflict resolution practitioners are discovering that such conflicts are not actually about power and resources, but about something much deeper, termed "basic needs" by John Burton. These are powerful needs for identity, security, respect and recognition, having more to do with the human spirit and relationships with others than with material resources and power. While land, resources, wealth and power are material issues around which conflicts appear to revolve, these are in fact not needs, but avenues through which people meet their basic needs. If ways can be found to meet the basic human needs which drive the parties, there is often more room for flexibility about the arrangement of resources and power than might at first seem possible.

> The challenge in conflict resolution, then, is not merely to negotiate new borders or re-arrangements of power and

wealth. Rather, the basic human needs driving the parties must be identified and ways found to meet them. This requires negotiation of material resources, but the most fruitful exchanges are in the way parties treat each other. The things that human beings crave the most – identity, respect, security, participation – have more to do with the human spirit than with matter.

The insights outlined above come from the conflict resolution field. A remarkably similar set of insights has emerged in the development field.

The traditional view of development is that it is about creating physical products, whether houses, schools, or training workshops. In this "product-centred" view, the major concern of government and public planners is to deliver products to citizens. But the world is littered with the rusting remnants of product-centred development programmes and this approach is widely acknowledged as having failed. Unless people are empowered in the development process, no number of products is capable of improving a community. In the words of the Chilean economist Manfred Max-Neef, "development is about people, not objects".

After years of development work in the Third World, Max-Neef believes people are motivated by a variety of "fundamental needs", including identity, freedom, subsistence, protection, affection, understanding, participation, creation, and idleness. The more of these that are met, the greater the chances that development efforts will succeed. Product-centred development does help meet some needs such as subsistence and protection, but because it ignores so many others, it is doomed to failure . . .

The task in development, then, in the view of Max-Neef and others, is not merely to deliver products to communities but rather to assist them in both identifying unmet needs and meeting them (Kraybill 1995: 6-7).

Meeting physical needs is an important goal in development, but social processes are far more important: "as long as they are living beyond a minimum threshold level of physical survival, how people are treated in social interaction has a greater impact on meeting their identity needs than the size of their house or the kind of transportation they use". The most critical factors that determine whether identity needs are met and destructive conflict is minimised, concern "how planning and decision-making about the future of a community are conducted. Who makes decisions? Who is informed? Who is consulted? How are the people in the community treated?" Basic development skills therefore include knowing how to design constructive human processes of interaction, plus an ability to prepare for conflict and use it creatively "as an energising force for encounter and joint effort, contributing thereby to development and healing" (Kraybill 1995: 7-8). The churches could play an important role in spreading this kind of understanding and skill.

All this must result in practical, well-researched and well-founded projects. Christians have shown they can easily initiate projects that embody co-responsibility between the advantaged and disadvantaged. Examples would be the use of church premises and personnel in basic adult education and training; housing co-operatives that bring those who need housing together with Christian business expertise and government subsidies; job creation through support of micro-enterprise with loans and training (examples are the SEED Foundation and Get Ahead).

We have suggested that a spirituality of reconstruction can be developed when a group involved in a task takes time out for sharing, meditation and prayer, establishing a pattern of action and reflection. As Desmond Tutu has emphasised, the same pattern is the way to growth for the individual person. In the life of Jesus "disengagement, waiting on God, always precedes engagement"; and to become Christlike we have to accompany Jesus in prayer, quiet, meditation and retreat, seeking the grace to bring God's word and action into human situations. Prayer shows its authenticity when its fruit is "some of the all-embracing generosity and compassion of God for all his children", expressing itself in actual service (Tutu 1991: 561).

Trevor Hudson develops this theme of the two poles of silence and involvement with people, exemplified in the life of Jesus. Jesus retreated into the silence of the desert; he prayed before sunrise; before his final test he retreated to Gethsemane; and then he went out into a life of intense involvement. These two poles "are crucial for an authentic expression of Christlike holiness: making space to be alone in God's presence and exposing ourselves to the suffering of others":

196

. . . These moments of silence and solitude were the secret of his life. In them Jesus was able to nurture his intimate communion with Abba, replenish his resources for compassionate ministry, wrestle with that dark, tempting voice intent upon enticing him into illusion, and renew his body in restful relaxation. If Jesus needed these spaces, surely our need is even greater (Hudson 1995: 87).

Trevor Hudson suggests noting where our life is hurried, asking how our daily activities can be rearranged to allow for calm moments, and making some small commitments such as:

pausing at the beginning of each new activity and reminding oneself of God's immediate presence; withdrawing before work or at lunchbreak for fifteen minutes of silence and prayer; replaying before falling asleep the day's encounters and noticing where God has been present in grace and blessing (Hudson 1995: 90).

Quiet is necessary; but any apparent piety that removes us from the reality of human suffering is not Christ-like holiness but a "false inwardness": "becoming holy opens eyes blind to Christ's presence in suffering people, increases awareness of our neighbour's pain and draws the Christ-follower into the human struggles of the day" (Hudson 1995: 91). Trevor Hudson describes a kind of active retreat, "pilgrimages of pain and hope", in which people mainly from a more affluent background entered into an eight-day reflective encounter with suffering and with people who, amid the suffering, "refuse to become prisoners of hopelessness . . . Encountering these 'signs of hope' challenges the pilgrims to examine their own faith-responses within the present historical moment. They learn that the future is open-ended and that their lives can make a creative difference" (Hudson 1995: 92). Such a deliberate exercise may open a door; but the reality in the end is to get involved in the work of reconstruction and development, the advantaged working together with the disadvantaged and seeking to grow together as citizens of a new and kinder nation.

It has been suggested that the success of a leader "depends on devising and transmitting 'stories' to their followers – stories that redefine the identity of the audience, telling them clearly where they are, where they are going, and what they have to do" (Snow 1995: 41). Desmond Tutu is a leading mind in just this sense, able to inspire and encourage, sharing his prophetic vision and making it fruitful in the life of the nation and the world. He has provided a paradigmatic image: the rainbow people. "We want peace, prosperity, and justice and we can have it when all the people of God, the rainbow people of God, work together" (Tutu 1994: v).

With God, all this is possible. "Now to him who by the power at work within us is able to accomplish abundantly far more than all we can ask or imagine, to him be glory in the church and in Christ Jesus to all generations, forever and ever" (Ephesians 3:20-1).

BIBLIOGRAPHY

CEP (Continuing Education Programme): *CEP News* No. 13, July 1995, published by CEP: Johannesburg.

Hudson, Trevor (1995), *Signposts to spirituality*, Struik Christian Books: Cape Town.

Kraybill, Ron (1995), "Development, conflict resolution and the RDP: Towards peaceful development" *Track Two*, Vol. 4 No. 3, September 1995: 4-8, published by the Centre for Conflict Resolution, UCT: Cape Town.

Jones, Cheslyn, et al. (1986), *The study of spirituality*, London: SPCK.

McGrath, Alister (1995), *Beyond the quiet time: Practical evangelical spirituality*, London: SPCK.

National Literacy Co-operation (1995), pamphlet on NLC, published, May 1995 by NLC: Johannesburg.

RDP (1994), *The Reconstruction and Development Programme: A policy framework*, Umanyano Publications: Johannesburg.

Snow, Peter (1995), "Leading Minds" in *Oxford Today*, Vol. 7 No. 3: 41.

Tutu, D.M. (1984), *Hope and suffering*, Glasgow: Collins.

Tutu, D.M. (1990), "A Christian vision of South Africa's future", in M. Prozesky (ed.) *Christianity amidst apartheid*, London: Macmillan, pp. 233-240.

Tutu, D.M. (1991), "The God of surprises", in K. Nurnberger (ed.) *A democratic vision for South Africa*, Pietermaritzburg: Encounter Publication, pp. 554-566.

Tutu, D.M. (1994), *The rainbow people of God*, New York: Doubleday.

En-gendering a theology of development: Raising some preliminary issues

These days in South Africa there is much talk about theologies of reconstruction and transformation. However, advocates of black theology, feminist theology, and other liberation theologies would argue that such talk is premature. There are others who would even argue that talk of liberation theologies was and is premature. For ordinary African women, talk of liberation, reconstruction and transformation are all premature: for the theology that they live by is a theology of survival.

Womanist theologian Delores Williams (1993) likens the experience of Hagar in the wilderness recorded in the biblical text with that of African-American women. The wilderness represents for Hagar, as it does for African-American women, a situation of near-destruction, a situation where survival becomes paramount. It is in this wilderness experience, in this struggle for survival, that God helps black women to make a way out of what they thought was no way (Williams 1993: 108).

Making a way out of no way is what ordinary African women in South Africa experience every day of their lives. It requires risk. It requires faith. It is a quest for survival. Thus this daily experience gives shape to a theology of survival. It is a working theology lived out in the shacks of the flooded Edendale valley, in the impoverished huts of the far-flung rural plains, and in the homes within crime-infested townships. Ordinary African women find a God who helps them each day to make a way out of no way; a God who is with them in their struggle for survival.

AFRICAN WOMEN IN SOUTH AFRICA

Domestic worker Sarah Khumalo has four children. She lives with her mother and sister and her sister's children in Newcastle, KwaZulu-

Natal. Her meagre salary supports them all. She says: "For me it is a big struggle every day. My sister doesn't have a husband so she has no money and she is too lazy to work. My husband – he works on the mines – sends some money every four months or so and things are a bit easier. Sometimes I speak to my madam – I say my children have got no clothes, or I must buy new schoolbooks or something. She will give some money, but usually I just don't know what to do" (Barrett et al 1985: 31). "Keeping a family, a home and a job going leaves most African women exhausted to the point of death" (Barrett et al 1985: 135).

Julia Kunoane says: "My husband he just look! He is reading the paper while I cook. He says he is tired. I am also tired but I must cook. I am used to it because it is our custom. On weekends I am not going anywhere, except to church sometimes, because I must wash and clean" (Barrett et al 1985: 135). "Everybody has died. My man has gone and died, as have my daughters. They took my land away. The Lord has gone – yes – I suppose he has also gone" (Barrett et al 1985: 181).

These stories of women were recorded during the 1980s. Similar stories were told in the decades before. The stories of African women in the 1990s would be no different.

Statistics show that African women consistently earn the lowest incomes, have the least wealth, and have worse jobs than men (Makgetla 1994: 7). The wage earned by the average African woman in 1991 was R300 a month (Makgetla 1994: 8). African women are usually relegated to the secondary labour market which includes the informal sector, agriculture and domestic work or to unpaid labour. They thus occupy a disadvantaged position in the economy. Makgetla (1994: 12) points out that discrimination in education has played a crucial role in sustaining this disadvantaged position. African women on average have had the privilege of only three years of education!

The disadvantaged economic position of women is exacerbated further by the unequal division of labour in the household. Women are expected to take care of the household chores, cook, clean and care for the children in addition to any paid work they do. Little time or energy is available to work overtime or take on more senior positions in the formal sector. These constraints result in a substantially reduced cash income (Makgetla 1994: 13). Furthermore, women in rural households have borne the brunt of the migrant labour policy which has left them economically impoverished, isolated and powerless. This powerlessness extends beyond the realm of economics. Wilson and Ramphele (1989: 155) vividly illustrate this in the following quotation from their foundational study on poverty:

> The vulnerability of a woman living alone, or possibly with her children, in the densely crowded, isolated resettlement areas whilst her husband is away as a migrant worker is one of the hidden realities of life in many parts of the country. In Ekuvukeni in KwaZulu[-Natal], for example, a graphic description was given to one of us when visiting the area, of how women would lie in fear in their homes whilst out-side the tsotsis would call, "Is anybody home?" If the woman would answer (or indeed not answer at all) then the gang would know that there is no man in the house and that it was safe to break down the door and rob the women and children inside. People have not yet, it would seem, learnt the survival technique of the American ghettos where a woman, caught in a similar situation, will bark like a dog.

The plight of South African women is not dissimilar to millions of other women in Africa and the rest of the Third World (or Two-Thirds World). Esther Boserup was the first to place gender issues on the international development agenda with the publication in 1970 of her landmark study *Women's role in economic development*. The invisible role played by women in the economic and social development of their countries was further and significantly highlighted during the United Nations Decade for Women from 1976 to 1985 (Moser 1989: 1799).

A school of thought committed to gender planning emerged in the Third World and came to be known as Women in Development (WID). Theorists such as Molyneux (1985) and Moser (1989), amongst others, differentiate between strategic and practical gender needs of women. Strategic gender needs "are formulated from the *analysis of women's subordination to men*" (Moser 1989: 1803) in order to achieve a more equitably organised society. Practical gender needs on the other hand, "are formulated from the concrete conditions women experience in their *engendered* position within the sexual division of labour, and deriving out of this their practical gender interests for human survival" (Moser 1989: 1803). These needs are based on what is termed the "triple oppression of women" where women in

low-income households are seen to have three roles, namely, repro-
duction, production, and community managing (Moser 1989: 1801).
WID theorists criticised international development agencies for not
foregrounding this triple oppression and for structuring development
planning according to the sexual division of labour without taking
strategic gender needs into account.

WID theory increasingly came under attack for the underlying liberal belief that "despite differences of culture and class, there is an universal and fundamental argument for the equality between human
beings" (Kabeer 1994: 27). It was argued that this stress on the equality of the sexes led to describing behaviour normatively and dualisti-
cally. Hence there was indifference "to the social implications of biol-
ogy for individual agency, choice and rationality" (Kabeer 1994: 28).

Furthermore, WID theorists advocated the notion of a global sisterhood. Just as they stressed the similarities between women and
men, they also stressed the similarities between women throughout
the world. The stress on commonalities between First and Third
World women was criticised because it "served to disguise and deny
material differences in power, resources and interests between women
themselves. It privileged a particular interpretation of women's needs
and interests over others which might reflect more accurately important differences in their social realities" (Kabeer 1994: 31).[1]

The notion of global sisterhood has also been critiqued from a postmodern perspective. Postmodernists argue that proponents of a global sisterhood speak of "the Third World woman". For Mohanty (1988:
62-63) "the Third World woman" is a composite and singular image –
an undifferentiated "other" – constructed by Western feminists that
does not exist. The image presented is of women uniformly poor,
powerless and vulnerable who have as a reference point modern, edu-
cated and sexually liberated Western women (Parpart 1993: 444).
African-American postmodernist, bell hooks [sic] (1984: 25) has argued against the notion of global sisterhood. She believes that in order
for the voices of the marginalised and displaced to be heard, it is the
difference and otherness of their experience that needs to be explored.

There are two important implications for the South African context
implicit in this postmodern understanding of the importance of difference and otherness. Firstly, there is no composite and singular
image of the "powerless" and "vulnerable" black South African wom-

1. See Kabeer 1994: 27-33 for a more detailed critique of WID theory.

an. Secondly, exploring the meaning of the powerless and vulnerability of black women must not be done within parameters prescribed by white feminists, but rather from within the boundaries of the lived survival experience of black women.

The danger of seeing African women as a composite and singular image is that "solutions" to their problems are postulated in a singular and normative way without any attempt to understand the complexity of their lived experiences, nor the resources these women have already cultivated in order to survive. This understanding is crucial to constructing an en-gendered theology of development. "An approach to development that recognizes the connection between knowledge and power, and seeks to understand local knowledges both as sites of resistance and power, would provide a more subtle understanding of Third World women's lives." Parpart argues further that "women's realities can only be discovered by uncovering the voices and knowledge of the 'vulnerable', and that once this is done, this 'vulnerability' is neither so clear nor so pervasive" (Parpart 1993: 456).

It was at the first South African conference on women and gender held at the University of Natal in 1991 that the issue of representation was foregrounded – who can speak for whom? The conference generated considerable reflection on this issue and was critiqued and analysed from a variety of perspectives (Agenda Collective 1991; Hassim and Walker 1993; Lewis 1993). Feminist discourse had up until then largely been in the control of white women. Black women argued strongly for allowing their experience, the voice of ordinary black women, to be heard.

In exploring the representation debate, Hassim and Walker (1993) note the constraints on white social researchers.

> The nature of African patriarchy, the meaning of motherhood for most women in South Africa, the social construction of gender identity and of sexuality in African communities are all examples of issues of Women's Studies where African women are able to draw on their linguistic and cultural insights to plot the contours of what womanhood means to African women and, from this to theorise about gender (Hassim and Walker 1993: 530).

However, they challenge the claim that only oppressed people can speak about their lives and argue against privileging experience as the sole arbiter of knowledge (Hassim and Walker 1993: 530).[2]

Difference in the South African context is the creative tool for understanding and theorising about gender oppression. Hassim and Walker (1993: 530) suggest that for difference (in the fullest sense of race, class, ethnicity, and culture) to have meaning, it must be rooted in a political commitment to change the structural oppression of women. "While sisterhood is not a useful concept, solidarity on the basis of common goals is" (Hassim and Walker 1993: 533).

But, I would argue, these common goals must be found in the as yet unspoken and inarticulated voices of the lived survival experiences of the majority of the women of this country.

Wilson and Ramphele (1989: 355) posed the following question in the final chapter of their study on poverty during the late 1980s: "Will political liberation necessarily be accompanied by a significant improvement in the material conditions and the quality of life of the very poor?" It is now the 1990s and political liberation has come – and the question remains. Will life be different for African women who are the very poor?

. The Reconstruction and Development Programme (RDP) was introduced in 1994 by the African National Congress in consultation with its Alliance partners and other mass organisations. It is an attempt to address the enormity of the poverty challenge (ANC 1994). To date, implementation has been slow, although there is already some evidence of changes to people's lives such as free health care for pregnant mothers and children under six. But the real success of the programme will depend on the extent to which people are truly enabled to participate as subjects in the process of development and as agents in their own organisation.

From a gender perspective, the RDP as outlined in the Draft White Paper (*Government Gazette*, 353, 1994) has already been criticised for the serious gaps in both the conceptualisation and implementation of gender issues (*Agenda Collective* 1995). While the document does attempt to address gender inequality, the most disturbing criticism is that women were peripheral in the process of drawing up the document (*Agenda Collective* 1995: 40). To rectify this omission the *Agenda Collective* argues for special measures to be adopted to ensure consultation with women throughout the RDP process (1995: 42).

The relationship between the state and development from a gender

2. For a detailed analysis of the complexities of this debate see Spivak 1988.

perspective has been equally problematic elsewhere in Africa, as high-lighted by Parpart (1987). She shows how colonial governments systematically attempted to disempower women, but argues that nonetheless there were individual and collective protests. Even though women did lose power during this period, "it was neither even nor linear" (1987: 198). However, in the post-colonial period their power was further eroded because "decolonization was essentially a transfer of power from one group of men to another" (Parpart 1987: 218).

Seidman (1993: 291) has argued that nationalist movements have consistently promised to improve the status of women before taking power, but these promises go largely unfulfilled once power is attained. She is hopeful that the situation might be different in South Africa. In analysing mobilisation and gender in South Africa during the period 1970-1992 she concludes:

> As women activists organize a broad constituency for gender-specific demands, it seems increasingly probable that the demands they make on the post-apartheid state will seek to create an unusual degree of support for women's economic independence and personal autonomy (Seidman 1993: 316).

For Seidman (1993: 316), women's potential for strategic organising lies within trade unions and community groups. Others such as the Agenda Collective (1995: 42) have specifically noted the church as a place where women are to be found. In the South African context, women meet in church groups of varying forms wherever they are struggling to survive. Surely, these are potential sites for those inarticulated voices to be heard? ". . . when all is said and done, [the church] is better placed than any other institution, religious or secular, to work with poor people" (Wilson and Ramphele 1989: 303) – or is it?

AFRICAN WOMEN AND THE CHURCH

There is not a great deal of literature written by African women which analyses their position in the church in South Africa today. What has been written presents the church as an oppressive, male-dominated structure that hinders rather than enables – disempowers rather than empowers women.

There can be no argument that the church is one of the most oppressive structures in society today, especially in regard to the oppression of women . . . Women are treated as minors, inferior to men, just as they are in society . . . Women are talked about not to (Ramodibe 1988: 16).

All the decisive decisions that have been made in the church have been made by men. Women have never been consulted. The church seems to be willing to re-educate people on every issue except the issue of the dignity and equality of women (Mosala 1986: 133).

Women seek to explore their own experience in religious terms, to view reality in a new way, to have a new consciousness. We must define ourselves in our own terms and not those of the institutional church, which has been controlled and dominated by men (Mncube 1991: 358).

The churches on the whole have taken our presence as women very much for granted and have not recognised with any seriousness that we have important ministries to offer within the church (Bam 1991: 363).

The church has made a very constructive contribution to the struggle for liberation in South Africa. The church has often taken over when the political parties were forbidden to organise. In this way, the church has taken the side of the oppressed people in their struggle for justice. But at the same time, it must be said that all is not well in the church. It has been an oppressor as well. When we speak about people in exile who are now coming back home, we should remember that there are women in exile because the church would not ordain them, so they chose to leave South Africa to fulfil their vocation as priests. So the church too has contributed to people fleeing the country to go and get what they could not get here (Mashinini 1991: 350).

The churches in South Africa are rich and powerful, owning land and investments. This undermines its willingness to pressure for change. Women must recognise that the church will not necessarily take their side. The church is as much a site of struggle as society (Mncube 1991: 361).

The church is not only a site of struggle for African women because of its institutional structures, but also because of issues related to tradition and culture. As the debate on the Africanisation of the church in South Africa grows in importance, so these issues take on critical significance for ordinary African women whose voices are marginal to this academic discourse, yet will be profoundly affected by its outcome.[3] The voice of African women must be heard. "African theology . . . has fallen into the trap of idolising African culture in an uncritical way . . . Because [it] starts from the context of African culture, which is patriarchal (in the static sense), it runs the risk of being party to the legitimization of the domination of women" (Ramodibe 1988: 15).

Research carried out in the informal settlement of Amawoti, outside Durban (Sibeko and Haddad 1996), powerfully illustrates how culture is used to dominate women. By means of the contextual Bible study process,[4] a reading of Mark 5:21-6:1 highlighted how ordinary African women experienced menstruation as a tool of oppression used by the leadership of the indigenous church to which they belonged. The reading illustrated the complex interplay of cultural and biblical arguments used by the male leadership to support the marginalisation of women in church life. Reading it contextually, the story of the woman with the haemorrhage in the biblical text had an empowering effect on the women of Amawoti. It enabled them to speak unspoken words and they clearly yearned for more unspoken possibilities.[5]

The oppressive potential of culture and tradition in church practice is not restricted to indigenous churches. Mpumlwana (1991: 375-376), writing as a member of a missionary-initiated church, lists culture, tradition, and biological functions (amongst others) as barriers to women occupying leadership positions in the church.[6]

3. A similar debate has emerged in the African-American church; see Sanders 1995.
4. For an explanation of this process see West 1993.
5. This discussion is developed in more detail in Sibeko and Haddad 1996.
6. The founding of the Circle of African Woman Theologians in 1988 at the World Council of Churches has borne fruit with the publication of The will to arise: Women, tradition and the church in Africa, Oduyoye and Kanyoro 1992. The volume reflects similar theological thinking to South African women, though notably the interface between gender, development and the church is not addressed.

And so, is the church better placed than any other institution to work with the poor?

CONCLUSION – OR A NEW BEGINNING?

The church has considerable resources – finances, land, buildings, and most importantly people – which are all crucial elements for the alleviation of poverty and for the development of a social infrastructure. However, the above discussion suggests that African women are at best ambivalent about the church's role in their lived experience of survival, and at worst cynical about the potential for the church to change. Why? Alleviation of poverty and the development of a social infrastructure have little meaning without all voices being heard and the accompanying empowerment that results. People, particularly ordinary women, need to feel that their voice is both heard and that it matters; then the church will become for them a place not of struggle, but of safety.

For the church to be a transformative agent in the development process, the church structures themselves need to be transformed. There has to be change. For change to take place there has to be a new vision. Hagar faced near-destruction in the wilderness. There, God helped her "to make a way out of no way" in her struggle for survival. God also provided her "with *new vision* to see survival resources where she saw none before" (Williams 1993: 198). Ordinary African women experience new vision daily. Theirs is a lived theology of survival. Will the church hear their voices?

BIBLIOGRAPHY

African National Congress (1994), *The Reconstruction and Development Programme*, Johannesburg: Umanyano Publications.
Agenda Collective (1991), "Impressions: Conference on 'Women and Gender' in Southern Africa", *Agenda: Empowering women for gender equity*, 9: 20-23.
Agenda Collective (1995), "Gender flaws in the RDP", *Agenda: Empowering women for gender equity*, 24: 40-44.
Bam, Brigalia (1991), "Seizing the moment: Women and the new South

Africa" In *Women hold up half the sky: Women in the church in Southern Africa*, Denise Ackermann, Jonathan A. Draper and Emma Mashinini, (eds.), pp. 363-68, Pietermaritzburg: Cluster Publications.

Barrett, Jane, Aneene Dawber, Barbara Klugman, Ingrid Obery, Jennifer Shindler and Joanne Yawitch (1985), *Vukani Makhosikazi: South African women speak*, London: Catholic Institute for International Relations.

Boserup, Esther (1970), *Women's role in economic development*, New York: St Martin's Press.

Hassim, Shireen, and Cherryl Walker (1993), "Women's studies and the women's movement in South Africa: Defining a relationship", *Women's Studies International Forum*, 16(5): 523-34.

hooks, bell (1984), *Feminist theory from margin to center*, Boston: South End Press.

Kabeer, Naila (1994), *Reversed realities: Gender hierarchies in development thought*, London and New York: Verso.

Lewis, Desiree (1993), "Feminism in South Africa", *Women's Studies International Forum*, 16(5): 535-42.

Makgetla, Neva Siedman (1995), "Women and economy: Slow pace of change", *Agenda: Empowering women for gender equity*, 24: 7-20.

Mashinini, Emma (1991), "Women between church and society, in *Women hold up half the sky: Women in the church in Southern Africa*, Denise Ackermann, Jonathan A. Draper and Emma Mashinini, (eds.), pp. 345-52, Pietermaritzburg: Cluster Publications.

Mncube, Bernard Sr (1991), "Sexism in the church in the African context" in *Women hold up half the sky: Women in the church in Southern Africa*, Denise Ackermann, Jonathan A. Draper and Emma Mashinini, (eds.), pp. 355-62, Pietermaritzburg: Cluster Publications.

Mohanty, Chandra (1988), "Under Western eyes: Feminist scholarship and colonial discourses", *Feminist Review*, 30: 61-88.

Molyneux, Maxine (1985), "Mobilization without emancipation? Women's interests, state and revolution in Nicaragua", *Feminist Studies*, 11(2): 227-54.

Mosala, Bernadette I. (1986), "Black theology and the struggle of the black woman in Southern Africa", in *The unquestionable right to be free*, Itumeleng J. Mosala and Buti Tlhagale, (eds.), pp. 129-33, Johannesburg: Skotaville.

Moser, Caroline O. (1989), "Gender planning in the Third World: Meeting practical and strategic gender needs", *World Development*, 17(11): 799-825.

Mpumlwana, Thoko (1991), "My perspective on women and their role in church and society", in *Women hold up half the sky: Women in the church in South Africa*, Denise Ackermann, Jonathan A. Draper and Emma Mashinini, (eds.), pp. 369-85, Pietermaritzburg: Cluster Publications.

Oduyoye, Mercy A. and Musimbi R. A. Kanyoro, (eds.) (1992), *The will to arise: Women, tradition, and the church in Africa*, Maryknoll, New York: Orbis Books.

Parpart, Jane L. (1987), "Women and the state in Africa", in *African futures: Seminar proceedings No. 28*, 185-227, Edinburgh: Centre for African Studies.

Parpart, Jane (1993), "Who is the 'other'?: A postmodern feminist critique of women and development theory and practice", *Development and change*, 24: 439-64.

Ramodibe, Dorothy (1988), "Women and men building together the church in Africa", in *With passion and compassion: Third World women doing theology*, Virginia M. M. Fabella and Mercy A. Oduyoye, (eds.), pp. 14-21. Maryknoll, NY: Orbis Books.

Sanders, Cheryl J. (ed.) (1995), *Living the intersection: Womanism and Afrocentrism in theology*, Minneapolis: Fortress Press.

Seidman, Gay W. (1993), " 'No freedom without the women': Mobilization and gender in South Africa, 1970-1992", *Signs: Journal of Women in Culture and Society*, 18 (Winter): 291-320.

Sibeko, Malika, and Beverley Haddad, (1996), "Reading the Bible 'with' women in poor and marginalised communities in South Africa", *Bulletin for Contextual Theology* 3(i).

Spivack, Gayatri (1988), "Can the subaltern speak?" in *Marxism and the interpretation of culture*, G. Nelson and L. Grossberg, (eds.), pp. 271-313, London, MacMillan.

West, Gerald O. (1993), *Contextual Bible study*, Pietermaritzburg: Cluster Publications.

Williams, Delores S. (1993), *Sisters in the wilderness: The challenge of womanist God-talk*, Maryknoll, New York: Orbis Books.

Wilson, Francis, and Mampela Ramphele (1989), *Uprooting poverty: The South African challenge*, Johannesburg and Cape Town: David Philip.

Theological education in the Church of the Province of South Africa (CPSA)

When the Federal Theological Seminary was opened at Alice in March 1963, I was the only black person on the teaching staff. In 1967, on his return from his studies in London, Desmond Tutu joined the staff of the Seminary to be the second black person on the teaching staff. Desmond left the Federal Theological Seminary at the beginning of 1970 to take up a lectureship in Theology at the University of Botswana, Lesotho and Swaziland, at Roma, Lesotho. After two years at the university, he was appointed Associate Director of the Theological Education Fund (TEF) of the World Council of Churches and was based in Bromley, Kent, in the United Kingdom, having responsibility for all Sub-Saharan Africa.

When I was asked to make a contribution to this *festschrift* I thought of his contribution in the area of theological education. I therefore decided to make my contribution in this area, with special reference to St Peter's College where Desmond was both student and theological tutor. Undoubtedly he is the most distinguished of all the alumni and teachers of St Peter's College. For this reason St Peter's College was a natural focus. Moreover, as far as the theological education of Africans in the CPSA is concerned, St Peter's was the best of the Anglican theological institutions. Before coming to this, however, I need to say something about the contribution of the Church of the Province of Southern Africa in the area of education in general and theological education in particular.

"Education and missionaries have always travelled together".[1]

1. Christoferson, A. F. (1967), *Adventuring with God,* Durban, p. 38.

This has been true of Christian missions the world over as well as of all missions that have laboured in South Africa. The achievement of the Church of the Province in the field of African education in this subcontinent is particularly remarkable because of the quality of education offered at its schools. The distinctive Anglican contribution was the work of its missionary orders in education.

With the arrival of Bishop Robert Gray, DD, in South Africa on Sunday, 20 February 1848, a new chapter opened, not only for the Anglican Church but for education as a whole in South Africa:

> [For him] as for many of our best pioneers that followed him, the founding of schools was every bit as important as the founding of churches . . . Robert Gray brought with him the conviction that the spread of true education was an integral part of the Church's obligation towards her children.[2] (Tugman)

The Anglican Church has built and run some of the best African schools in the country. St Peter's College, Rosettenville, Johannesburg; Zonnebloem, Cape Town; St Augustine's, near Dundee; St Matthew's, Keiskamma Hoek; and St John's, Umtata, (as they all used to be) speak of only part of the story.

As regards theological education Bishop Smithies once said:

> We are more and more convinced, as the years go on, that if Africans are to be converted in any large numbers, it must be by the ministry of Africans themselves.[3]

A Principal of St Peter's College, Rosettenville, Johannesburg, said:

> If the growing Native Church is to express native ideas and meet native needs; if it is to bring any special contribution of its own to the fullness of Christ it must be more and more taught, built up and held together by men of its own race.[4]

2. Tugman, C. "What the Church has done for European education", in the *Gray Centenary Pamphlets*, First Series, No. 2.
3. Victor, O. (n.d.) *The thin black line*, Johannesburg, p. 5.
4. Ibid. Quoted from an article by C.F.G. Goodall in the *Gray Centenary Pamphlets*, First Series, No. 2, p. 3.

With these convictions the Anglican Church proceeded to train African men for the Christian ministry. In the Anglican Church, as in the Methodist and other churches, three stages have been noted in the development of an African ministry:

1. There emerged from mission schools men with a sufficient knowledge of the English language that enabled them to interpret the sermons of the missionary.
2. These men began to exhort their own people and to preach the Word:

> thus arose a class of the simple, barely-literate evangelist, Catechist or Reader – the nursing fathers of countless little congregations to whom the European priest could bring the Sacraments only at rare intervals".[5]

Some of these men were given further training and ordained.

3. There was the type of man who had sufficient general education and a sense of vocation to the full-time work of the ministry to be trained at a theological college.

For a number of years promising African students were sent to St Augustine's College, Canterbury, England, "to complete their education",[6] without necessarily being committed to join the ministry. Indeed, some of these men were never ordained. The usual period of study at St Augustine's was two years. One of these students, Hami, was found on his return to South Africa, "reading a treatise of St Cyril of Alexandria against Nestorius, in the original Greek for pleasure!"
This experiment broke down for two reasons:

1. The students found the British climate too severe for them; they did not get good advice as regards suitable clothing; therefore, some of them died from pneumonia and tuberculosis.
2. The church authorities who sent them to Canterbury believed that some of them got "spoiled" by the way they were treated and the

5. The Net, 1st October 1870, p. 152; The Net, 1st October 1889, p. 158.
6. Goodall, C.F.G.:"The church and the ministry", in the Gray Centenary Pamphlets, First Series, No. 2.

kind of life they experienced in England. As a result on their return they were unable to fit into the kind of life "allotted to the Native" in South Africa. A few of them, however, returned "unspoilt" and made the necessary adjustments.

Towards the end of the nineteenth century a group of men began as catechists, and if their education was good, say up to standard 4 or 5, and if in the judgement of their priests and bishops they were considered worthy, they were ordained deacons and later priests. Thus they had no formal theological education but were trained by the senior clergy under whom they worked, and then moved on to ordination. Such men were Peter Masiza and Jemuel Pamla (St John's), Titus Mtembu and John Ncamu (Zululand), Paulus Masiza (Grahamstown).

DIOCESAN COLLEGES

Some catechists of long standing had proved themselves to be able and devoted pastors, and missionaries believed that such men needed further training in the environment in which they lived and worked. Thus the era of diocesan colleges began, training three or four students at a time for the same neighbourhood and speaking the same vernacular.

> At one time there were eleven of these colleges in existence, domestic and patriarchal in character, the students closely in touch with the Bishop who would eventually ordain and licence them.[7]

THE IDEA OF ONE CENTRAL THEOLOGICAL COLLEGE

The Church of the Province had several poorly staffed, financially starved colleges with a few students. It was following the pattern in England where most dioceses had their own colleges. While there might have been some advantages in running small diocesan colleges geared towards the needs of each diocese, the advantages of having one central college for the whole Province outweighed the disadvantages.

7. Victor, O. (n.d.), *The thin black line*, Johannesburg, pp. 7-8.

In 1934 the Heads of Theological Colleges met in Johannesburg and agreed that the smaller colleges be closed; that St Bede's, Umtata, should cater for the southern part of the country, and St Peter's College for the north. The church was thus able to concentrate its resources on two Provincial colleges.

An important development at this conference was the recognition that ministerial training was a provincial rather than a diocesan concern.

ST PETER'S COLLEGE, ROSETTENVILLE, JOHANNESBURG

The Anglicans found in the Transvaal what the Methodists had already discovered before them in the same province as well as in Zululand, that the work of evangelism had been started by a band of untrained, untutored, but dedicated African men. Towards the end of the last century African work in the Church of the Province fell on the shoulders of one man, Canon Farmer. He reported as follows:

> When I came to the diocese I was surprised to find there were no less than sixty native men working hard for the Church. They had been amongst those who at different times had gone from the Transvaal to work in other parts of South Africa for money to pay their taxes or supply their needs. They had gone away from locations or villages on Boer farms, some to Kimberley, others to Maritzburg, Grahamstown or Cape Town, and while there they had come under the influence of some of our Missions, been converted and baptised.
>
> Then they went to their own homes in the midst of heathenism, and instead of falling away, as might have been expected – without a thought of pay, and with no other idea but the glory of God and the salvation of souls – they set to work to preach the Gospel to their fellow creatures . . . I found that I had to register in the Church books thousands who had been converted by means of these men. Each year my baptisms exceeded 500, and just before the war broke out, I went round the Missions to administer the Holy Communion to all I could reach, putting down their names in a book. When the tour which took a month, was

over, I found I had the privilege of administering the Holy Communion to over 2 000 natives.

. . . I was also surprised in going up and down the country to find that these natives had built for themselves, without any outside promptings or assistance, rough buildings for *churches*. These buildings were only of rude structure, with walls of mud and roofs of thatch, with holes for windows and a rough screen of reeds for doors. They were often decorated inside with crude ornamentation in coloured earth, and on the wall at the further end would be drawn a large Cross in some coloured pigment.

These churches were some of them quite small, but often were capable of holding from one to two hundred people. They had done this in the midst of a great amount of difficulty in finding time and means of building as well as from opposition on the part of their Boer masters . . . I must say I could conceive of no more valuable help than these laymen gave, and no more devoted band of workers.

Canon Farmer continued:

These men were very capable missionaries, even though they were uninstructed and laymen. There can be no doubt that the very best missionary must be the properly trained native, and the end of our work must be a Native Ministry . . . But to ordain natives without their being properly trained would be fatal to the spiritual life of the Church. This training we must set ourselves to give.[8]

Canon Farmer began to do just that. With financial help from the SPG (Society for the Propagation of the Gospel) and the SPCK (Society for the Promotion of Christian Knowledge) he built a "really decent church" for the African congregation in Pretoria. Next to it he put up another building which he called St Cuthbert's College. Here he made a beginning by training about a dozen men "in habits of *prayer* and *study* and *work*". Some of these men had been accepted by the bishop as candidates for the ministry when the outbreak of the Boer War (1899-1902) stopped the whole venture.

8. Reproduced by Winter, A. (n.d.), *Till darkness fell*, p. 56.

Canon Farmer thought that "a College of English Clergy and Natives" was needed. The dream came to fruition in a rather different way. It was imperative to restart in Pretoria after the war. But meanwhile the Community of the Resurrection had established a community house and mission centre at 10 Sherwell Street, Doornfontein, Johannesburg. To this they attached a theological college, St Peter's College, which was opened in April 1903, with one student, Matthew Mntande. Later in the year he was joined by Titus Malape, Stephen Mashupye, Michael Mpumlwana and Apollos Monare, all of whom had begun their training as catechists at St Cuthbert's College, Pretoria, before the war.

THE TRAINING OF CATECHISTS, DEACONS AND PRIESTS

Having begun with the training of catechists, St Peter's went on to train deacons and priests. The training of catechists was discontinued in 1937. From that date St Peter's trained only ordinands. By 1937, 88 catechists and 75 ordinands had gone through St Peter's.

The training course for deacons lasted two years at the college, and included Old and New Testament studies, church doctrine based on the creeds and some articles. Church history covered the early church, English and South African church history. Students were also trained in pastoralia, devotional life and the use of the prayer book as well as the constitution and canons of the church. Later English and Latin were added. After five years as a deacon, each candidate for the priesthood had to undergo a further year of training. English had to be learnt as it was the medium of instruction and examinations.

ACADEMIC STANDARDS

When St Peter's started in 1903 the educational facilities for Africans in the Transvaal were very poor. Indeed, a letter written to the Community of the Resurrection by the Secretary for Education in the Transvaal, dated 22 February 1909, stated: "There is no provision at present for carrying the education of natives above standard 3".

In view of this low level of education in the Transvaal, African men went to St Peter's College on the recommendation of their priests and the bishop, to be trained mostly as catechists. Only those students who came from the Cape or Natal had qualifications higher than Standard 3. In addition to their low standard of education the students were elderly married men who were interested in qualifying as catechists or deacons.

In order to improve general educational standards the Community of the Resurrection took over St Peter's Day School and raised the standards until in 1925 they started secondary school classes and in 1927 the school produced its first two Junior Certificate "graduates". In 1932 matriculation classes were started.

In 1922 the theological school fixed Standard 6 as the minimum entrance qualification. In 1934 a Conference of Heads of Theological Colleges agreed:

1. That the Junior Certificate or a Teacher's Certificate be the minimum standard accepted;
2. That the Deacons' Course be lengthened from two to three years;
3. That such candidates as were capable be encouraged to read for the Provincial Licentiate in Theology (LTh).

Since then many St Peter's students have qualified for the LTh.

In 1938 John Tsekiso went to St Peter's with a BA degree from Fort Hare. The following year Alphaeus Zulu entered St Peter's, with a BA degree also from Fort Hare. Zulu had been teaching at Umlazi, near Durban, for some yars. When the call to the ministry came he decided that he must first study for a university degree. Thus he went to Fort Hare where he graduated in 1938 with majors in Ethics and Social Anthropology. At St Peter's he read for the LTh which he received at the end of two years. In December, 1940, he was ordained deacon and was appointed to St Faith's Mission, Durban. Two years later he was ordained priest and continued there, becoming rector in 1953, until 1960 when he was appointed assistant bishop of St John's, Umtata.

Then he was appointed diocesan bishop in Zululand and Swaziland, thus becoming the first African diocesan bishop in the Church of the Province of South Africa. His university and theological studies as well as his gifts and personality fitted him well for the distinguished leadership role which he played in the life of the church in this country and in the world church as a member of the Praesidium of the World Council of Churches. In 1974 he received an honorary Doctor's Degree from the University of Natal and in July, 1975, he retired to Edendale near Pietermaritzburg.

There is no doubt that St Peter's was the best theological college for Africans in the Church of the Province of Southern Africa. Compared with St Bede's, whose students came mainly from the Diocese of St John's and the Order of Ethiopia, St Peter's attracted students from all over the country. Staffed by members of the Community of the Resurrection, St Peter's had a larger teaching staff (usually three or four) and, therefore, more specialisation in the teaching was possible.

Financially St Peter's was built and maintained by the Community of the Resurrection, though bishops paid for the students they sent there for training. St Bede's, on the other hand, was a one-teacher theological school supported financially by a poor diocese. Whereas St Peter's stopped training catechists in 1937 and concentrated on the training of ordinands, St Bede's continued training catechists until recently. Many St Peter's students qualified for the LTh examinations whilst very few St Bede's students qualified for these examinations.

Theological training at St Peter's College, Rosettenville, Johannesburg, continued until the end of 1962, when as a result of the Group Areas Act, the South African government forced the College to close because it was training and accommodating black students in a "white group area". The Community of the Resurrection joined other churches which faced a similar plight to seek another site for the training of ministers. So at the beginning of 1963, after a period of negotiation, St Peter's College became one of the four constituent colleges of the Federal Theological Seminary which was established at Alice, in the Eastern Cape, and opened its doors on 1 March 1963.

In this way St Peter's College shared "the slings and arrows" that afflicted the seminary until it was expropriated by the South African Government on 26 November 1974. In March 1975, the seminary community moved to Umtata where it shared facilities with St Bede's College and the Ncambedlana Training Centre which was run by the Methodist Church of Southern Africa. But this was only a temporary home for St Peter's and the seminary community, for the Matanzima government, under pressure from the Nationalist government in Pretoria, forced the seminary to leave Umtata at the end of 1975.

From the beinning of 1976 to the end of 1979, the seminary community was accommodated in mobile tents and other buildings at the Edendale Lay Ecumenical Centre, while negotiations were afoot for the building of a permanent home for the seminary at Imbali near Pietermaritzburg. The year 1976 saw the appointment of the first black principal of St Peter's College in the person of the Rev. (later Dr)

Sigqibo Dwane who was the first married principal of the College and the first principal of the College who was not a member of the Community of the Resurrection. The new campus of the seminary was opened in 1980. Here St Peter's, as part of the seminary community, continued until the constituent colleges of the Federal Theological Seminary united to form a united seminary in 1991.

Through a series of unfortunate events the seminary was closed at the end of 1993. And this meant the death of St Peter's College as well, and the end of a noble dream.

THE FUTURE OF THEOLOGICAL EDUCATION IN SOUTHERN AFRICA

The present trend towards regional and denominational colleges or centres of training is an unfortunate retrograde step. The churches must look seriously at theological education and not make it a step-child in their programmes and financial provisions. No-one should be accepted as a candidate for the ministry if she/he does not have qualifications that would enable her/him to study at university level. Training should be ecumenical and nonracial and should be in close proximity to a university. Training should be located in an urban area where it would be possible for students to do practical work side by side with their academic studies.

APPENDIX 1

The following have been Principals of St Peter's College from its inception until 1990:

Fr Latimer Fuller	CR	1903-1909
Fr Francis Hill	CR	1909-1910
Fr Osmund Victor	CR	1910-1916
Fr Aidan Cotton	CR	1916-1924
Fr Gregory Evans	CR	1924-1936
Fr Eric Goodall	CR	1936-1942
Fr Christopher Millington	CR	1942-1952
Fr Phillip Speight	CR	1954-1957
Fr Godfrey Pawson	CR	1958-1960
Fr Aelred Stubbs	CR	1960-1972
Rev. Dr T.R. Simpson	CR	1973-1975
Rev. Dr Sigqibo Dwane		1976-1983
Rev. Victor Mkhize		1984-1990

APPENDIX 2

In the Chapel lobby at St Peter's College, Rosettenville, Johannesburg, there is a tablet with this inscription:

Glory and Thanksgiving to God

For this College of the Resurrection and St Peter
Opened at Sherwell Street, April 1903, and
Moved to Rosettenville, April 18th, 1991.
Also for the completion of the Quadrangle and for the
Blessing of it by + JOHN, Archbishop of Cape Town,
and for the Consecration of this

Chapel of Jesus the Good Shepherd

by + GEOFFREY, 2nd Bishop of Johannesburg,
October 15/16, 1941.

"Was there no-one left to give glory to God except this foreigner?" Breaking the boundaries in Luke 17:11-19

ARCHBISHOP TUTU AND THE BIBLE

The speeches and sermons of Archbishop Desmond Mpilo Tutu reveal a life spent in continuing reflection on the Bible. The Bible informs his world view and often shapes his vocabulary. But this reflection on the Bible is determined by his conviction that liberation is its central theme, its hermeneutical key. It was a conviction he and other key South African leaders, lay as well as clerical, learnt from the Community of the Resurrection at St Peter's, Rosettenville and developed futher. This is highlighted by the ringing statement he made to the Eloff Commission (1981-1984) when he was General Secretary of the SACC:

> You do not want biblical exegesis every time you ask me a question, but I think I have to indicate to you that liberation, setting free, is a concept of the Bible. The paradigmatic event in the Bible is the Exodus, the setting free of a rabble of slaves . . . we are participating in God's glorious movement of setting his people free (Du Boulay 1988: 182).

This epitomises a characteristic movement in his thinking from an understanding of the liberatory axis of the Bible as historical text to an application of it to Christian praxis today. It is what the Kairos Document calls "Biblical Theology" (Kairos 1986) and what others have called "contextual exegesis" (Draper 1991: 235-257).

BIBLICAL INTERPRETATION FOR LIBERATION

Biblical interpretation for liberation implies a constant reflection on

222

Scripture in the light of experience, so that each sheds light on the other, in a dialectical tension. This process of critical reflection is most effective when analytical tools are brought to bear on both the Bible and the social matrix of the experience of the reader. The Bible is not exempt from the "hermeneutic of suspicion" to which society is subjected, or else readings will simply be determined by the received and accepted tradition and new insights will be lost.

For instance, the adoption of the Exodus as the liberatory hermeneutical key to interpreting the Bible forces the South African reader to question the narratives of the conquest of Canaan. Could not the systematic elimination of the indigenous population of Canaan by the victorious Hebrew settlers be called genocide or colonialism? Would South African readers wish to adopt without question the royal ideology of some of the Psalms and Book of Kings, which suppressed the Israelite peasantry? Can the subjection of women in the Pastoral Epistles be reconciled with liberation, and particularly with Paul's statement of Galatians 3:28? When South African Christians under apartheid became acutely aware of the manipulation of language by the government to mask their oppression, they could also become aware of the potentially oppressive dynamics of scriptural language. Itumaleng Mosala, for instance, believes that the Bible was written by the ruling classes and can only be liberatory when it is read against the grain (Mosala 1989; cf. West 1995: 60-82; Draper and West 1989: 34-37).

In terms of Gerald West's typology of reading, Archbishop Tutu reads the Bible "on the text", at the level of the narrative, whereas Itumaleng Mosala reads "behind the text" to uncover the struggles of the poor and oppressed communities which may be masked by the dominant classes who wrote the text (West 1995: 131-173). However, both Archbishop Tutu and Itumaleng Mosala take liberation as their fundamental principle of biblical interpretation.

In this paper, we will explore the well-known story of the healing of the ten lepers in Luke 17:11-19, taking liberation as the hermeneutical key. Surely, we might argue at first sight, this is a story of miraculous healing and does not give us much insight into society and Christian life beyond that? But a systematic interpretation of this passage in the way suggested by Archbishop Tutu's paradigm can provide us with a fresh perspective on faith and life.

"PURITY RULES" IN APARTHEID SOUTH AFRICA

The starting point of the interpretation is our South African experience of boundaries drawn by society, separating people from each other. Apartheid was about drawing boundaries to exclude people perceived as "impure", in a racial sense, in order to preserve a "pure" white society. To most white people, safe within the protective walls of the "pure" prosperous white society, the rules seemed self-evident and right. However, to those excluded from wealth and prosperity, and stigmatised on account of their "blackness", these purity rules were experienced as oppression. Since no-one is able to change their race and colour, the purity rules of apartheid often led to a sense of hopelessness and despair among the oppressed black majority. Many even internalised their oppression and accepted that white was somehow superior or "pure" compared to their blackness.

Purity rules are, however, arbitrary, even when they seem natural, derived from creation. Dirt is only "matter out of place":

> As we know it, dirt is essentially disorder. There is no such thing as absolute dirt: it exists in the eye of the beholder. If we shun dirt, it is not because of craven fear, still less dread or holy terror. Nor do our ideas about disease account for the range of our behaviour in cleaning or avoiding dirt. Dirt offends against order (Douglas 1966: 2).

Purity rules are a matter of control exerted over others. They derive their power over us from our belief that they are "the way things are", that they are "natural" or God-given, but at the end of the day they are mere human constructs designed to control. An example would be rules which are made about whether women are "clean" or "unclean" during their menstruation. The very different ways different societies view this matter show that it is not a matter of "nature" but of "culture". Even in the matter of clean and dirty hands, this is true. If my hands have soil on them when I am planting beans, then no-one would call it dirt on my hands. But if I sit inside eating a meal with soil on my hands, then people would say I have dirty hands. Yet it is the same soil in both cases. Only the social situation defines what constitutes dirt.

Those who control the definition of what is clean and unclean thus have enormous power, but a power which only exists as long as that human construct can be held in place.

What has happened in South Africa is that the "purity rules" based on race have been shown up for their falsity and unjustness. Apartheid was built on the premise that separation of the races was merely preserving the natural order of things, and that if the boundaries were not maintained, the result would be catastrophic. So sexual relations between those of different races were described as "immorality", even if they were between husband and wife. The apartheid laws have now been gone for several years and the world has not ended. They have been shown up for the oppressive lie that they were. But is this the end of the matter? Are we likely to face new problems related to such human boundaries and purity rules?

TEN LEPERS COME TO JESUS

It is no accident that the story of the ten lepers who come to Jesus is located in the border area between Samaria and Galilee. The text is a little unclear exactly what "between Samaria and Galilee" means, but we can be sure that there would be a "no-go zone" between the two population groups. We learn from the Jewish historian Josephus that Jews under John Hyrcanus, the Maccabean priest-king from Jerusalem, had captured and destroyed the Samaritan temple about 150 years before Jesus' ministry and utterly destroyed their capital city of Samaria (*Jewish wars* 1.61-63; *Antiquities* 13.249, 254-256). This produced a lasting suspicion and hatred between Jews and Samaritans, which we see reflected in Luke 9:51-56, where the Samaritan villagers will not allow Jesus and his disciples to stay because they were on the way to Jerusalem.

So the border area between Samaria and Galilee would have been full of ambiguity and danger. Both sides would regard it as in some sense "impure" or "out of bounds", because neither could control it properly. Such an area is the refuge of the lepers, who have been declared ritually unclean by both communities. Their disease was regarded as incurable and contagious, although some forms of skin disease classified as leprosy could be cured and there were rituals prescribed to enable such persons to return to society (Leviticus 13-14). These included showing themselves to the priest, who would determine whether the person was in fact healed. However, persistent leprosy led to the demolition of the home of the leper and his or her expulsion from society. Leprosy could only be dealt with by driving

225

the unclean person out into the wilderness. Leprosy seems to have been regarded as a punishment for sins (*b.cArakin* 15b, 16a), so that the act of driving the person out of the community was justified also as morally grounded. In Luke 17:11-19, ten lepers approach Jesus together outside a village, standing at some distance from him, aware of their uncleanness and hopelessness.

And yet, there are ten of them together. Their common "impure" position outside the bounds of society, in the no-go area between Galileans and Samaritans, has brought them into a solidarity of affliction. Not only does this solidarity defy the separation and loneliness of impurity, but it makes them strong. A group of ten standing together and shouting attracts attention and response; a group like this would be regarded with fear and awe by the villagers. There is power and danger in the margins beyond what society declares clean and unclean. One might say that their solidarity is the beginning of the undoing of the oppression of their "impurity".

A further significant detail in the story is that they themselves, in their oppression, rejected the normal boundaries which separated them from other human beings. In their liminal situation on the margins of their own society, they were free to discover a new fundamental human community (Turner 1969). So their number includes both Jews and a Samaritan, who would not normally have anything to do with each other. The ten cry out to Jesus together, from this most basic and unpretentious community of need and solidarity: "Jesus, Master, have mercy on us."

JESUS' CHALLENGE TO FUNDAMENTAL HEALING

Jesus' response to this cry is unexpected. He does not pronounce healing or do anything. He simply instructs them to go and see the priest to confirm that they are healed, as prescribed by the Torah. In one sense, this is a recognition that their discovery of a new human community has already begun its healing work. In another sense, it is a challenge to make a public stand together, to publicly witness to the healing effect of their new human community which has overcome the oppressive force of human "purity" rules. As with so many of Jesus' healing miracles, the concern is with the creation of human community and reconciliation. It is another form of Jesus' instruction to the healed demoniac at Gerasa to go home to his own village in Luke 8:39: "Return to your household and tell everyone what God has done for you, and he went through the whole city proclaiming what Jesus had done for him." The healed person is restored to his/her community and relationships are rebuilt.

What follows in the story of the ten lepers describes a counter-movement. Once the ten realise that they have been healed, that the oppressive effect of the purity laws has been lifted from them, their human solidarity breaks down. The nine Jews who had easy access to the temple and the priesthood part company with their Samaritan companion. A new marginalisation takes place and the Samaritan is excluded and alone. The old boundaries are re-established and the nine seem to have failed to understand the true meaning of their heal-ing. They do not return with the Samaritan to accord recognition of the real nature of their healing as the transcending of oppressive human purity laws, but are only too eager to fit neatly back into the old boundaries.

It is only the Samaritan, excluded and oppressed because of his race, who comes back to Jesus and recognises the source of his heal-ing. Despite the fact that Jesus is a Jew, a member of the society which continues to exclude him, he returns to thank him. His experience of fundamental community with the other nine has transformed his life and he no longer thinks within the boundaries of racial purity. He is the one on whom Jesus pronounces the blessing of healing, of which no word has yet been spoken to the others: "Get up and go, your faith has healed you." We hear no more of the other nine, but perhaps we are meant to think that their healing was superficial or ineffective in that it did not go beyond the physical removal of leprosy. The Samaritan, on the other hand, receives the healing which is described by the word which is traditionally translated by the word "saved". His healing is a holistic restoration which goes to the roots of the human experience of alienation.

THE CHALLENGE OF COMMUNITY RECONSTRUCTION IN SOUTH AFRICA

We should beware, of course, of simplistic applications of the Bible to society. There is no one-to-one correspondence between the world of the Bible and our own society and, in any case, all our readings of the text are necessarily conditioned by our own context. In one sense the context determines what we will see in the text, but in another sense the text projects a world and challenges us to be transformed by it. The relation of text to context is not that of blueprint to a construction but of road map to a journey. The relationship is dialectical.

In the story of the ten lepers we can see many parallels to our experience of apartheid and our deliverance from it. In the margins of the old South Africa, where people were excluded from resources and power by racially constructed purity rules, there emerged a solidarity and fundamental experience of human community. For many in the struggle against an oppressive government this involved an acceptance of others from other racial groups in a way that created the potential for a new, transformed society. In the first place, the various groups classified as "non-white" (referred to then as Africans, Coloureds, Cape Coloureds, Other Coloureds and Indians and so on) began to discover their commonality in "blackness". What emerged was a refusal to be defined by what they were not and an insistence on being defined by what they shared. So what was enforced as a "purity rule" became a source of rediscovering fundamental solidarity.

Beyond this, a common commitment to the struggle enabled whites to abandon their "purity" and identify with the non-racial movement. This meant, for instance, that what are sometimes called "white liberals" had to learn the hard lesson that they were not being asked to lead, to control or to work "for" the oppressed, but to fight "with" or to be in solidarity with them.

The new South Africa has provided the potential for an inclusive new community, which carries over the potential of human solidarity into the process of reconstruction. This does not mean ignoring the injustices of the past, which must be confronted and healed. This also does not mean ignoring the cultural contributions and languages of different groups in South Africa.

On the other hand, it does mean that a deep healing cannot emerge for our society if the nine go off to the high priest and abandon the tenth member of their community. That is, if the fundamental community and solidarity which was discovered in "blackness" and non-racialism in the struggle against apartheid are abandoned by a return to the old divisions, then the healing will be only superficial. It could not provide the foundations for a new community and a new nation. Likewise, if a new rich and powerful elite forget the poor and marginalised people they found solidarity with in the struggle and construct new walls or "purity rules" to protect their privilege, then there can be no lasting reconstruction.

This question has emerged as a major one confronting our new "rainbow nation", and it is one which Archbishop Tutu himself has been outspoken about. Reading the biblical text from this perspective could provide rich resources for a Christian response to the challenge.

BIBLIOGRAPHY

Douglas, M. (1966), *Purity and danger: An analysis of the concepts of pollution and taboo*, London: Routledge.

Draper, J.A. (1991), " 'For the Kingdom is inside of you and it is outside of you': Contextual exegesis in South Africa", in P. J. Hartin and J.H. Petzer (eds.), *Text and interpretation: New approaches in the criticism of the New Testament*, pp. 235-257, Leiden: Brill.

Du Boulay, S. (1988), *Tutu: A voice of the voiceless*, London: Hodder & Stoughton.

The Kairos Document: Challenge to the churches (1985), Braamfontein: Skotaville.

Mosala, I.J. (1989), *Biblical hermeneutics and black theology in South Africa*, Grand Rapids, Michigan: Eerdmans.

Turner, V. (1969), *The ritual process: Structure and anti-structure*, Ithaca, New York: Cornell University Press.

West, G.O. (1995), *Biblical hermeneutics of liberation: Modes of reading the Bible in the South African context*, Pietermaritzburg: Cluster.

Gay liberation in scripture and theology

INTRODUCTION

One of Archbishop Desmond's most consistent traits has been his defence of the position and rights of those who appear to be oppressed, deprived or, to use modern jargon, marginalised. While specially engaged in the struggle for black liberation in the years of apartheid he argued that whites could not be truly free unless blacks too were free. In a different context he was asking Shelley's question: "Can man be free if woman be a slave?".[1] Those who try to restrict the freedom or rights of others simply because of their innate characteristics of sex, colour, language or suchlike, find themselves similarly limited in the exercise of their own freedom. So God shows his sovereignty in allowing human beings a share in his absolute freedom. He is almighty, especially in the sense that his plans and purposes will prevail in spite of all human attempts to thwart them. Human beings therefore, made in the image of God, can likewise find their freedom only in so far as they allow others the same degree of freedom as they claim for themselves.

In the new South Africa the church is summoned to uphold the rights of all people and to protect their dignity as children of God. Among the minority groupings in society today are those whose sexual orientation is directed to a partner of the same sex. Many people, Christians and others, harbour a strong prejudice against gay behaviour, and often feel that nothing can be said in its favour. In the face of this Archbishop Tutu has urged the Constitutional committee "to include the sexual orientation clause in the Final Constitution" for South Africa,[2] and has likewise condemned President Robert Mugabe

---

1. *The revolt of Islam*, line 1045.
2. Letter to members of the Constitutional Assembly, 16 August 1995.

of Zimbabwe for claiming that gay persons have no rights. In view of the common prejudice, it seems worthwhile to consider, from a biblical and theological point of view, the attitude which the Christian church ought to adopt towards gay persons. This brief essay is therefore offered in gratitude for Desmond Tutu's ministry to all who seem to have been treated as less than human.

THE EVIDENCE OF SCRIPTURE

The two passages most frequently quoted regarding homosexuality (Genesis 19:1-14 and Judges 19:16-30) are concerned not with homosexual intercourse by consent, but with homosexual rape. What is condemned is the abominable treatment of guests who would have expected to receive the hospitality customarily offered in early Semitic societies. The accounts have nothing to say about the legitimacy of homosexual intercourse by consent, and indeed suggest that this was not unusual. They rather describe the attempts of rapists to use force against visitors to satisfy their sexual urge. It is unfortunately misleading that sodomy gets its name from the Genesis story, which for many centuries was not connected specifically with homosexual behaviour (Boswell 1981: 93-98).

Deuteronomy 23:18-19 notes that male prostitutes were to be found at heathen sanctuaries. The term "dog", a literal rendering of the Hebrew, as found in the AV and RSV, was widely used in the Near East to refer to male prostitutes. Modern versions render it accordingly.[3] Sacral prostitution, both male and female, was a regular practice in the whole of the ancient East. It was this which was regularly condemned, rather than simple homosexual intercourse, as is shown by the references in 1 Kings 14:24 and 2 Kings 23:7. Such ritual prostitution effected a relationship with the deity which the prostitute represented. The male and female prostitutes were called respectively *qadesh* and *qedeshah* (Deuteronomy 23:18), the root meaning of which is "one who has been separated, or consecrated", and so holy to the deity.

The Law of Holiness (Leviticus 17-27) condemns sodomy and connects it with bestiality (18:22-23; 20:13-16). The adoption of this post-exilic position may well have been due to the close link between

3. The term is used again in Revelation 22:15, where GNB and REB render "perverts", while AV, RSV and NRSV retain "dogs".

homosexuality and the heathen shrines. The regulations of the Law of Holiness are what sociologists call "boundary markers". They indicate the practices which had to be observed if Israelites were truly to be seen, and were to see themselves, as the people of the Lord. Even the prohibition of stealing, cheating and deceiving concerns only actions against fellow-Israelites (19:11-13, where neighbour [re'ah] refers to a fellow-citizen, not to everyone, as in the New Testament). Similarly, fornication is prohibited only with the wife of a fellow-Israelite, not with an alien (18:20). Not surprisingly, Leviticus was rarely cited by early authors as evidence for Christian behaviour, for which its regulations are scarcely relevant.[4] Boswell considers that homosexual practices were branded as "ceremonially unclean rather than inherently evil" (1981: 102).

The evidence of the Old Testament is therefore far from clear. Approval of erotic homosexual relations seems to be given by the story of David and Jonathan (1 Samuel 18:1-4; and especially 2 Samuel 1:26).

In the New Testament the important passage is Romans 1:24-27, where homosexual intercourse is seen to be the result of idolatry (verses 21-23,25).

> For this reason God handed them over to dishonourable passions. Women changed natural intercourse to that which is against nature, and men likewise abandoned natural intercourse with women and burned in their lust for one another, men working shamelessness with each other and receiving in themselves the recompense which their error demanded (verses 26-27).

The meaning of "nature" and "natural" is not clear. Sometimes "nature" refers to conventionally acceptable behaviour, as in 1 Corinthians 11:14, where Paul holds that "nature" teaches that it is dishonourable for a man to have long hair. Paul may also have been aware of the belief that homosexuality represented a congenital physical (i.e., natural) characteristic of some people, just as he described God's action

---

4. G. B. Shaw said of them: "The most fanatically observant Jew could not now obey them without outraging our modern morality and violating our criminal law. They are mere lumber nowadays." *The black girl in search of God*, Penguin, 1946, p. 14.

in grafting a wild olive (Gentiles) onto a cultivated olive (Israel) as being "against nature" (Romans 11:24). If so, he would be referring not to homosexual *persons*, but to homosexual behaviour of people who were naturally heterosexual (Boswell 1981: 108-113). The normal understanding, however, that Paul is referring to God's purpose in the Genesis account of the creation of man and woman seems more likely, and was so understood by early Christian writers such as Clement of Alexandria (Fox 1988: 355). Even so, as Chrysostom noted in the fourth century: "Paul did not talk of those who loved and desired each other, but of those who burned in their lust for one another" (Boswell 1981: 117).

There are few other references to homosexuality in the New Testament. In 1 Corinthians 6:9-10 Paul lists those who "will not inherit the kingdom of God" – fornicators, idolaters, adulterers, *malakoi* (male prostitutes, NRSV), *arsenokoitai* (sodomites, NRSV), thieves, greedy persons (*pleonektai*), drunkards, slanderers, robbers. In this comprehensive list the meaning of the two words which NRSV and most modern versions take to denote practising homosexuals is far from clear, as Boswell (1981: 335-353) shows in his detailed investigation. Until fairly recently *malakoi* (a Greek word with a very wide meaning – "soft", "gentle", "effeminate", "cowardly") was usually taken by Christian writers to refer to those who indulge in masturbation.

Similarly *arsenokoitai* is a rare word, and may refer not to sodomites but to male prostitutes prepared to offer their services to women. Though it is likely that the NRSV rendering of both words is correct, their exact meaning is uncertain. It should be noted that Paul's most vehement strictures against sexual offenders appear in his letters to Corinth, where male and female prostitutes were associated with the worship at the temple of Aphrodite. He recognised (1 Corinthians 6:11) that some of his converts had been among those whom he described in the previous verses, perhaps in the service of the goddess, but "you were washed, you were sanctified (i.e., you became God's people), you were put right with God in the name of the Lord Jesus Christ and in the Spirit of our God". Because they now belong to Christ they cannot cleave to a prostitute (verses 15-16), since their bodies are "a temple of the Holy Spirit who is in you" (verse 19), and therefore they may not have any connection with a heathen temple. The term *arsenokoitai* recurs only in 1 Timothy 1:10, where its meaning is again not clearly defined. Apparently it was not a word to which later Greek authors referred when attacking homosexual practices.

In view of the general acceptance of homosexual conduct in the predominantly Gentile communities of early Christianity (Greenberg 1988: 151), it is surprising that the New Testament has so little to say about it. Most inhabitants of the pagan world regarded their sexuality as part of their human nature, and though restrictions were placed on its exercise, sexual conduct was regarded as reprehensible only if it harmed others. In Roman society especially the passive partner in homosexual acts was held in low esteem, unless he were a slave. Various philosophical schools certainly advocated strict restraint in sexual behaviour, but even among philosophers in the early centuries there were differences of opinion with regard to both heterosexual and homosexual behaviour. R.L. Fox (1988: 340-374) has illustrated the wide divergence of Christian attitudes to sexual behaviour in the first few centuries of the church's life from that of secular society, pointing out that Christianity "went beyond anything practised by Jews or pagans and its teaching has troubled consciences ever since".

THE BASIS OF THE CHURCH'S TEACHING

In spite of its importance, the evidence of scripture is only one of the factors involved in determining the Christian attitude to this and other ethical issues (Suggit 1994: 11-16). The wide divergency in methods of interpreting scripture today should remind us that the Bible was never meant to be a legal code for Christians as the Koran is for Moslems. The teaching of the church (*traditio*), considered in its widest sense, however, may never be ignored. Nor can we afford to neglect either the place of human reason or the contemporary context. When reason is exercised on the witness of scripture and the teaching of the church in the contemporary context, we get theology. These four factors must always be considered together. Undue stress on the biblical witness leads to an arid fundamentalism which does not make room for the continuing activity of the Spirit in the church, while neglect of the Bible leads to subjectivism or ecclesiastical tyranny.

There is no doubt that as the Christian faith spread among Gentiles, due especially to the work of the Christian teachers of Alexandria, such as Clement and Origen in the second and third centuries, there was a growing tendency to devalue the worth of material things. This was in line with Greek philosophy in general as well as the teaching of Gnostic schools. The great Greek philosopher Plotinus expressed it

234

succinctly: "The cause of the weakness of the Soul and of all its evil is Matter."[5] Writers like Origen effected a revolution in the understanding of the Christian gospel. What had originated as the faith of some Jews now began to be the faith of the pagan Roman Empire, and then moulded the thought of the whole Western world. Origen, said Prestige (1948: 58), "made it possible for the intelligent Christian to believe the Bible, and so for intelligent people to remain Christians". But this context of Greek thought conditioned the way in which Christian thinkers viewed sexual behaviour. The ideal was considered to be total abstinence from sexual relations. Origen went so far as to castrate himself in pursuance of Matthew 19:12. It was in this period that the title "ever-virgin" was given to the mother of Jesus, and the great monastic movement began in the deserts of Egypt and Syria as thousands of men and women committed themselves to a life of celibacy. From then on the human sexual instinct was regarded as a snare of the devil rather than as God's good gift to humankind. Celibacy and permanent virginity were praised, even though such conduct was contrary to nature, in the biblical sense. The fiery Jerome, for example, in the early fifth century, considered that the only advantage of marriage was that it produced virgins who could be consecrated to God (*Epist* 22: 20).

Many writers, therefore, in the early centuries condemned human erotic experience in general, whether heterosexual or homosexual. Since this attitude was largely due to the prevailing philosophical climate, there are sufficient grounds to justify a fresh consideration of the Christian attitude towards sexuality in the light of the modern understanding of the value of material things and of the world-affirming nature of the gospel. This is especially necessary in view of the tremendous technological development in the last fifty years which has inevitably brought about a profound change in the way in which people regard themselves and their relationship with others, particularly in the sphere of their sexuality. The words of Jesus are specially apposite: "Every interpreter of scripture who has been initiated into the kingdom of heaven is like a householder who brings out from his store things new and old" (Matthew 13:52). New teaching must retain what was good in the old, while recognising the impact of changed conditions. Human sexuality, rightly regarded as a good, is to be used in ways which express love for God and for one another. The traditional teaching that this is to be expressed in monogamous heterosexual life-

5. *Enn* 1:8:11, as rendered by S. MacKenna and B.S. Page.

long marriage must still remain the ideal, without roundly condemning all other forms of sexual activity. Gay and lesbian couples who are unable to express their sexuality in any other way must be welcomed and encouraged by the church. As in the case of heterosexual unions, they are called by Christ to express in their life together their love for God, for one another and for others.

THE MEANING OF FREEDOM

This does not mean subscribing to the permissiveness of modern secular society, which holds that any kind of behaviour is in order if it leads to greater self-fulfilment. The Christian is to find true freedom in obedience to God, "whose service is perfect freedom", as Cranmer's collect had it.[6] Freedom does not give people the right to do exactly as they like. That leads to slavery to their passions and desires, so that they fail to be truly human. Their behaviour is to be guided by reason (*logos*), which is God's gift to human beings enabling them to control their passionate desires. The insistence both of Greek philosophers and Christian teachers that human passions and lusts were to be subject to reason did not imply an unhealthy repression of natural instincts, but a recognition that human beings are not beasts guided by irrational passions. They are rather persons created in the image of God, called by his grace to share in the true image of God, his word (*logos*) made flesh in Jesus (John 1:1). The statement that the *logos* became flesh (*sarx*, John 1:14) is the great affirmation of the gospel. Not only does it express the sanctity of the human physical body and indeed of the material world as a whole, but it views the value of creation always in relation to God's purpose for it as expressed in the person of Jesus Christ. The problem in human life is to overcome the difference in human beings between what they were created to be and what they in fact are. The doctrine of the atonement can well be considered as a description of the way in which this difference can be overcome. In the person of Christ, and through his expression of the love of God for humankind shown in the cross and resurrection, he enables human beings to develop their latent possibilities, and to respond to him in free obedience. Though this possibility is due to

6. The original Latin (*cui servire regnare*) literally means "to be his [God's] slave is to be a king".

God's action (his grace), it cannot be achieved without an act of the human will. It was Abelard (1079-1142) who was particularly insistent that an action can have moral worth only if it results from a free intention of the human will. He argued that this was made possible by the love of God displayed in the passion of Christ which had the power to arouse the human will to respond in love so as to reflect God's love in human action. True freedom is to be found by those who enter by faith into the redemption won by Christ and who have allowed their wills to be changed by him (Suggit 1974: 31-37). This has much to say concerning the church's attitude towards gays.

THE ATTITUDE OF THE CHURCH TODAY TOWARDS GAYS

In any community it seems that on an average there are some seven or eight per cent of people whose sexuality can be expressed only in a homosexual relationship (Carson et al 1988: 439). This may be due either to genetic factors or to the environment of their developing years. In either case there is nothing "unnatural" in their behaviour. They are responding to their natural affections planted in them by God, or to circumstances over which they have had no control. Their sexual orientation is not due to an intentional act of will. No blame can be attached to them for being what they are, and as a minority group they are to be accepted and welcomed as members of the church, the body of Christ, and encouraged to take a full part in its life and witness. This does not give gays, or anyone else, the right to do just what they like with impunity. There must be guidelines for sexual behaviour applicable to all who belong to Christ. It is here that difficulties arise. What limits are to be placed on forms of sexual activity once it has been agreed that human sexuality is to be used not solely for the procreation of children but also for expressing love and commitment, as well as for mutual pleasure and enjoyment?

In interpreting the claims of Christ the church needs to be guided by the twin scriptural principles of the steadfast love or faithfulness of God towards his people (Hebrew *hesed*) and his righteousness, his deliverance (Hebrew *zedeq*) (Suggit 1994: 75-81). Both are reflected in the person of Jesus. In his incarnate life he displayed the steadfast love of God for his human creatures and his world. The New Testament calls this the act of God's grace (*to charisma*, Romans 5:16), and in the New Testament grace (*charis*) approximately represents what is denot-

237

ed by the Hebrew *hesed* in the Old Testament. In a similar way Jesus revealed God's righteousness (*zedeq*, Greek *dikaiosunê*), by which human beings are put in the right relationship with him (1 Corinthians 1:30; 2 Corinthians 5:21), and so are brought to discover their true place in God's creation. These two attributes of God are to be reflected in the lives of those who have been brought to be his people in union with Christ. As the prophets put it: "It is steadfast love (*hesed*) in which I delight, not sacrifice" (Hosea 6:6); "Listen to me, all who pursue what is right (*zedeq*), who seek the Lord" (Isaiah 51:1). The two themes are united in the commandments of Jesus to love God and to love one's neighbour as oneself. Any interpretation of scripture, said Augustine, which fails to build up love for God and for others is bound to be wrong (*DocCh* 1: 40).

In displaying his love to the world (John 3:16-17) God accepted people as they were. Sanders (1985: 206) has even suggested that the real offence of Jesus in the eyes of the Pharisees may have been his acceptance of sinners *without first requiring their repentance*. If this is so, there is all the more reason for the church to welcome gay persons (who are no worse sinners than anyone else), without demanding that they change their lifestyle. But if the church is to bear witness to the value of sexuality as a gift of God, its exercise must be subject to the same principles as guide other human actions and activities. It must reflect love for God and for fellow human beings. Sexual behaviour (whether heterosexual or homosexual), as a way to satisfy one's passions and lust, is not only foreign to the gospel (Matthew 5:27-28), but devalues the sexual instinct, usually at the expense of the other partner. The principle that a human being should never be treated *merely* as a means to an end needs to be respected especially in sexual relationships.

For this reason rape, whether homosexual or heterosexual, can never be condoned by Christians, as it entails using a human being to gratify lust. Since the sexual act is meant to reflect an attitude of love and commitment of the partners to one another, gays and lesbians have the same responsibility as heterosexual couples to commit themselves to one another on a permanent basis. Casual promiscuity has no place in the Christian understanding of the proper use of human sexuality. This may be a characteristic of many animals, but human beings are differentiated from beasts by the possession of reason, which renders them morally responsibile to control their natural instincts. The virtue of self-control (*enkrateia*, Galatians 5:23) is a gift of the Spirit, given by God's grace to all who will to seek it. "Give me continence," prayed Augustine as a young man before his conversion, "but not just yet!" (*Conf* 8:7[17]). He was afraid that the Lord might hear him too soon and cure what he called the disease of lust. The ability to use our will to direct our conduct is a mark of our humanity. Augustine knew well enough that moral behaviour depends on an act of will.[7] In this he shared the view of the Stoic philosopher, Seneca.[8] Right behaviour must be learnt, and the church has the responsibility of teaching it, especially by helping parents to teach their children their Christian responsibilities. This is particularly needed when their children turn out to be gay or lesbian. So often the rejection which they experience from their family affects and impairs not only their own welfare, but also the contribution which they can responsibly make to the whole community, Christian and secular.

Much harm is inflicted when society rejects gay persons, and (especially if they are Christians) when the church rejects them, as though they are worse sinners than anyone else. The New Testament frequently links sexual sins with *pleonexia*, which simply means greed, wanting more than one's due.[9] Few of us are free from all forms of covetousness. All of us are weak insignificant creatures, enabled nevertheless by God's grace to achieve great things. As a consequence, gays and lesbians need to be encouraged by their local congregation, and by the church at large, to discover themselves as loved by God and to recognise that their conduct needs to be guided by their love for God and their love for others. The support already given by Archbishop Desmond needs to be reflected in the life of the church as a whole.

7. "No-one does good against his will." ("*Nemo enim invitus bene facit, etiamsi bonum est quod facit*") Conf 1:12 [19].
8. *Epist* 123: 16: "*Nemo est casu bonus. Discenda virtus est.*" ("No-one is good by chance; goodness must be learnt").
9. Ephesians 5:3; Colossians 3:5. *Pleonektēs* ("a greedy person") is found in similar contexts in 1 Corinthians 5:10-11; 6:10; Ephesians 5:5; and *pleonektein* ("to be greedy") in 1 Thessalonians 4:6.

BIBLIOGRAPHY

Boswell, J. (1981), *Christianity, social tolerance and homosexuality*, Chicago: University of Chicago Press.

Carson, R.C., J.N. Butcher and J.C. Coleman (1988), *Abnormal psychology and modern life*, 8th ed., Illinois: Scott, Foresman and Co.

Fox, R.L. [1986] (1988), *Pagans and Christians*, London: Penguin.

Greenberg, D.F. (1988), *The construction of homosexuality*, Chicago: University of Chicago Press.

Patterson, T.J.M. (1984), "An introduction to the ethics of homosexuality" in *Journal of Theology for Southern Africa*, pp. 48, 45-54.

Plummer, K. (Ed.) (1981), *The making of the modern homosexual*, London: Hutchinson.

Prestige, G.L. (1948), *Fathers and heretics*, London: SCM.

Sanders, E.P. (1985), *Jesus and Judaism*, London: SCM.

Suggit, J.N. (1974), "Freedom to be", in *Journal of Theology for Southern Africa*, 8, pp. 31-37.

Suggit, J.N. (1994), *The Word of God and the people of God*, Fish Hoek: Celebration of Faith.

Living in multifaith South Africa

INTRODUCTION

The prerogative of starting a sermon, speech or lecture by telling a joke belongs to Desmond Tutu! I would therefore rather start my contribution to this most appropriate tribute by relating a parable which Desmond himself composed more than a decade ago:

> Light Bulb used to shine and glow wonderfully. Everybody was attracted to brilliant Light Bulb until Light Bulb grew with pride and arrogance. He thought his brilliance was self-generated. He disdained the flexes hidden away in the ceiling which connected him to the dynamo, the source of his energy. Then one day someone unscrewed Light Bulb from the socket and placed him on the table. Try as he would, Light Bulb just remained black and cold and people then passed him by without paying him the slightest attention.

The context in which I came across this parable was the inaugural Desmond Tutu Peace Lecture organised by the South African Chapter of the World Conference on Religion and Peace and scheduled for 14 September 1985. Since this lecture was banned in terms of the emergency regulations in force at the time, it was never delivered. Tutu (1994: 11) used this parable to to put on record the fact that he owed so much to the contributions and prayers of others.

In the present context I now have the privilege to pay warm tribute to Desmond Tutu for the formative influence he has had on my life during our friendship which has now lasted for almost two decades. He became a real role model to me through his remarkable ability to strike a balance between a deep spirituality and a genuine commitment to social justice. He has also exposed me to the international interfaith scene and has greatly supported and inspired me to work towards increasing awareness of the multifaith reality of South African society.

In this essay I would first of all like to highlight the contributions which Tutu has made towards the understanding of religious pluralism in our country. Then I would like to attend to some of the implications which living together as people of different faiths could have for the future.

DESMOND TUTU AND OTHER FAITHS

It is not clear whether Tutu has always been aware of and sensitive to the multifaith reality of our world, and, in particular, of our country. However, being a son of Africa, where religious diversity is part of life, he most probably shared the generally tolerant attitude towards people of other faiths. Be it as it may, in 1966 he obtained the degree MTh in Islamic Studies at the University of London. Studying under the well-known Geoffrey Parrinder, he no doubt had to think through the presence of other faiths and in the process develop his own "theology of religions".

In what follows, a brief attempt will be made to trace Tutu's thinking on the theological significance of other faiths. Attention will also be given to his views regarding religion and society and religion and the state.

It will be noted that the earliest statement by Tutu on the presence of, and interaction with, other faiths dates back to 1984. It is quite possible that he expressed similar opinions, unknown to me, at an earlier date. However, since the interfaith movement in South Africa came off the ground in 1984, it constituted a framework within which Tutu's pronouncements became very relevant and noticeable.

Tutu's "Theology of Religions"

Knowing Desmond Tutu, I can well imagine that he will be quite surprised to find that what he has said in a few papers, speeches and interviews is suddenly used to construct a theology of religions! To present the thoughts which he has expressed over a period of time as his complete and final opinion on the matter will therefore be both presumptuous on my part and unfair to him. However, even if what is

242

presented below is looked upon as a broad outline, it becomes evident that much original thought has been devoted to this very vital issue.

Certainly one of the most provocative statements which Tutu has made, and that on television, was his pronouncement that God is not a Christian! He later elucidated this statement as follows (1994: 128):

> Everybody knows that Christianity is just under 2000 years old. If God is a Christian, what was he before Jesus Christ came to earth? We surely will not say God did not exist before the advent of Christ.

The contexts in which both his statement and explanation were offered were those of societal co-existence and dialogue with people of other faiths. He further states that:

> God is too great to be apprehended only by a finite Christian.

He is, by implication, appealing to all people of faith to apply a measure of modesty in the claims they wish to press for their particular faiths. This becomes even clearer when we find him (1994: 10) agreeing with John Hick that "we should move from a Christianity centred to a God centred understanding of the nature of religions".

Whilst he stopped short of asking the same from the adherents of Hinduism, Islam and Judaism amongst others, I have no doubt that Tutu would, as a matter of consistency, extend his view to include these traditions.

In addition to the discussion on the idea of God, which often features in interfaith dialogue, Tutu picks up another matter which invariably surfaces when people of other faiths are encountered. He (1994: 127) is faced on the one hand with the *unarguable goodness, probity and holiness* of adherents of other faiths. On the other hand he finds himself confronted by many Christians who hold that *non-Christian faiths are devoid of all truth.* Categorising the latter attitude as a hostile refusal to acknowledge the validity of a plurality of religious faiths, he remarks as follows:

> Somehow it seems God is diminished if we should acknowledge the undoubted verities and goodness that reside in non-Christian faiths and the virtues to be found among their adherents.

243

It is clear that Tutu respects other faiths as ways and means to grapple with ultimate realities. He (1994: 129) allows for the possibility that other traditions have seen something of the "divine splendour" and he wants to listen to what they have to share in this regard. In advocating the necessity of interreligious dialogue, Tutu (1994: 9) however denies that such an enterprise boils down to religious relativism in terms of which all religions are really the same.

Whilst expressing the view that his convictions do not require offensive behaviour towards people of other faiths, he (1994: 129) makes a clear statement of faith:

> Jesus Christ for me is the full and final revelation of God. I will not compromise my belief in his absolute uniqueness.

When the above statements are evaluated, it would at first glance appear that Tutu's viewpoint bears resemblance to that which the Vancouver Assembly of the World Council of Churches expressed in its report "Witnessing in a divided world":

> While affirming the uniqueness of the birth, life, death, and resurrection of Jesus, to which we bear witness, we recognize God's creative work in the seeking for religious truth among people of other faiths (Gill 1983: 40).

However, the resemblance ends when it is noted with Braybrooke (1992: 260) that the leadership of the WCC at the time denied that the statement acknowledged God's presence with people of other faiths. Tutu on the other hand clearly implies that other faiths do not merely represent a searching for the truth, but also signify that something of the "divine splendour" has been found. It was only in 1990 that at least part of the WCC constituency "caught up" with Tutu. During a consultation held at Baar, Switzerland, the Sub-Unit on Dialogue with People of Living Faiths, (now called the Office on Inter-Religious Relations), resolved; amongst other affirmations, the following:

> We affirm that God has been present in their seeking and finding.

Religion and society

Tutu's understanding of the role of his own tradition, i.e. Christianity, in society has always been that obedience to Christ implies identification with, and concern for, the victims of society. Whilst he has always considered social justice to be an essential part of the Christian message, he has also acknowledged the fact that Christianity does not have a monopoly on values such as equality, justice, peace, truth and virtue (1994: 127). These were rather to be viewed as human values shared by all religious traditions. Tutu (1986: 20) shows full awareness of the fact that all faiths claim social justice as belonging to their essence:

> To be concerned for justice and human dignity as well as for peace are not optional extras which we may take up or abandon as the whim strikes us. It is integral to being a religious person, for the consummation to which most of our faiths look, is a condition of unalloyed bliss, fellowship, unity and true joy.

Like several others, the year 1984 will be remembered as significant in South Africa's painful journey to full democracy. This particular year was marked, on the one hand, by uprisings in the Vaal Triangle which eventually contributed to the infamous Delmas Treason Trial. On the other hand, 1984 marked the establishment of the so-called Tricameral Parliament which gave Coloureds and Indians representation in parliament, albeit in separate chambers. The latter event had particular bearing on religious pluralism in South Africa.

In the pre-1984 period it was mainly Christians, inside and outside of parliament, who could be blamed for promoting or supporting apartheid. In so doing they had the support of at least part of the Jewish electorate. In 1984 the situation changed in the sense that, for the first time, Hindus and Muslims actively participated in the apartheid structure. Many of them did so with the conviction that their respective beliefs were providing them with the necessary justification.

Against this backdrop, the Interfaith Colloquium on Apartheid, organised by Archbishop Trevor Huddlestone, took place in London in 1984. Realising its importance and relevance for all religious people in South Africa, Tutu, then still General Secretary of the South African Council of Churches, ensured that an interfaith delegation from South Africa attended. With the Colloquium sounding a strong note on the incongruity between the dehumanising system of apartheid and all living faiths, Tutu applied himself to the establishment of an interfaith organisation in South Africa. His endeavour in this regard paid dividends when the South African Chapter of the World Conference on Religion and Peace (WCRP) was established during that same year.

At the World Assembly of WCRP held in Nairobi in August 1984, Tutu (1986: 19) was able to express himself as follows on the moral responsibility of people of all faiths, not only in South Africa but all over the world:

> If people of faith are to uphold the integrity of their religious profession, then we must consistenly condemn injustice, exploitation and oppression, arbitrary arrest and the execution of innocents who happen to be the ones who are pushed to the periphery of society outside the corridors of power.

Religion and the state

Two aspects of the relationship between religion and the state are dealt with below, namely the equal treatment of religions by the state and the separation of religion and the state.

Equal treatment

The right for all religions in South Africa to have access to the publicly owned media, such as radio and television, has been strongly advocated from several quarters. Tutu added his voice to this campaign when he said (1992: 2):

> Christians have unlimited access to the media, including the electronic media, which is supposedly owned by the entire nation. When last did you see on TV, for instance, a Muslim or a Jewish service?

The Archbishop has no doubt noticed with approval that this inequality has been rectified. The fact that devotional talks, services and festivals of other faiths are now also screened certainly acknowledges the presence of the different traditions in our society and will hopefully foster understanding of, and respect for, our neighbour's faith.

The Peace Convention, which took place on 14 September 1991, was the first state function in South Africa ever to have featured prayers by representatives of four different traditions. As one of the twelve facilitators, this arrangement was strongly supported by Tutu. Amidst controversy, the same pattern was repeated at Codesa I and II. Chairing a subcommittee on the religious arrangements for the inauguration of President Nelson Mandela on 10 May 1994, Tutu ensured that together with the Christian faith, Hinduism, Islam and Judaism were duly represented. Criticism of the fact that people of other faiths participated at the aforementioned events invariably raised the point that South Africa was a "Christian country". Tutu (1994: 128) addresses this assertion as follows:

> Often we hear that South Africa is a Christian country. I do not know what that means unless it is to tell us that the majority of South Africans claim to be Christians. It certainly cannot mean that South Africa is a country which lives by the highest Christian principles.

At an earlier occasion, Tutu, looking at the fact that Christianity is decidedly pluriform in belief, in worship and in expression, stated (1992: 4):

> It becomes obvious that we could not apply the appellation "Christian country" univocally so that its meaning was obvious and identical to all who were interpreting the term. If the meaning is so idiosyncratic, is there any useful purpose being served by using such a confusing description?

Whilst Tutu has pleaded for equal treatment of the different faiths, and, as we will see below, for the separation of religion and the state, he is obviously in favour of the continued, visible role of religion, not only in society but also at state occasions. Commenting on the present practice of observing silent prayer in Parliament, Tutu (1994: 130) does not hesitate to criticise:

> I hope we will restore the custom of starting Parliamentary sittings with prayer. The new practice is a cop-out which I condemn strongly. People can still observe their reverent silence as prayers were offered by ministers of different

faiths by rotation. Perhaps Christian prayers might be offered more frequently to reflect the demographic reality.

Separation between religion and the state

In the process of mapping out a new constitution for South Africa, members of the Constitutional Assembly have been arguing that the best route to take in determining the relationship between religion and the state would be that of the so-called secular state. In contrast to, on the one hand, a theocratic state and, on the other, an atheistic state, the secular ideal seems best suited to meet the need for tolerance and freedom in a situation of religious diversity.

However, it would appear that a misunderstanding prevailed on the exact meaning of a secular state. This concept was misconstrued by some as signalling the end of religious activities in state institutions and of religious personalities holding public office. Matters were brought to a head when, in 1995, the African Christian Democratic Party and an organisation called "The Christian Voice", organised a protest march of thousands of Christians to Parliament. The members of the Constitutional Assembly were, among other things, accused of planning a "Godless" state.

Reacting to the consternation which the idea of a secular state has caused, Tutu in a pastoral letter to Anglicans (quoted in Constitutional Talk 9, 1995) added his voice to the debate:

> A secular state is not a godless or immoral one. It is one in which the state does not owe allegiance to any particular religion and thus no religion has an unfair advantage, or has privileges denied to others.

A secular state will then ensure equal treatment as far as different religious traditions are concerned. Minority religions will certainly welcome the disappearance of discrimination from the side of the state. On the other hand, the so-called majority religion will also gain from such an arrangement in the sense that separation between religion and the state will prevent it from losing its credibility.

The close association which existed between the apartheid regime and the Christian church, albeit by and large with one particular denomination, brought the credibility of the Gospel of Jesus Christ into question. The loser in this case proved to be not the state but the church, whose message of love, peace and justice became tarnished by an inhumane and sinful ideology. With this history in mind, Tutu (1992: 5) earlier questioned the advantage of a country having a religious tag attached to it:

> Almost always the adherents of that particular dominant faith in that country fall disasterously short of the high ideals of their professed faith, which tends to be brought into disrepute by its association with the state in such an intimate way.

A final matter which has already caused much debate, and which is bound to cause even more in months to come, is the question of whether the name of God should be referred to in the preamble to the Constitution or not. In order to put this debate into perspective, we need to look at the fairly recent history of the Constitution of our country.

The constitution adopted in 1961 when South Africa left the Commonwealth and became a republic was in force until 1983. It was then replaced by a new constitution which provided for the establishment of the so-called tricameral parliament, in terms of which separate chambers were created for Coloureds and Indians.

The preamble of both these constitutions acknowledged the sovereignty of Almighty God. Since the tricameral system brought Hindus and Muslims into parliament this acknowledgement in the 1983 Constitution was interpreted in certain circles to have meant that the diversity of culture and religion was now recognised and that the term "Almighty God" could no longer be identified with the Triune God of Christianity. On account of such an interpretation it could be concluded that even the legislators were accepting religious plurality as a given fact of South African society.

However, the above conclusion seemed to have been contradicted when, in the same Constitution, it was stated that one of the national objectives would be "to maintain Christian values and civilised norms and to recognise and protect freedom of worship".

Whilst some Christians want to see the authority of the Triune God of Christianity clearly acknowledged in the Preamble, there are other views held in this regard. Proponents of other views, inter alia, point to the fact that South African society is made up of people from different faiths and of no religious faith. They further hold that the Constitution of a democratic South Africa should therefore be free from any compulsion or imposition of a religious or anti-religious

249

nature. Referring to this debate, Tutu (Constitutional Talk 9, 1995) warned that Christian morals and standards were clearly not guaranteed just by mentioning God in the Constitution :

> The old constitution invoked the name of God and then the apartheid government totally ignored God as it carried out unGodly, unChristian and immoral laws. It was blasphemy to use the name of the Lord in vain.

IMPLICATIONS FOR THE FUTURE

In coming to grips with religious diversity and turning it into an asset, the role of the dominant faith in a particular society is of the utmost importance. The sociological laws operating in majority-minority relations suggest, amongst others, that the extent to which a minority can strive toward emancipation, thus becoming a full partner in societal life depends on the dominant force.

In South Africa's case it has been of great importance that a Christian leader of the stature of Archbishop Desmond Tutu has been dealing with those issues which have caused minority faiths through the years to feel tolerated rather than free. He has challenged the "Christian monopoly" of many sought-after human values and shared in destroying the myth that South Africa is a Christian country and added his voice to the campaign for the separation of religion and the state. In so doing he has greatly contributed to the societal shift from the mere acknowledgement of religious diversity to the building, even if ever so slowly, of relationships between people of different faiths.

If it can be said that an atmosphere conducive to the emergence of real tolerance and freedom in the area of religion has been created due to the efforts of Tutu and others, a valid question is: what implications does this hold for the future? Although clear-cut answers are impossible, an attempt will be made to outline areas which could have an effect on, or be affected by, people of different faiths living together in one country.

Religion and society

Religion has always formed a part of South African society and will continue to do so. Even as our society becomes more industrialised and experiences an explosion of scientific knowledge, religion will persist. Here, as elsewhere in the world, religion is concerned with fundamental questions about human existence, and it does this in a way that differs radically from the rationalism of modern, industrialised society. Thus, there will always be an affinity for religion in South African society and its basic functions, while religion, in turn, will continue to influence our behaviour.

Like any other society, the South African one requires a cohesive value system that is capable of controlling the conflict that emerges from opposing interests. Religion can then benefit its adherents and our society by giving emotional support to the fundamental values which our society requires.

As the democratisation of our society has reached the religious scene, a number of things have become evident. In the first place the so-called "tyranny of religion" has come to an end. Together with the plea for, and the reality of, the separation between religion and the state, it would appear that it is admitted, more readily than ever before, that not all people in our society are religious nor adhere to a particular faith. The designation "people of no faith" is therefore becoming more and more acceptable when religious rights and freedom are being discussed. Contrary to what we would have believed before, such an acknowledgement constitutes a liberating experience for religion as such. No longer are people "forced" to be counted as religious, nor is religion any longer a "state sponsored" affair. Whilst everybody is granted freedom of association, religion is given the opportunity to demonstrate its credibility and relevance uninhibited and free from any obligations

Linked to the first, a second development is the fact that religion in our society has now become largely unsheltered. But this, of course, does not mean that religion is now disregarded, since, as we will see below, the proposed constitution clearly makes provision for religious freedom. However, the promotion and protection of religion or religious requirements are no longer a state responsibility. The deregulation of commercial and recreational activities on a Sunday is a case in point.

Minority faiths such as Hinduism and Islam have, in a rather strange way, also become "unsheltered". The repeal of the notorius Group Areas Act, although widely welcomed, has in reality meant that the Muslim and Hindu communities are no longer the "closed" communities which they used to be. They have therefore become much more exposed to the missionary efforts of Christian churches than ever before. The reverse is of course also true in the sense that many Christians are now for the first time having real encounters with their neighbours and colleagues of different faiths.

The matter of missionary outreach is a very sensitive area which, if not correctly handled, can affect the creation of an atmosphere of co-operation and interaction very negatively. In general it should be said that religious liberty does include the freedom of religious groups to propagate their respective faiths. In fact, both Muslims and Christians regard this as inherently part of their religious obligations.

On the other hand our Hindu and Jewish partners in dialogue have been telling us that genuine respect for other faiths excludes all missionary efforts, since the latter implies that other faiths are regarded as inferior.

It may be helpful if religions in a particular area could come to an agreement on a code of conduct for missionary outreach. Such a code should then contain certain ground rules for acceptable practices in this regard. A matter which will have to be squarely faced is the role of humanitarian aid in missions. Although such a code would most probably not be enforceable by law, the discussion leading up to it could be highly significant and productive in itself.

The fact that residential areas and educational facilities have been opened to all will hopefully lead to more frequent and normal contact between people of different faiths. This may in turn lead to an increase in marriages where the marriage partners belong to different faiths. Whilst the different religious communities will no doubt inform their members about the additional problems in terms of compatibility which such a union may cause, "mixed" marriages will nevertheless still take place. The different religious communities will therefore need to be prepared to render special pastoral care to their members in such cases. This kind of pastoral care may even at times have to take place in consultation with a spiritual leader from the other faith.

The issue of religious instruction and religious education at school may prove to be another sensitive area. Ideally such instruction should be undertaken in the parental home and by the particular religious institution. However, since it has been part of the school curricula of the greater part of the South African educational establishment, it will most probably be retained. If handled in a responsible way, such a subject or subjects could make a significant contribution towards a better understanding of, and respect for, the different faiths in South

African society. However, before this can happen, the educational authorities will have to gain clarity on the status of such a subject and also ensure the availability of professionally trained teachers. Faith communities should, on the other hand, contribute positively to the whole process, if the gains in terms of nation-building are properly evaluated over against the perceived threat which exposure to other faiths may constitute.

A last remark concerning the multifaith nature of our society deals with the importance of joint projects in terms of social services. It is fairly obvious what impact a programme of support, directed by people of different religious persuasions, can have in a particular neighbourhood. However, before joint projects can begin, relationships of trust should first be established. Building such relationships between people of different religions is the unique contribution which uninhibited contact and constructive dialogue across the religious divide can make.

Religion and the Constitution

The Working Draft of the New Consitution gives clear evidence that the Consitutional Assembly is indeed taking cognisance of religious realities in South Africa. Chapter 2 (of the Bill of Rights) deals with fundamental rights which include provisions for the recognition and protection of religious freedom in South Africa. In offering a view of what is in the interest of religion in South African society, a brief critique will now be offered on the provisions made for religious freedom in the Working Draft. Some of what is offered below may be described as ideal and may not necessarily be deemed essential for a constitution. It is however intended to serve as a gauge for the religious community regarding the measure of constitutional protection which it will enjoy.

Section 8: Equality

Since all the sub-sections are not relevant to our discussion, only sub-section (3) is quoted, which reads as follows:

> (3) Neither the state nor any person may discriminate directly or indirectly against anyone on one or more grounds including race, gender, sex, marital status, ethnic or social origin, colour, sexual orientation, age, disability, religion, conscience, belief, culture, language and birth.

The above article is phrased in such a way that it seems to apply only to individuals. The question is therefore whether religious communities, like individuals, enjoy equality before the law. It is sincerely hoped that the state will uphold the equality of all religious communities before the law. It is a further question whether 8(3) adequately protects religious communities against slander and denigration.

Section 14: Freedom of religion, belief and opinion

(1) Everyone has the right to freedom of conscience, religion, thought, belief and opinion.

(2) Religious observances may be conducted at state or state-aided institutions provided that –

    (a) those observances follow rules made by an appropriate authority;

    (b) they are conducted on an equitable basis; and

    (c) attendance at them is free and voluntary.

(3) The Constitution does not prevent legislation recognising the validity of marriages concluded under a system of religious law or a system of personal and family law adhered to by persons professing a particular religion to the extent that the system is consistent with the Bill of Rights.

The right to freedom of conscience is explicitly guaranteed in 14(1). This safeguards the religious convictions that people hold. On the other hand, the right to change one's religious allegiance is merely implicitly provided for in 14(1). One would have hoped for a more explicit statement in this regard. Another shortcoming of 14(1) seems to be the fact that the right to profess, practise and propagate the religion of one's choice is not explicitly recognised.

Subsections 14(1) and 14(2) together seem to guarantee the arrangement that the state should not identify with or favour any particular religious tradition. However, against the backdrop of South Africa's past, it is a question whether there should not be an explicit stipulation in the Constitution that the conduct of the state will be free from identification with or bias towards any specific religious tradition.

Subsection 14(2) makes provision for religious communities to conduct "religious observances" in a state or state-aided institution. However, in the light of the recently reported intentions of the South African Defence Force to review religious observances at official occasions, one needs to ask whether this subarticle adequately guarantees the religious rights of an individual in such an institution.

Section 15: Freedom of expression

(1) Everyone has the right to freedom of expression, including –
    (a) freedom of the press and other media; and
    (b) freedom to receive and impart information and ideas.

The above subsection guarantees every person the right to freedom of speech and expression, a right which surely also applies to religious groups. Religious communities are not given a special place as the "conscience" of society; the state should take cognisance of the fact that religious communities feel called to act as watchdogs of social justice, even to the extent of criticising and challenging social and political structures and policies.

CONCLUSION

In 1987 Archbishop Tutu led an interfaith delegation to consult with the ANC in Lusaka on the future of religion in a post-apartheid South Africa. This consultation ended with a very clear message from our partners in dialogue to religious leaders and their communities: "We are busy building a house. Don't ask us to reserve a room for you; join us in completing this dwelling."

When the question is therefore asked whether a new South Africa will be kind to religion, it should at the same time be asked whether religion will be kind to the emerging new society. Given the constructive role which Desmond Tutu and other religious personalities have played during the National Peace Initiatives, and are bound to play in the search for truth and reconciliation which is presently under way, the latter question can be answered in the affirmative. An affirmative answer to the question as to whether the new South Africa will be kind to religion can certainly also be given. Exactly because they will function as separate entities, sound interaction, to the benefit of our entire society, will result.

BIBLIOGRAPHY

Braybrooke, Marcus (1992), *Pilgrimage of hope: One hundred years of global interfaith dialogue*, London: SCM.

Gill, D. (ed.) (1983), *Gathered for life: Official report VI, Assembly World Council of Churches*, Geneva: WCC.

Jack, H.A. (1993), WCRP: *A history of the World Conference on Religion and Peace*, New York: WCRP.

Tutu, D.M. (1995), "Secular State not Godless" *Constitutional Talk*, Official Newsletter of the Constitutional Assembly, 30 June 1995 – 10 August 1995.

Tutu, D.M. (1986), "World religions for human dignity and peace" in J.B. Taylor and G. Gebhardt (eds.) *Religions for human dignity and world peace*, Geneva: WCRP.

Tutu, D.M. (1992), *The secular state and religion: Archbishop Naidoo memorial lecture, July 1992*, Cape Town: Salesian Press.

Tutu, D.M. (1994), "The religious understanding of peace" in G. Lubbe (ed.), *A decade of interfaith dialogue*, pp. 9-17, Johannesburg: WCRP.

Tutu, D.M. (1994), "Let us celebrate our diversity" in G. Lubbe (ed.), *A decade of interfaith dialogue*, pp. 124-130, Johannesburg: WCRP.

Where do we go from here?

The essays in this book range over a wide variety of theological issues. To a large extent, they reflect the breadth of Desmond Tutu's career and his multiple contributions to theological education, the church and society. We all owe a great debt to him.

As one reads these essays, one becomes aware of the tremendous and exciting challenges facing theological education, the church and society, today. On the one hand, there is the challenge of re-evangelising South Africa, and transforming it by God's creative power in the light of the realities of the church and society. Some church leaders have argued that re-evangelisation must be high on the list of priorities for the church in South Africa. Saayman, who is an ardent proponent of this view, lists at least three interdependent dimensions of re-evangelisation: conscientisation, empowerment and liberation. The process of conscientisation, he argues, implies becoming aware of and making others aware of the sinfulness involved in living according to a system of life which prided itself on being "Christian", but was not. Empowerment implies creating the conditions to be fully human in community, nurturing the courage to overcome the inhumanity of being either oppressor or oppressed, either sinner or sinned against. Liberation implies becoming fully human, realising what has been promised for us in the life, death, and resurrection of the new human being, Jesus of Nazareth. According to Saayman, attaining full political and economic rights, the right to equal and proper education and housing, and the right to celebrate together our common identity, are very important dimensions of this full humanity (Saayman 1995: 3). Re-evangelisation should target in particular racism, sexism, religious fundamentalism and authoritarianism, which threaten to suffocate both the church and society in the new South Africa.

But this is not the only challenge facing South Africa. There is also the challenge of responding to the urgent need for sustainable justice and peace; and the question of the church and human sexuality, the church and development, the church and women, and the church and people of other faiths. Related to this is the fundamental question of the relationship of the church to the state. A theological response to these questions has vital practical implications, not only for South Africa but also for many countries in the southern hemisphere.

Ecumenism is another pressing challenge in our part of the continent. There is a desperate need to rethink and rebuild ecumenical co-operation and theological formation in Africa. The collapse of the Federal Theological Seminary (FEDSEM) in Pietermaritzburg symbolises the crisis in ecumenism and theological education both within South Africa and universally. FEDSEM was the focal point of black theology in South Africa, and it was the most significant ecumenical theological seminary in the region. Perhaps the recent African consultation, under the auspices of the Ecumenical Theological Formation (ETF) desk of the World Council of Churches (WCC), held at the Kuruman Moffat Mission in August 1995, is the hope for the future of ecumenism and theological formation in South Africa. The Kuruman Consultation established a task force to develop a Strategic Plan for Ecumenical Theological Formation in Africa, and with the various subregions of the continent, including South Africa. The task force has the responsibility of making specific proposals to the WCC about how the Kuruman report may be implemented. According to this report, issues which are clearly priorities are the development of appropriate curricula for Africa and its regions; the production of suitable textbooks; accreditation; the training of theological educators and the development of centres of graduate training in the region; the development of both an ecumenical consciousness and commitment within the churches and institutions, as well as providing education which is ecumenically oriented (De Gruchy 1995: 2). Thus the immediate challenge for the church in South Africa is to establish a mechanism which can work with the task force to develop an ecumenical policy for the future.

And last, but not least, is the challenge of the reality of Africa for interpreting reality. Closely connected with this issue is the question of the relationship between the Scriptures and African cultures. This challenge calls for an ongoing attempt to find new ways of reading the Bible in Africa, especially in a community that is continuing to struggle to find what it means to be both African and Christian. In its use of Scripture, Black theology in South Africa epitomises this challenge. South African Black theology is primarily concerned not so much with exegesis of the text of the Bible in its original context and time of writing, as with its immediate existential relevance to the situation of the reader and the hearer. The relationship of the biblical world to the concrete realities and immediate experiences of African readers, and of listeners to the Word of God, therefore, constitutes one of the important aspects on the way ahead.

Accordingly, another of Desmond Tutu's significant contributions, especially in theological education, was the facilitation of the process of a paradigm shift from Eurocentrism to Afrocentrism in academic pursuits and in the interpretation of reality. He affirmed the presence of the black people and reversed the historic devaluation of Africa and the African world, both in academic and in non-academic circles. Out of this Afrocentric approach came African and black perspectives as the basis for understanding reality. Thus the European experience became to him no longer normative for interpreting African reality and the Bible. He elevated the African world to a level of importance heretofore unknown to the African world. Therefore, the reality of Africanism and the interpretation of the Bible constitute as formidable a challenge today in South Africa, and the world, as ever they did. Some important work in this regard is being done already, especially by the School of Theology at the University of Natal, Pietermaritzburg (LeMarquand 1995: 2).

Women play a vital role in the daily life of the churches in South Africa, but are by and large excluded from its centres of power and influence. They have seldom, if ever, been regarded as having a contribution to make to theology. The same has been true within society more generally, despite the fact that women have often initiated and been at the forefront of political resistance and protest, both within African nationalist and labour movements. However, signs of change have begun to emerge in the recognition of the role of women in the life of the church and society. In the church, this change has found expression in the development of feminist theology within the country. Regrettably though, there are still few women theologians and clerics in South Africa, notwithstanding the number of black women elsewhere in the workplace. Feminist theology in South Africa needs to challenge vigorously not only patriarchalism but also the authoritarianism which prevails in the formal structures of the church. However, the new constitution in South Africa has entrenched women's rights, and as a result women are visibly represented in most structures of the civil service. These are signs that a new generation of women is emerging in spite of the obstacles facing them.

There is also the question of religious pluralism in South Africa. Despite the fact that South Africa is a predominantly Christian country, it is also a religiously plural society. All religions represented in the country play a significant role in that society, even though the number of its adherents may be small. As a democratic society, we have to take more seriously our religious differences, and begin to see how the various religions can critically relate to each other within the life of the society. We need to begin to see how each religion, while maintaining its own legitimacy and integrity, can contribute to a wholeness of perception, faith and action, and perhaps in the process transform even the adherents. There is profound wisdom in Charles Villa-Vicencio's observation that:

> What the interfaith debate teaches us is that particular cultures, religions and other forms of social identity contain within themselves the possibility of a pluralistic universal. As a relationship of understanding emerges between the particulars, what is "different" is seen to be descriptive not merely of others but also of ourselves. Pluralism which is central to thoughtful interfaith dialogue, constitutes an insight to the character of the national soul that could be indispensable. It is about the many in the one. It concerns the possibility of a national identity that is culturally plural, without giving way to counter hegemonic rivalry. (Villa-Vicencio 1994: 38).

This serves as a reminder that there are still horizons ahead of us. God's activity of revelation will never be over (John 16).

Archbishop Desmond Tutu, in whose honour these essays have been written, played a pivotal role in giving expression to all the challenges we have just mentioned. One of Desmond Tutu's most significant contributions to theological education, the church and society is that he offered leadership of an inspirational kind. He was prepared to take the risk of going against the current, thereby exploring alternatives to the prevailing order. He may be said to be a latter-day prophet; and we desperately need inspiration from his ilk if we are to have any hope of changing the dominant and oppressive models in theological education, the church and society. After all, such models must become fair and balanced for all, rather than unbalanced, unjust, and exploitative, favouring a minority at the expense of the majority.

Furthermore, to take on the task which Desmond Tutu pioneered is not an optional extra which the church and society are free to choose or ignore. It lies at the heart of the mission of the church, the mission of making redemption a reality. It is the translation of the Good News into the reality of our world. Therefore, if the church is serious about evangelising and transforming South Africa, then we need to devote much of our energy to the formation of leaders to carry out that task. If the church is to offer the kind of inspiration which is needed, it needs to make full use of all available resources to help it provide a more inspired leadership. We still need women and men who can inspire us to believe that what seems unrealistic or even impossible is not necessarily so. Other ways of proceeding are conceivable. Both the church and society must make, among other things, a resolute commitment to produce such leadership as a matter of course. Can it be that Desmond Mpilo Tutu is the kind of person given to humanity only once in many centuries? Perhaps a more serious challenge is upon Christians, individually and corporately, to devote their lives to showing that a more just and humane way is possible, both in the church and society in South Africa. Christians can be sure that God will continue to send us prophets; and to make us prophets both to challenge us in our complacency and to comfort us in our trials.

If we are to meet these challenges, then we need also what Denise Ackermann calls "a spirituality of risk" (Ackermann 1994: 125). Why?

> Because [our struggle against] the deeply entrenched power of racism and sexism [fundamentalism and authoritarianism] . . . makes formidable demands without the promise of lasting and convincing victories . . . Because a spirituality of risk has to struggle to weave together times of active involvement in the work of justice and liberating praxis with times of withdrawal, silence and prayer, often a politically unpopular activity. Because there is ambiguity in making allowance for mystery away from the certainties of life. Because we know that maturity needs growth, truth demands change, and freedom entails making choices . . . A spirituality of risk responds to such challenges and objec-

tives with the willingness to trust the Holy One who is, intimately and inclusively engaged in the renewal of the whole world (Ackermann 1994: 125-126).

This requires us to participate with all due theological and moral responsibility in the shaping of our latter-day church and society, without forgetting the limitations of both our vision and our actions.

BIBLIOGRAPHY

Ackermann, Denise (1994), "A spirituality of risk for Christian witness in South Africa", *International Review of Mission*, LXXXIII: 328, January 1994.

De Gruchy John W. (1995), "ASATI and the future of theological education", An unpublished paper presented at the Annual General Meeting of ASATI on Friday, 8 September 1995.

LeMarquand, Grant (1995), "A bibliography of the Bible in Africa: A preliminary publication", *Bulletin for Contextual Theology in Southern Africa and Africa*, 2: 2, August 1995.

Pato, Luke Lungile (1994), "African theologies", in John de Gruchy and C. Villa-Vicencio (eds.), *Doing theology in context: South African perspectives*, Orbis Books: Maryknoll, New York; David Philip: Cape Town and Johannesburg.

Saaymaan, Willem (1995), "Re-evangelising the new South Africa", *Journal of Theology for Southern Africa*, 92, September 1995.

Villa-Vicencio, Charles (1994), "The quest for a national identity", *Journal of Theology for Southern Africa*, 86, March 1994.

List of contributors

Denise M. Ackermann
Professor of Practical Theology at the University of the Western Cape

Michael Battle
Visiting Professor of Christian Ethics, School of Theology, The University of the South, Sewanee, Tennessee, USA

E. D. H. (Liz) Carmichael, MBE
Chaplain and Tutor in Theology, St John's College, Oxford. Previously an Anglican priest involved in peace and reconciliation work in Alexandra township and responsible for the promotion of spirituality in the diocese of Johannesburg

Francis Cull
Anglican priest, formerly Desmond Tutu's spiritual director

Jonathan Draper
Professor of New Testament in the School of Theology, University of Natal, Pietermaritzburg

John W. de Gruchy
Robert Selby Taylor Professor of Christian Studies, University of Cape Town

Simon Gqubule
Bishop of the Queenstown district, Methodist Church of Southern Africa

Beverley Haddad
An Anglican priest in the diocese of Natal, currently undertaking doctoral studies at the School of Theology, University of Natal

Janet Hodgson
Advisor in Local Mission, Diocese of Durham, England. Previously a lecturer in the Department of Religious Studies, University of Cape Town and a member of the Board of Mission, CPSA

Leonard D. Hulley
Professor of Theological Ethics, University of South Africa

Libuseng Lebaka-Ketshabile
Lecturer at John Wesley College (Methodist Church of Southern Africa)
Kilnerton, Pretoria

G. J. A. (Gerrie) Lubbe
Senior Lecturer in Religious Studies, University of South Africa

Edward L. King
Dean Emeritus, St George's Cathedral, Cape Town

Louise Kretzschmar
Senior Lecturer in Theological Ethics, University of South Africa

Simon S. Maimela
Vice-Principal (Tuition), University of South Africa

Njongonkulu Winston Ndungane
Bishop of Kimberley and Kuruman, CPSA

Livingstone Ngewu
Senior Lecturer in the Department of Biblical and Religious Studies,
University of Transkei

Luke Lungile Pato
Principal of the College of the Transfiguration, CPSA, Grahamstown

R. Neville Richardson
Associate Professor in the School of Theology, University of Natal,
Pietermaritzburg

J. N. Suggit
Emeritus Professor of New Testament at Rhodes University

Caroline Tuckey
Director of Professional Child Care College, completed an MTh in the
Department of Systematic Theology and Theological Ethics, UNISA, in
1994

Charles Villa-Vicencio
Professor of Religion and Society, University of Cape Town. He is presently
Director of Research in the Truth and Reconciliation Commission.